TAROT
FOR THE
WILD SOUL

TAROT FOR THE WILD SOUL

A Trauma-Informed Approach to the Cards for Growth, Healing, and Grounding in the Present Moment

LINDSAY MACK

RUNNING PRESS
PHILADELPHIA

Running Press
Hachette Book Group
1290 Avenue of the Americas, New York, NY 10104
www.runningpress.com
@Running_Press

First Edition: May 2026

Published by Running Press, an imprint of Hachette Book Group, Inc.
The Running Press name and logo are trademarks of Hachette Book Group, Inc.

Print book cover and interior design by Jenna McBride

Library of Congress Cataloging-in-Publication Data

Names: Mack, Lindsay, 1984– author.
Title: Tarot for the wild soul : a trauma-informed approach to the cards for growth, healing, and grounding in the present moment / Lindsay Mack.
Description: First edition | New York, NY : Running Press, 2026. | Includes index. | Summary: "From respected intuitive card reader and podcaster Lindsay Mack, Tarot for the Wild Soul is a trauma-informed, soul-led, compassionate approach to tarot for self-reflection, healing, and growth" —Provided by publisher.
Identifiers: LCCN 2025022422 (print) | LCCN 2025022423 (ebook) | ISBN 9780762488971 (hardcover) | ISBN 9780762488995 (ebook)
Subjects: LCSH: Tarot.
Classification: LCC BF1879.T2 M3225 2026 (print) | LCC BF1879.T2 (ebook) | DDC 133.3/2424—dc23/eng/20250909
LC record available at https://lccn.loc.gov/2025022422
LC ebook record available at https://lccn.loc.gov/2025022423

ISBNs: 978-0-7624-8897-1 (hardcover), 978-0-7624-8899-5 (ebook)

Printed in China

1010

10 9 8 7 6 5 4 3 2 1

To Chase and Lynx, the two great loves of my life.
Nothing would be possible without you.

And to the Reverend Richard G. Rento III, who gave me the gift of a radically loving, inclusive, and critically thoughtful foundation around God and spirituality, without which this book wouldn't be possible.

No Artificial Intelligence of any kind was used in our writing or creation of this book, or in its illustrations.
—Lindsay Mack and Chelsea Granger

CONTENTS

INTRODUCTION

MY STORY

As a highly sensitive, anxious, traumatized kid growing up amid physical and psychological abuse, I was stretching my arms out to some kind of God for as long as I can remember, searching for meaning in the world however I could.

When I discovered Tarot in a used bookstore in New Jersey at the age of 12, it seemed like a dream come true. A deck of cards that could offer me a path out of my pain and fear (and maybe even a glimpse at the future!)? I was delighted. I bought the Tarot deck and all the Tarot books the store had to offer, setting out to teach myself how to read and interpret these cards.

Some of my first memories of that tender time of teaching myself Tarot surround how baffled I felt by the interpretations. The Court Cards were always representative of other people in your life? The Tower was always traumatic disaster? Ten of Swords meant that someone was going to stab me in the back? As someone living in a highly dysfunctional environment, I found these meanings very activating, as well as largely inaccurate. I often noticed that I would pull a card and find no correlation between the interpretations in these books and the reality of my day—an observation that would become a strong foundation for my work with the Tarot as a much older person.

I didn't feel comfortable with the sweeping generalizations the books made about the meanings of these cards. I was especially uncomfortable with how fear-based they could be.

Somehow, instead of discouraging me, this dissonance made me curious. Even at that young age, I knew there had to be another way to work with these archetypes. The authors of these books (brilliant and trailblazing as many of them were) were humans themselves, prone to their own unchecked or unexamined biases and belief systems, just like me. Perhaps they had never thought critically about what they were passing along with their interpretations of the cards.

I started to slowly allow my own experiences to inform the way I was reading. I would notice what came up during my day and how that related to what cards I pulled. I began opening myself to something more intuitive and free-flowing, which was a marked deviation from the antiquated books I had been reading.

At age 30, I experienced a nervous breakdown, born of decades of untreated PTSD from severe abuse, that completely transformed my life and brought Tarot back into my hands after many years of not using it regularly.

I began to realize, through pulling cards during my healing process and reaching for my deck in moments of despair, that the Tarot could help me anchor back into myself and the present moment—no matter how unpleasant it might be. Tarot could be a stabilizing force for me, one that was highly effective when combined with all the other rings of support and care around me (like therapy, medication, and work with my amazing mentor) that I was lucky enough to have access to at the time.

Every time I needed a gentle reanchoring, I turned to my deck. Formally and informally, in restaurants, on bathroom floors, on the subway, anytime I needed to pull an Anchor Card, it was there.

In those very contractive moments, the Tarot allowed me to connect to and engage with something larger than my emotions and the anguish of my PTSD, even as it encouraged me not to discount or run away from those feelings and experiences. It helped me to come back home to myself.

The cards that were traditionally described as scary or unfavorable were some of the most helpful to me in my growth. Reversals held a whole universe of wisdom that had nothing to do with being out of alignment. The Tower was a true friend and ally. I welcomed the presence of The Swords. The more I said yes to my intuitive understanding, the more the cards began to sing to me. It was a truly magical initiation.

Slowly but surely, I began to realize that I had different things to say about the Tarot than other folks did. My readings were different, and my approach was different—not just some select alternative interpretations of cards, but a whole new perspective on how to use the Tarot as a radical helping tool, gained through the personal journey work I had been doing with my own deck. This was the birth of Soul Tarot, which is the kind of Tarot that I developed, practice, and teach.

As I deepened into giving readings professionally, I found that my clients were changing in extremely profound ways, their potential unlocked by the soft guidance that could emerge when the present moment was honored and witnessed.

I began to teach Tarot both to people in one-on-one settings and to very intimate groups. That quickly blossomed into larger workshops and retreats all around the country. Since opening the doors to my Soul Tarot practice ten years ago, I have had the privilege of training and teaching tens of thousands of students (many of whom have gone on to become fantastic Tarot readers and teachers in their own right) and have reached tens of millions of listeners through my podcast, *Tarot for the Wild Soul*.

The concept of Soul Tarot is simple, practical, and revolutionary: Rather than treating the cards as a tool for the future, it honors Tarot as a tool for the *present moment*, one that can help us find our way back home to ourselves amid any emotion. It honors the way each card brings medicine for our continued self-tending and evolution, rather than something predictive that is happening *to* us. It can help us stay with ourselves when we would rather run. It is a gentle road map that can lead us back to our innate intuition and wildness. It helps us keep our hearts open to ourselves no matter what might be arising, which allows for radical personal growth to occur.

This book invites folks to open themselves to each of the cards in the deck, seeing every Tarot card as a helpful ally and anchor through whatever might be arising in their lives. It offers compassionate and practical treatments of the cards, perfect for beginners and seasoned readers alike who are seeking a soul-led, evolutionary perspective on the Tarot that can assist in expanding our capacity for joy, self-love, and perpetual growth.

HOW TO USE THIS BOOK

There is no right or wrong way to engage with this book. You might feel called to read it from cover to cover, or you might feel drawn to use it as a guidebook, flipping to particular sections as the need arises.

If you want to use it as a quick reference for your Tarot readings, feel free to flip to the back of the book for an index on all corresponding page numbers for each card.

If you want more clarity on how to put the fundamentals and frameworks of this style of reading into practice, part 3 of this book has what you are looking for.

An important final note: The references to my readings and clients in this book come from real experiences, but identifying details have been changed to honor their privacy.

PART ONE

THE FOUNDATIONS OF SOUL TAROT

CHAPTER ONE

WHAT IS SOUL TAROT?

The power has been out for over 12 hours. There is no estimate as to when it will be restored.

It is 10:45 p.m., and my daughter, my husband, and I are trapped in our freezing house due to a sudden ice storm. Chase and I are thinking only of our two-year-old. How will we keep her warm all night? Will we be able to make it to a hotel in the morning? There is no one to call, no one to reach out to. Everyone around us is also buried in the snow.

I keep praying through the day. Praying for the power to come back on. Praying for help. Praying for guidance. Praying for an intervention of some kind. I go to my Tarot deck a few times and ask for guidance on what to do. I don't get a very helpful response from the cards I pull.

I do all of this with equal parts desperation and half-hearted skepticism. I know that it is unlikely for the power to come back on for the next few days, given the severity of the storm, and it feels foolish to even ask for that kind of irrational miracle. Now I am scared that we will freeze to death in the night, *and* I'm beating myself up. Why didn't we plan better for this? Why didn't we try to leave our house sooner?

It is 2 a.m. in front of the fire, and my daughter is finally asleep, curled up next to me under a blanket. I feel my heart soften, and something in me shifts. The nature of my prayer shifts.

> Spirit, please be with me. Please help me to stay calm. Please help me to navigate this experience. How can I be present with what's arising in this moment?

I reach for my Tarot deck across from me and pull a card: Nine of Swords. I feel a click in my soul, the kind of click I feel when I've touched in with an inquiry that my deck can actually respond to. Nine of Swords is a beautiful and affirming response to my question, offering both a deep acknowledgment of the terror that I feel around this situation, and a helpful and useful message:

> This is so hard and scary. We're with you. Tend to the fear. Talk to the frightened parts of you. Be gentle with yourself as you navigate this.

I close my eyes and send this message to my inner kiddo, acknowledging and honoring their fears. I sit with my feelings. I sit with how hard this is, how painful it is that we're experiencing it, and I continue to feel a shift. Grief starts to flow. This is still so hard and scary, but my relationship to it has changed. I feel more space around me, if even just for this moment.

Pulling Nine of Swords didn't fix the situation I was in. It didn't turn the power back on, and it didn't give me a clear estimate as to when it would be back on. It did, however, offer a balm for the situation that made it easier to bear. It held me, witnessed me, and offered gentle guidance on how I could hold myself (and my child, by extension) through it. It is also a beautiful example of how we might engage with our decks from a Soul Tarot framework.

Soul Tarot is, essentially, a reinterpretation and intentional utilization of the Tarot as a nonpredictive helping tool, one that can assist us in differentiating the noise of our thinking mind from the truth of our heart and soul.

It is an approach to the cards for folks who desire to learn to read Tarot from a soul-centered, inclusive, trauma-informed, nonpredictive, evolutionary perspective, rooted in common sense and critical thinking. It is an invitation to learn how to read Tarot for anything that arises, to show up to our decks in the present moment and engage with them as integral helping tools in moments of uncertainty, chronic pain, or grief.

When I speak of the *soul* in Soul Tarot, I'm speaking about the truth of us. The soul is that deep, heartfelt, quiet compass within all of us that cannot be ignored, brushed aside, or bypassed—at least, not for any true length of time. The soul self is here to leap, fly, evolve, grow through discomfort, and perpetually expand. The soul connects us with our Spirit Helpers, beloved dead, ancestors, and Guides, the otherworldly beings who have our back, and can hold a much more present, calm, loving, spacious perspective than we might be able to do for ourselves.

Conversely (and this is painting with a fairly broad brush for the purposes of this book), the mind wants to keep us safe, alive, and in what feels familiar and known. It actively eschews leaping and flying, loving us enough to try to keep us in what seems to be safe territory. All of us experience this kind of moment-to-moment paradox, this dissonance between our mind and soul. This dual experience (as my former teacher Michelle refers to it) can be incredibly confusing. We may long to try something new but feel doubtful, worried, or insecure. What if we fail, or make a fool out of ourselves? What if we're rejected? What if our heart gets broken?

Soul Tarot reconciles this duality somewhat by helping us understand and honor the mind without necessarily letting it run the show, so to speak. At the same time, it helps us acknowledge the pull of that deep-soul knowing that lives within all of us at any given moment.

When we consider reading the Tarot from a Soul Tarot framework, it also allows the cards to become a gentle and spacious reflection of our Spirit Helpers, Guides, and beloved ancestors.

In Soul Tarot, the cards, like our Spirit Helpers and Guides, *invite*—they never demand or command. Similarly, all the cards in the Tarot (in my humble experience, anyway) help us come home to our own heart, to tend to ourselves through whatever might be arising for us. They can help us repair, forgive ourselves, and pause when we would rather run, holding an unconditionally loving space for us all the while, just as our Spirit Helpers do.

Both our Spirit Helpers and the Tarot can help us remember that we are not linear beings, but rather "spiralic" ones. When we feel frustrated that we aren't healing, recovering, or moving through our lives in the ways we expected or hoped to, our Guides and the Tarot can gently hold us in those feelings, and remind us that we are cyclical, containing multitudes, moving slowly but surely through our process. They can remind us that we are rosebud, rose, rose hip, and thorn in one gloriously imperfect and ever-learning embodiment.

Of course, Soul Tarot is not the only way to read or work with Tarot, nor is it necessarily the best fit for everyone. I have great respect for my colleagues teaching and reading Tarot from different perspectives, and for many of the folks who paved the path for this work. I wouldn't be here without them.

What Soul Tarot *does* do is offer an alternative framework for how we work with the cards and our practice as a whole. It allows the Tarot to become a humble tool for our growth and can be a gentle assistant in releasing identification with fear, ego, and contraction. It enables the Tarot to become a gentle yet fierce anchor amid collective devastation, heartbreak, loss, and revolution.

What role does a Tarot practice play in crushing, unimaginable times? How can it be of service to us when we've lost everything? How can it be an ally to us the in the midst of racism, systemic oppression, loss of our rights, or the wild grief of climate change unfolding before our eyes? Indeed, the Tarot cannot reliably tell us when something will end or how something will turn out. It doesn't consistently fix, heal, or tell us precisely what will happen or when it will happen. But it can be medicine in the face of deep pain. It can help us come home to and stay with ourselves, no matter what might be arising.

CHAPTER TWO

THE PILLARS OF SOUL TAROT

The pillars and principles of Soul Tarot are not meant to be strictly upheld and are constantly evolving, just like the Tarot itself. These pillars can help to ground us in the ethos and spirit of the framework for Soul Tarot as a practice, allowing us to understand what exactly we are working with, but they can be shifted or deviated from flexibly.

I also think it helps to have sturdy foundations for our Tarot learning process. The Tarot is ultimately a tool of and for the people. A great number of folks who use the Tarot are self-taught and form their own unique meanings through its continued use. These pillars (or Soul Tarot as a whole, for that matter) can be the foundations of the house we build with our Tarot practice.

If we feel challenged around some aspect of our Tarot practice, these pillars can offer some scaffolding. If they resonate with you, you are welcome to come back to these pillars as a gentle compass in your practice anytime you are struggling with a card or feeling blocked in your relationship with any of these archetypes.

1. **There are no "bad" or "good" cards in the Tarot. All cards bring medicine.**

   In Soul Tarot, we are invited to consider *each card* in the Tarot as a benevolent friend bringing a basket of tea, a vessel of wild honey, some warm muffins, and a good book to our door.

   No matter how spiky the image on the cards may be, they all offer some useful medicine. Whether the medicine is sweet or bitter, it is helpful to assume that the cards we pull in a reading bring us something we need, even if we don't immediately know what that is.

With that said, we don't have to like or prefer all the cards in the Tarot. But it is our job to gently challenge ourselves to stay open, curious, and nonjudgmental around the cards that show up in readings for ourselves and those we are reading for. The more we do this, the more the reading or card pull will soften and expand for us, helping us to see new things about the card that we hadn't considered before. Despite its sunny and welcome reputation, The Empress card can occasionally be extremely challenging and activating for folks. The Tower can be a relief for others. If we tend to lean on judgment-based qualifiers in our readings, automatically assigning cards as "good" or "bad," we can inadvertently miss the mark in our interpretations.

This pillar of Soul Tarot invites us to consider befriending all the cards, which, in my experience, drastically enhances our skills as readers.

2. **The present moment is all there is, and the present moment is where Tarot shines most brightly.**

There is no fixed future. All we have is this moment. When we are truly willing to come home to that understanding, we will be able to lean on the Tarot as a humble tool that can help us be with what *is*, rather than one that swings us from the past to the future. This is part of why we root Soul Tarot in this moment, rather than what was, or what might come. *What is needed right here, right now?* What is asking for our attention? What seemingly small (and perhaps even pesky!) thing in our lives might actually be a catalyst for change, or a bridge to what we're longing for?

Rather than consistently focusing our questions on what might come to pass, or when the current moment might come to a close (both of which are valid questions, but ones that the Tarot may or may not be able to consistently answer), we might consider asking, *"What support can I call upon to help me to be present with whatever this moment is bringing me?"* or *"How can I respond when I find myself wanting to get out of the current moment?"*

There are absolutely folks who read Tarot in a more predictive, future-based method, some by way of a closed and/or inherited practice with the cards, which is beautiful. For the rest of us, however, this alternative way of considering the cards can help us be present with ourselves, no matter what might be arising.

3. **Each card that we pull is an *invitation* (not necessarily a decree or harbinger of what is to come).**

No card ever commands, demands, forces, points a terrifying finger, or offers a harsh, point-blank telling of how it's going to be. Never, ever.

Each card is an invitation, one that we are welcome to accept or reject, one that we have agency around working with. This is a subtle but powerful shift in perspective. The pressure for Tarot readers to be psychic and tell the future is enormous, *and not all Tarot readers are psychic, nor do they need to be.* Sometimes Tarot readers can cave to that pressure without even realizing it, feeling like they need to know everything, or have all the right answers for their client or friend. It is not to say that Tarot cards or Tarot readings cannot be predictive or cannot give you a sense (sometimes a very clear sense) of the overall cycles of time and the seasons to come. Even if we do get a sense of what's to come, the thing we focus on in Soul Tarot is *how you are being invited to work with that information.* What support can you call upon to be with you now, and as you go through it? How might this upcoming season *feel* to you? We could pull The Tower card and then pull The Sun for how it might feel to move through our Tower experience. Those details matter enormously and require that we as Tarot readers expand our awareness and flexibility around what the cards are capable of being.

If our client or querent's nervous system is activated (in other words, if they are anxious and afraid of what might be coming around the bend), *they will not retain a word we have said.* If we are seeking to offer a trauma-informed, heart-led Tarot reading (the bare minimum for a Tarot reading, in my opinion), we must provide context, clarity, and bolstering around our Tarot pulls—not just what the client has pulled, but how to work with it, what support might be useful in doing so, and where we might place our attention when doing so. When we consider the Tarot as an invitation—rather than something that is fixed, static, or predestined—we place the power, autonomy, sovereignty, and dignity back into our own hands or the hands of the folks we read for, and take unnecessary pressure off our plates as readers.

4. **We're allowed to be messy when we go to our Tarot decks.**

   In Soul Tarot, we really emphasize that we're allowed to be upset, jealous, anxious, and/or "messy" when we go to our Tarot decks.

   The importance placed on cleansing oneself before reading Tarot is a holdover from organized religion, insisting on purity to have an audience with God or the Divine. I would like to humbly remind you that a relationship with Source, Spirit, God, Divine, your higher self, spaghetti monster, etc., is your *birthright*, should you choose to work with energies like these. You don't need to push or clear away your humanness to sit with the numinous. In fact, in my experience, Spirit welcomes us at our dirtiest, most raw, most broken, most confused, and most tender.

   If we are reading for other people, then this is a little different. If we're in the depths to the point where we can't really function, then of course we should reschedule with our client and tend to ourselves. But as querents or clients, or in moments when we're reading for ourselves, we should be able to bring it all to the table. The process and practice of Soul Tarot invites us to show up to our decks with whatever we've got going on and then engage with a Drop-In (more on that in part 3) to help create a gentle filter around what we'd most like to receive before we pull cards. But, honestly, showing up to our decks and saying, *"Spirit/cards, I'm really in it. I'm so angry, I'm so contracted, I hate everything, and I don't know what to do. What anchor can I work with in the deck to help me to come back home to myself right now? What am I needing most at this moment?"* is enough for us to receive a beautiful and solid reading. We are encouraged to start at the messy, broken place and let the cards nourish us from there, rather than trying to clean it all up before we ask for help.

5. **The Tarot is spiralic (and so are we).**

   As much as we might try to deny this, we are wholly and utterly cyclical, seasonal, flexible, ever-changing, spiralic beings. We encompass it all—the good, the abhorrent, the wistful, and the cynical; the robin's egg, the lilac bush, the mycelium, and Douglas fir in one very human package. This is just a mirror for life and everything in it, which is spiralic, too. Death and dying is a spiral. Aging is a spiral. Our growth and evolution through life is a spiral. Healing in all its forms is a spiral.

   If you've ever recovered from surgery, you likely understand this. You seem to be going in a "good" direction with your healing, then have a complication, or experience some hard days, then things get better, then possibly challenging again. Sometimes we get the gift of a smooth, easy, linear process in this life, but mostly, it is as described above. Tarot tends to align with this rhythm, too.

   I think this is important to name and acknowledge for a few reasons.

   One, we deserve to remember that we are spiral beings, living a spiral existence. Two, if we aren't willing to consider the fact that the Tarot is a spiral, it can inadvertently lead us to believe that we might have pulled the "wrong" Tarot card for ourselves, which can lead to doubt in ourselves and our skills. If you've ever had a client ask about a particular subject, and had the reading you pull for them be about something completely different from what they asked about, you will understand this. The Tarot reading we receive is the one that is meant for us.

   I'll offer an example of this.

Many years ago, I went to my deck for what felt like a very pressing question about my work. I dropped in, asked my Guides for clear guidance about how to proceed with a decision I needed to make, and got Queen of Pentacles.

Queen of Pentacles is an invitation to take sweet, tender care of ourselves and our bodies—to rest, nourish, hydrate, and allow ourselves to be held in whatever ways we're needing most. A lovely card, but not necessarily a clear answer to my question about work. I assumed that I might not have been clear enough with my question, so I popped Queen of Pentacles back into my deck, dropped in again, and pulled again. This time: Queen of Pentacles *reversed* (aka, "Helloooo, we are inviting you to tend to yourself and you're not listening . . .").

I felt frustrated. What the hell did this have to do with the question I was asking? And then I realized: It was 10 a.m., and I had only had coffee. I was hungry, dehydrated, wildly overcaffeinated, and in need of a few deep breaths (along with a shower). My Guides and my Tarot deck didn't give me the answer I asked for, but they did give me what I needed at the time, and took me on a spiral journey to get there. After tending to my body, I went back to my Tarot deck and asked the question for a third time, and actually got a resonant response.

Tarot is a spiral, just like you, me, and everything else in life. Understanding this can allow us to pause and reflect when we pull a Tarot card that doesn't immediately make sense to us. It's possible that it just might not make sense—that can happen. But it also might be pointing us to a need or longing that we didn't necessarily center in our question, which happens a lot with this work.

6. **No Tarot card requires an external element to exist.**

   There is no windfall card, no soulmate card, no disaster card, no harmony card. No Tarot card can be predictive of any one person's feeling state, either. I wish that The Sun card automatically brought happiness, or that Ten of Cups hand-delivered our deepest wishes to us.

I don't say this to burst anyone's bubble but to gently draw attention to the degree of shorthand assumptions that have been collectively placed on certain Tarot cards; if we aren't careful, this shallow, less complex way of considering the cards can become a Tarot reader's whole framework for reading. It might seem like a smart way to work with the cards, but it doesn't yield to consistently accurate readings over time.

We can also rest comfortably in the fact that if any Tarot card could consistently tell us when we will receive a windfall, or when we will meet our beloved, we would absolutely know by now. How do we consider another way? In Soul Tarot, we aim to respectfully divorce Tarot card meanings from external elements, so we can really connect the cards to a much softer, more consistent invitation to focus inward. If The Lovers doesn't mean that we're going to meet our beloved (and it's not to say that it cannot indicate that; it just doesn't *automatically* indicate that), what might it mean to us then? It kicks off a whole journey of rewilding the Tarot for ourselves, redefining the cards and approaching them in a completely different way.

And while we are on the subject:

7. **Are we being inclusive or exclusive with our Tarot interpretations?**

   What do The Court Cards become once we remove the binary of age, gender, and hierarchy from them? What does The Hierophant become when we move away from the idea that it is about meeting an external teacher or guide, and consider it as a road back home to our own brilliant and deep intuitive knowing? How do you imagine that might empower someone who has survived a cult, or has experienced abuse at the hands of a spiritual teacher? How are we centering aromantic, asexual, and/or celibate folks when we talk about The Cups or The Lovers? How are we making space for chronically ill or disabled folks when talking about The Pentacles, which are rooted in the marriage between the body and our soul-led work in the world?

In Soul Tarot, we aim to be as inclusive as possible with our considerations of the Tarot, because a big part of the older paradigm and shorthand way of interpreting the cards is rooted in a great deal of exclusion, whether intentional or unintentional. One example is gender. There is no gender binary in the Tarot. None of the cards are linked to any kind of gender identity as a rule. The Empress is not an exclusively feminine card, nor is The Emperor an exclusively masculine card, regardless of how the figure on the card is visually presented.

If The Empress is an incredibly important card to you as a woman, nonbinary femme, mother, and/or parent, *that's beautiful and doesn't need to go away*. You get to keep and cherish that connection. However, it is crucial that you do not allow your own personal connection with the card to cloud how you work with it for your clients. Not everyone will have that particular connection with The Empress, nor will that kind of treatment of the card be appropriate for them to receive. When we remove these constructs from certain Tarot cards, what do we have left? *So much medicine*—a glowing center from which to work, which we will explore in this book.

8. **Everything in a Tarot practice is flexible and mutable. There truly are no rules.**

The last pillar is an invitation and a reminder that nothing is hard and fast here. Soul Tarot is, again, not an end-all, be-all practice. No method or framework for Tarot reading is. You will inevitably disagree with me, deviate away from this work, take what works and leave what doesn't, which is precisely what a healthy, seasoned Tarot practice is all about.

CHAPTER THREE

THE BONES OF THE TAROT

In part 2 of this book, we're going to explore the Tarot in a seasonal, spiralic way, deviating from some of the expected order and structure of the deck. This section is meant to offer folks a little bit of that structure before we go ahead and break from it.

In Soul Tarot, the Tarot is divided into three fundamental parts: **The Major Arcana, The Minor Arcana, and The Court Cards.**

THE MAJOR ARCANA: THE MACROCOSM

The Major Arcana consist of 22 cards that encompass the journey from The Fool to The World. These cards are *macrocosmic, big-picture energies that we cannot control or create ourselves*; the sun rising and setting, the tidal shifts of the ocean, the phases of the moon, the weather. Because we cannot create a Major Arcana energy (they come to us, not the other way around), the key to working with any of the Majors is *surrendering* to them, allowing them to assist us in evolving on our soul's path.

Working with The Majors does require a willingness to surrender, but it doesn't take away our agency. There are many ways to work with an ocean wave. We can surf the wave, duck under the wave, or leap up into the wave, letting the water sparkle over us. Sometimes we cannot get into the ocean at all or need to run as far as we can from the shoreline. We can expect that each of the Major Arcana cards will show up a little differently from one another and will variate from reading to reading.

We can further deepen into our understanding of the Major Arcana by leaning into Rachel Pollack's brilliant way of viewing them: *in three lines of seven, with The Fool on top of the three lines.*

The Fool lives on its own, away from the other Majors, because it is card zero: both of the world, and not of the world. It represents a big leap and invites us to lean into our courage and willingness to try something new. When the mind begs us to stay on familiar, seemingly safer ground, The Fool will be there, calling us to leave behind what no longer serves us and take the next bold, brave step into a new cycle. The Fool is the golden thread that links all the cards in the Major Arcana together, and when it shows up, it's a clear signal that we are ready to evolve into something new.

Line One of the Major Arcana: The Magician to The Chariot

Line One of the Major Arcana is the journey that takes us from The Magician to The Chariot, one that is kick-started by our leap into The Fool. *In Soul Tarot, we view this as the line of the caterpillar, a time of growing, building, and preparing.*

The cards in Line One are all about foundation and formation of core identity: who we are, how we align ourselves, and what we believe in. Regardless of our age, our work in Line One of the Major Arcana can be mapped back to our journey from birth to young adulthood. That time in our lives is crucial for learning, making mistakes, exploring, individuating, and blossoming into ourselves. We journey through the same themes when we work with the Tarot cards in this line.

Once we reach The Chariot, the last card in Line One of the Major Arcana, we usually begin to feel a little restless. Like a full-term baby, or a bird that is ready to hatch out of a too-tight egg, we've outgrown the container we are in but have no clue what lies on the other side. The Chariot marks the beginning of a deeper journey into the realm of the soul, and ushers us into Line Two of the Majors.

Line Two of the Major Arcana: Strength to Temperance

Line Two of the Major Arcana is the journey that takes us from Strength to Temperance, one that is initiated by our willingness to leave our Chariots behind in Line One. *In Soul Tarot, we view this as the line of the chrysalis, a time of deep processing and inner growth.*

Line Two is an underworld journey, one that invites us to surrender to the unknown and turn deeply inward. The cards in this line call upon us to befriend the things that frighten us with an undefended heart, shift our relationship to time, release egoic control, shed aspects of ourselves that we've outgrown, and open to a more collaborative ongoing relationship with Spirit and our soul.

Once we've moved into Temperance, the last card in Line Two of the Major Arcana, we have been profoundly shifted. We are freshly liberated from the chrysalis, waiting for our wings to dry in the sun. Now that we've gone through this process of transmutation, we are ready to move into an even deeper level of personal work. This is the beginning of our journey through Line Three of the Major Arcana.

Line Three of the Major Arcana: The Devil to The World

Line Three of the Major Arcana is a journey that takes us from The Devil to The World, one that is sparked by our willingness to say yes to our soul work in the Temperance card. *In Soul Tarot, we view this as the butterfly line, where we emerge transformed, and move from a creature that crawls to one that flies.*

Line Three is a journey of becoming, an initiation that assists us in cutting the chains of attachment to anything that separates us from our soul self. The cards in this line call upon us to say no thank you to the stories that keep us small and contracted, raze and rebuild the structures in our lives that aren't serving us, heal the wounds that we've carried, befriend the void, allow ourselves to truly be seen, and awaken to what is ready to be acknowledged in our lives.

After a wild and profoundly transformative journey, we finally greet The World—the last card in the Major Arcana. We have gone as far as we're meant to go in this iteration of our soul's journey. Now, The World is going to help us to simultaneously release and clear out this cycle of lessons, hard knocks, and awakenings we've experienced, and be birthed into a completely new paradigm on the wings of The Fool.

The spiral keeps turning, and we keep growing, shedding, and rebirthing again and again and again.

THE MINOR ARCANA: THE MICROCOSM

In Soul Tarot, the Minor Arcana represent the *microcosm*, the day-to-day lessons and invitations that help to support us through our big, messy, imperfect human experiences.

The Minors are where we learn to love and reparent ourselves, honor our rage, make space for our grief, pause and take responsibility when we have caused harm to ourselves and others. They invite us to choose ourselves, to make space for rest and pleasure without apology, to learn and grow, to fuck up and forgive ourselves, again and again. They are all tools in our hands that we're encouraged to learn to use through *experience*. The key to working with the Minors is to *collaborate* with them—to lean into whatever invitation they happen to be bringing us.

The Minor Arcana Suits: Wands, Cups, Swords, and Pentacles

The Wands are ruled by the element of Fire. In Soul Tarot, The Wands help us work respectfully and creatively with our current energetic capacity and the organic pace of our bodies. The Wands honor that, depending on the season, we might be a tealight, an ember, a bonfire, or any iteration in between. The awareness and distinction around the kind of fire that's running through us, or that we have access to right now, is crucially important. Rather than pushing, forcing, or attempting to control these parts of ourselves, The Wands help us keep things as tempered as possible during big births, creative processes, initiations of any kind, and/or deadlines. The Wands also help us learn how to work with our passions, big ideas, and artistic practices in right relationship with our current energetic reserves. They center, honor, and encourage us to unapologetically engage with rest, play, and magic as means of supporting our creative and intuitive processes.

The Cups are ruled by the element of Water. In Soul Tarot, The Cups guide and invite us to radically love ourselves and make space at the table for everything that might arise within our lived experience. We are encouraged to take our time in The Cups, to reparent ourselves and honor whatever process we might be moving through. We're also invited to get really vulnerable in The Cups, to be honest about what it is we're longing for, and open to the love that surrounds us. We want to take care to remember not to center our readings with The Cups around romantic relationships, as not everyone is romantically or sexually inclined, nor can The Cups cards predictably tell us when we might meet someone or venture into an intimate relationship of any kind. The Cups are really about our relationship with ourselves, which can then trickle out and inform the relationships we have with others.

The Swords are ruled by the element of Air. In Soul Tarot, The Swords suit invites us to witness (rather than believe) our mental stories, and engage with our communication, actions, and thoughts in radically new ways. We're also invited to get curious about what we might be needing in each of these cards—if we're really anxious or in our head about something, we want to consider the kind of balm, care, or support that might benefit us. Each card in The Swords suit is its own deep, spiralic journey into self-tending: The mind invites us into a story, we notice that story without identifying with it, and we give ourselves the care we need and deserve. We also want to make sure not to frame The Swords cards as frightening or otherwise negative. That is not their truth, nor is it a worthy honoring of the brilliant complexity they bring to a reading.

The Pentacles are ruled by the element of Earth. In Soul Tarot, The Pentacles suit invites us to bring our soul work more fully into this material world and calls us on a journey of reclaiming our resources, our bodies, our boundaries, our pleasure, our space, our devotion, and our attention. These cards can be inclusive of work, money, and finances (which is how they are often characterized), but this is definitely not the rule. We are truly gardeners when we work with The Pentacles suit: planting, sowing, harvesting, composting, and tending to a deep vision for our lives, careers, creations, and anything else these cards might show up around. We learn deep and important lessons in The Pentacles suit—how to navigate fallow times, how to savor the fruits of our labor, how to wait for things to ripen in their time, and how to work with aligned timing, to name a few.

THE COURT CARDS: THE WISE INNER TEACHERS

In Soul Tarot, we look to The Court Cards as the wise, soul-led teachers that live within us. They are our compasses (**The Pages**), currents (**The Knights**), coves (**The Queens**), and contributors (**The Kings**).

Rather than being representative of other people, we view The Court Cards in Soul Tarot as sacred reflections of our own brilliance, a part of ourselves reaching out to be reclaimed. It doesn't mean that these cards cannot be other people—that's just not where we start in this particular framework for Tarot.

In Soul Tarot, The Court Cards are not bound to or relegated by hierarchy, age, sex, or gender identity. The Kings, Queens, Knights, and Pages can be any age, can identify and express themselves flexibly, and are generally quite fluid. They are all of us and belong to all of us. While I believe that they work together and support one another, they each have different zones of genius, different roles to play inside of that collective process.

If you help or are of service in the world (or desire to be); if you rally, organize, disrupt, and amplify; if you teach, hold space, or walk between thresholds, The Courts are anchors and allies to you in your life's work, all coming together to support, guide, and nourish you on your path. We work best with these cards' energies when we *embody* them—imagining ourselves literally meshing with them, and allowing them to show us the way forward.

In Soul Tarot, **The Pages** are ruled by the element of Earth and are our *compasses*—our sacred foundations and root systems that tether us to our humility, purpose, and soul service. Each of these wise beings has moved through the journey from Ace to Ten, and each possesses a newfound sense of connection and intimacy with their respective elements. Whenever we feel ourselves removed from this root and need to come back home to ourselves, The Pages will point us back to true north.

In Soul Tarot, **The Knights** are ruled by the element of Air and are our *currents*. They represent four beautifully unique rhythms of medicinal movement, each inviting us to *feel* into our relationship with aligned timing, and the ways in which we take up space in the world. Whenever we are unsure about the unfolding of something, or of the ideal rhythm, speed, and pace of a particular season of our lives, The Knights will help us sense into that.

In Soul Tarot, **The Queens** are ruled by the element of Water and are our *coves*. These four cards represent our inner essence, and the energy, intention, and magic that emanate from us organically, without effort or explanation. Whenever we need to return to that deeply nourishing center within ourselves, to retreat and refuel, The Queens will be there to help us do so.

In Soul Tarot, **The Kings** are ruled by the element of Fire and are our *contributors*. They represent our aligned leadership, the way we show up and express our soul work in the world or to the community around us. The Kings are an outward expression of our intuitive knowing, of our rooted connection to our Queen, Knight, and Page. Whenever we are of service, guiding others, or being asked to help in some way, The Kings will show up to help us support ourselves in that process.

KEY TAKEAWAYS

- **The Major Arcana** = macrocosm. We work best with these cards' energies when we *surrender* to them, letting them guide us.
- **The Minor Arcana** = microcosm. We work best with these cards' energies when we *collaborate* with them, letting them show us where we might need to refine our actions, or make an internal or external adjustment.
- **The Court Cards** = wise teacher within/inner calling. We work best with these cards' energies when we *embody* them—imagining ourselves literally meshing with them and having them show us the way forward.

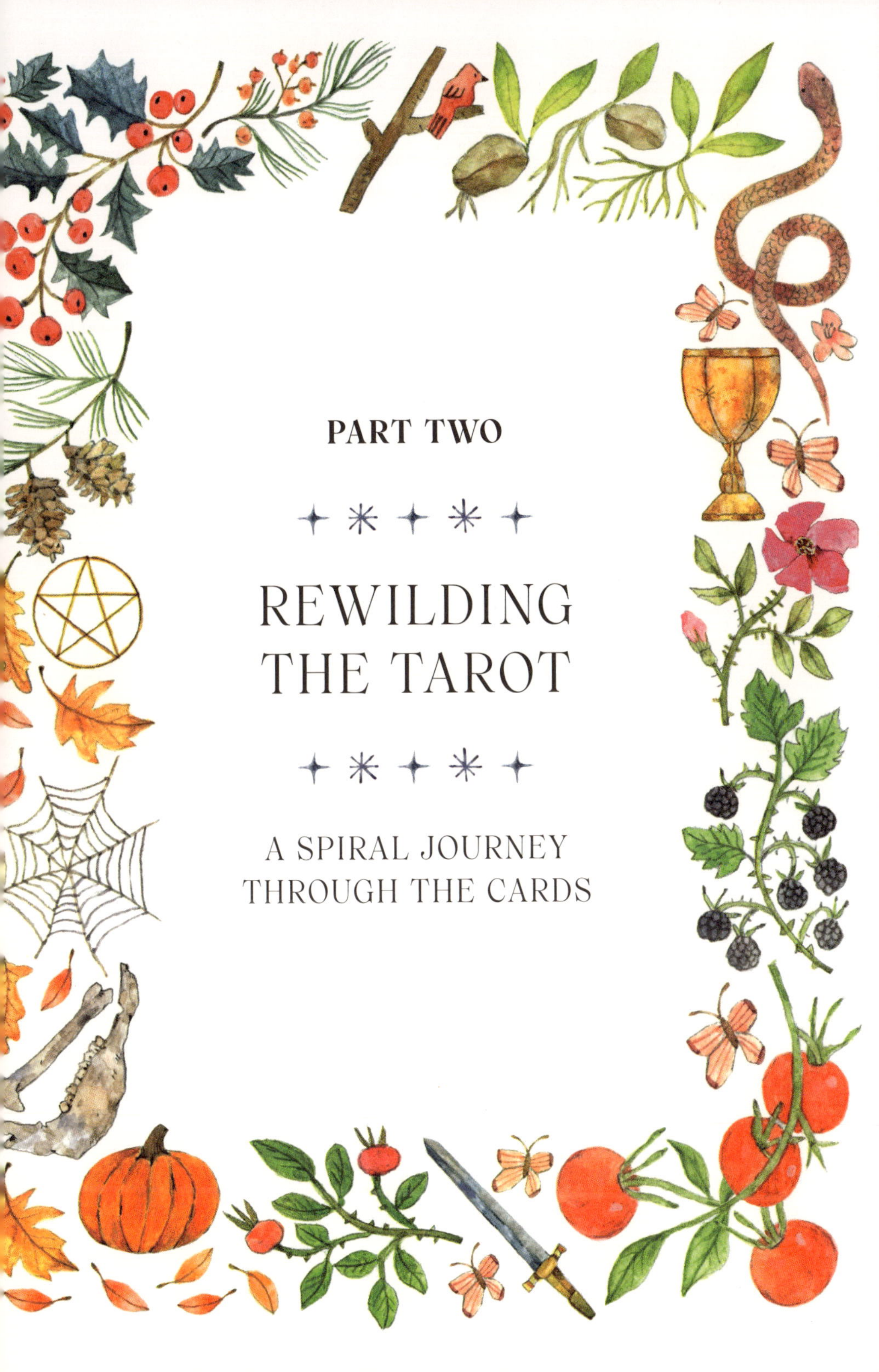

PART TWO

REWILDING THE TAROT

A SPIRAL JOURNEY THROUGH THE CARDS

The term *rewilding* refers to a form of ecological restoration in which the emphasis is on humans stepping back and returning an area to nature. It's a term that was first coined by Jesse Wolf Hardin and was later expanded on by conservation biologists Michael Soulé and Reed Noss.

Rewilding Europe, a Netherlands-based nonprofit organization dedicated to creating rewilded landscapes throughout Europe, describes rewilding as *"letting nature take care of itself, enabling natural processes to shape land and sea, repair damaged ecosystems and restore degraded landscapes. Nature knows best when it comes to survival and self-governance. We can give it a helping hand by creating the right conditions—by removing [dikes] and dams to free up rivers, by reducing active management of wildlife populations, by allowing natural forest regeneration, and by reintroducing species that have disappeared as a result of man's actions. Then we should step back and let nature manage itself."*

In part 2 of this book, we will be using the framework for rewilding as a guidepost in the gentle and lifelong process of untethering ourselves from old paradigms, interpretations, and definitions of the Tarot that can be regressive, patriarchal, exclusionary, capitalist, and altogether out of alignment.

In the ten years that I have had the privilege of teaching Tarot students professionally, I have come to believe with all my heart that each person already has their own unique, beautiful, brilliant relationships with all the cards, even if they are at the beginning of their journey with the Tarot. I believe that all the cards already belong to you. I do not believe that you need anyone to tell you what Tarot cards mean—teachers and books will always be available to us, but we can and will all find our way to that knowing in our own way, even with those guideposts. Even the students who really resonate with Soul Tarot as a framework eventually shed that skin and come into their own meanings and relationships with the cards, which is ideal and delightful.

What I *do* think many of us desperately crave is a framework that gives us permission to think beyond the collective assumptions and traditional perceptions that have been placed on the Tarot. This is, in essence, the "helping hand" that the folks at Rewilding Europe speak about. It is the removal of blocks and dams that enables our own wild and glorious knowing to begin to flourish, applied to our Tarot practice.

When we rewild our Tarot practice, which is work that takes place over our lifetime, we make space for our own brilliant and beautifully unique ways of approaching, understanding, and befriending the cards. This section of the book is a gentle invitation to begin sensing into some different ways of reclaiming that knowing.

In the following 10 chapters, we will explore the Tarot through a more spiralic, seasonal framework, deviating slightly from the traditional order of the Tarot. This is both to help us rewild and reframe our relationships with the cards, and to allow us to consider *living* our relationship with them. After all, we are profoundly cyclical beings. Shouldn't the Tarot be able to assist, support, and bear witness to us within those seasons?

Two final notes, before we dive in:

1. If you are seeking more support around how to pull cards, read for yourself, and generally begin to put some of these frameworks into practice, you will find guidance on this in part 3 of this book.
2. I also want to remind you that you can engage with this book in any way that feels most supportive to you. Feel free to read everything in order, or jump around, or use it as a guidebook of sorts, where you touch in with the card interpretation you need in the moment that you need it. If you'd prefer a more organized layout of how to find the card meanings in this book, refer to the index at the back of the book for the specific page numbers that correspond to each Tarot card.

Let us light the lantern and begin the journey.

CHAPTER FOUR

WHEN YOU'RE A SEED

Tarot Cards for New Beginnings

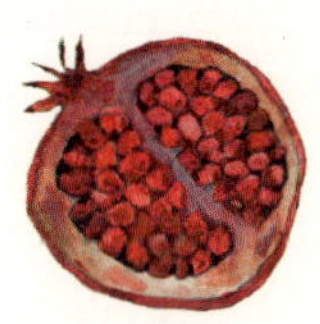

THE FOOL

THE MAGICIAN

PAGE OF WANDS

THE ACES

THE FOOL

THE MAGICIAN

PAGE OF WANDS

ACE OF WANDS

ACE OF CUPS

ACE OF SWORDS

ACE OF PENTACLES

How does one begin something great and new? To show up to the chair, the easel, the patch of bare dirt, or the blank page is formidable and often terrifying. There have been books, movies, musicals, and poems written on this holy, messy subject since time immemorial: How do we create the things that are in our heart to bring forth? And once we've arrived at doing so, how do we keep showing up?

When we feel like a seed—like something full of potential but not yet in form—we might consider calling upon or working with the Tarot cards we will be exploring in this chapter, namely: **The Fool, The Magician, Page of Wands,** and **The Aces.**

Each of these cards holds a powerful portal of medicine for us around this humbling potent invitation, should we choose to accept it: to break out of our comfort zone, show up to the project or act of creation that's been keeping us up at night, and, by extension, show up to ourselves in the process.

BLOSSOMING IN GROUNDLESSNESS WITH THE FOOL

The Fool is Card Zero in the Major Arcana. It is the radicle, the first part of a seedling, emerging in the first phases of germination. It is both here and not here, seamlessly and gracefully traveling through this world with one foot in this realm and another behind the veil. The Fool card is, for all intents and purposes, the representative for the soul in the Tarot. This is the journey we embark on as we travel through the Majors, commune with the Minors, and open to The Court Cards. With each breath, each step, we move side by side with The Fool.

When we've stayed too long in one Tarot energy, The Fool is the golden cord that tugs at our heart, letting us know that it's time to keep moving, keep growing through the experience that we are in. It calls upon us to eschew what is comfortable and familiar for the sake of appearances or perceived safety. It invites us to say yes to the whisper of the soul that lives within us, despite our frustrated, exasperated, repeated attempts to stuff it into oblivion, or at least submission. The Fool is like a beach ball that we try to shove under the water, but it bubbles up and pops us on the nose. There is no quieting it, no getting rid of it—and thank goodness for that.

The Fool card is often spoken of as a fresh start, a new cycle, one that is ripe and rife with many blessings. When we receive this card, we are invited to leap into this new chapter and take a chance on something novel, even if it feels scary. All of this *can* be true about The Fool card; it's just not always true.

It is absolutely the case that The Fool often brings a sense of newfound energy into our lives, and shows up when there is an act of commitment to be made in some significant way, even if it's an internal process rather than an external one. But the idea of a big, momentous leap often requires access to resources, financial or otherwise, or privileges that not everyone is afforded either in their life or in a particular season of their life.

In truth, working with The Fool is much more about our willingness to be the seed that is available to crack open, to blossom in groundlessness, and to die back over and over again. In the majority of situations, The Fool card is less of a big, momentous wave than it is a quiet, moment-to-moment experience.

Working with The Fool in a moment-to-moment way reminds us clearly that there are no guarantees in this life. None of us know when we will die. We don't know if the person we love will ever love us back. We don't know if the thing we toiled to create will ever be liked, engaged with, or consumed by even one single person. When meditating on this, it initially might seem like it's the safer choice *not* to leap—to never love, never be vulnerable to losses, never create anything that could be rejected—but in truth, a soul-led life begins when we are willing to do the brave thing.

The Fool can't really leap, because there is no ground under them to begin with. The ground is the illusion of safety that the ego provides. Leaving it is the real work we do in The Fool. It is the initiation of a soul-led life. This card knows that we aren't getting out of this alive, so why not try? Why not say a courageous and loving yes to ourselves? Why not give that thing that we've been dreaming about a real shot, to the extent that we're able? Even if we fall flat on our face, it will still inform our overall experience. It will still build character and foster wisdom. It calls upon us to be the seed that is willing to be blown away from the tree in the hopes of blossoming into something beautiful. It is a rebirth, the start of a new life.

When The Fool shows up in a reading for us, it's a signal that a new cycle is beginning in our lives, and it is partially initiated by our willingness to say a courageous, deep, and meaningful yes to it. How can we be brave enough to allow ourselves to crack open, to evolve in the direction that our heart is longing to go?

The Fool Reversed

When The Fool shows up reversed, it's not necessarily indicating that we shouldn't leap, evolve, grow, or try out that new thing. It's letting us know that, most likely, some part of us is feeling really worried and/or scared about this leap, or moment of soul-led groundlessness. With The Fool card, there is normal, expected contraction, and there is *fear*—terror and true dissonance in which the nervous system really needs a parachute in order to say yes to what's being asked. In this case, part of our work with The Fool is to sit next to that scared part of ourselves at the edge of the proverbial cliff and tend to it. What is that part needing from us, or our support systems? What are they feeling most scared about? How can we help?

BEING THE VESSEL WITH THE MAGICIAN

The Magician is, in many ways, a natural extension of everything that The Fool brings to our door. The Fool card is the seed, the soul. It is pure essence without full form, the willingness to say yes and try something new. The Magician is the seedling, the creative, collaborative process that enables that growth to be made manifest. It is the willingness to embody and express the ephemeral in earthly form.

The Magician is here to help us learn not only how to be a vessel for creation, to open to the magic, medicine, and inspiration that lives within each of us, but also to have the courage to bring it into form. We don't have to channel down the next great novel or tap into the secrets of the universe. We can start our work and relationship with this card from a much more tangible place.

When we commit ourselves to being a vessel for creation, we are stating that we are available to receive brilliance, new ideas, and artistic impulses from whatever numinous place they happen to originate. It is the beginning, or the deepening, of our willingness to be a channel for the muses, inviting imagination to move through us. Acting upon the inclination to create, write, paint, sing, compose, speak, or express the thing that's knocking at the door to our soul is what The Magician is here to help us work on. The essence of this card can be found in the last lines of "Finishing the Hat," from Stephen Sondheim's *Sunday in the Park with George*:

> Look, I made a hat
> Where there never was a hat

The Magician invites us to create, allowing inspiration to flow through us and be expressed into earthly form. This card isn't interested in perfection when it comes to the creative process. We are allowed and encouraged to play, try new things, expand out in new ways, and share it with no one, or everyone. The Magician decenters the value of gaining something from what we've shared, and focuses our attention on just making what our heart is longing to make manifest.

How can we do this?

Greater and more experienced writers and artists have written better words than I ever will be able to on this subject. *The War of Art* by Steven Pressfield, *Bird by Bird* by Anne Lamott, *Big Magic* by Elizabeth Gilbert, and of course *The Artist's Way* by Julia Cameron are all great places to begin. Each of these brilliant authors invites us to show up to the proverbial page—even when we seemingly have nothing of interest or significance to say—and watch as something much more magical and unexpected gradually begins to unfold.

When we show up to the "page," we show up for ourselves. We show up for our soul, our inner artist, our inner creator. This is much of what The Magician card helps us to touch into. Connecting and working with The Magician card is an opportunity to remember that we are vessels for imagination, innovation, and inspiration just by virtue of our existence. We don't need to be chosen, selected, given an award or approval. We are already card-carrying members of the club.

For a plant to flourish, it needs sun, dirt, water, space, air. Our creative selves need much of the same things. To be witnessed, warmed to; a space for us to build our strengths and expand our root systems; to be watered and nourished; to have the freedom to try, to fail, to succeed, to try again; to have the gift of spaciousness: of time to do nothing, to reflect. When we allow ourselves to meet those conditions for our creative selves, we will thrive. We simply need to give ourselves the permission to express what lives within us when it taps us on the shoulder to get our attention.

When The Magician shows up in our readings, we're being invited to create and express with abandon. If we are a sweet seedling, what is needed at this moment to help us continue growing? What gives us light? What waters and feeds us? What helps us strengthen our roots and feel more tethered in the world? With this card, we're not creating for accolades or approval. We're creating to move and channel out some of the energy that's living within us. This card gently reminds us that we never have to show anyone what we've made, and we don't have to be amazing. Let the painting, the writing, or the song be shitty. It's not your job to judge it—your only job is to express it.

The Magician Reversed

When perfectionism, resistance, or limiting stories rear their heads, The Magician encourages us to show up and allow ourselves to be deeply and unimpeachably imperfect. Write for 20 full minutes about how you suck at writing. Slap paint onto a canvas and let it be messy. Sing like shit. Even if it's terrible (which is not something we will ever be able to judge accurately for ourselves anyway), you will still be writing, painting, and singing. Sometimes when The Magician shows up reversed in a reading, it can feel like we are blocked or stuck. Often, just giving ourselves permission to move things around or try something new can help to move the needle. If it doesn't, please feel free to give yourself the grace of time and space. We can always try again tomorrow.

TUNING IN AT THE CROSSROADS WITH PAGE OF WANDS

When Page of Wands shows up in a reading, it's usually an invitation to pause and check in before we decide to engage or participate in something. Is the matter at hand a yes or a no in our bodies? Can we leave a space, or a pause to reflect on all aspects of the crossroads before we commit in one way or another?

Some of us might be acquainted with the process and practice of tuning in with ourselves before we commit to something. For most of us, however, this might seem somewhat out of reach for many good reasons.

Many folks do not have the luxury of choice and need to do what's necessary for themselves or their families, whether they want to or not. Some of us (especially those of us who have experienced abuse and/or gaslighting) struggle to trust our bodies and lean into our agency. Some of us might feel so pressured to say yes to something, or so worried about saying no, that we talk ourselves into something we don't really want (or talk ourselves out of something we really *do* want). To everyone who identifies with one or more of these descriptions, I bow to you in empathy, witness, and solidarity. Page of Wands isn't an invitation to bypass any of these experiences, or somehow magically heal these wounded places. Working with this card, however, can be an incredibly soft and gentle way to begin to wade into the waters of this kind of check-in.

Page of Wands usually shows up in moments when there actually *is* some kind of agency available to us, whether it seems that way or not. The point of working with this card is not to necessarily always get perfect clarity on our next steps, but to gain some awareness and practical knowledge of what wisdom our bodies offer, and how they communicate that wisdom to us. In that way, Page of Wands can be a beautifully subtle and humble helper in reclaiming our intuitive knowing and bodily autonomy. Not because the card itself holds any kind of special powers, but because of the potency of its invitation. Checking in with ourselves is something that builds over time. The more we do it, the clearer and stronger those responses become, and the more attuned we begin to be.

Page of Wands is a very important energy to work with during big seed or gestation seasons. It's such a tender and unique time, one when it can feel like nothing is happening even though so much is occurring under the surface. It is during these seasons that we run the risk of inadvertently overloading ourselves, or of planting additional things on top of the bulbs and seeds that are currently in the process of sprouting under the earth. Page of Wands can help us slowly get more clarity at the crossroads, begin to trust more deeply in our knowing, and foster more connections with ourselves.

Page of Wands Reversed

Are we rushing forward without checking in? Piling too much on our plate? Page of Wands reversed wants us to tune in to that and inquire as to whether there's anything we can do to change it. We're always allowed to change our minds, even if it might disappoint another person. It's also never too late to check in with ourselves and try to get further clarity on a situation. This card showing up reversed is a strong call to do just that.

THE SPARK AND THE SEED WITH THE ACES

The Aces are the ignition, the spark that kicks off our journey into the Minor Arcana, which in and of itself is a beautiful and sacred landscape of lessons and opportunities for growth.

One of the most common misconceptions about The Aces that I see as a Tarot teacher and practitioner is the belief that they automatically indicate expansion and forward momentum or are a signal of a new pathway opening up for us. It's not that that cannot be true about The Aces; it's just not automatically true.

The Aces are seeds—the promise of some great adventure, a huge *yes* that sets a whole new cycle into motion. They are whispered dreams and hopes, nudges from the soul, intentions of the heart. Where do these seeds come from? Where do our great ideas and deep longings come from? What is the source of our inspiration, of that pull and nudge we get when we know we're being invited to expand in some way?

I believe for myself that there's some sense of Spirit, of God, of ineffable knowing and belonging at play with those seeds, those nudges. I also believe that we have access to incredibly deep wisdom in our own being, and that makes up an important part of those seeds, too. When that deep knowing within ourselves gets woven together with that deeper call from Spirit, an Ace usually appears.

The Aces are not, explicitly, harbingers of concrete, tangible events. They are not a guarantee that we're getting all we want, or that everything we are dreaming of is being handed to us on a platter. They bring New Moon–like energy to the spiral of the Tarot, offering us a gentle opening into the garden of movement and growth. They are, in short, the lighthouses that blink back from the ocean, letting us know that the time is ripe for some kind of new evolution within ourselves, that the cosmic winds are favorable for a new beginning.

This is a huge part of what The Fool and The Magician bring, too. Each of these cards help us in times when we are seeds, full of potential, eternally evolving, ready to be transformed, cracked open, and carried into the next season of our lives.

Ace of Wands: A Seed of Collaborative Creation

The Wands are all about passion, creativity, and movement. They are the champions we want and need in our corner when embarking on anything that feels really meaningful and potentially exciting. The Wands can run hot. They want to move fast and have fun while they do it. The real, deep soul-level work we do with The Wands is rooted in our willingness to wisely and respectfully work with this fire from a grounded place.

Ace of Wands is the spark that lights up a whole new cycle of exploration around these themes, the kick that calls us into a period of new and deliciously fiery growth.

When we receive Ace of Wands in a reading, it is an invitation to check in with our inner flame, and the fuel that we currently have in the vessel of our being for this embarkation. Is our gas tank full, empty, or somewhere in between? Are we a candle stub, barely flickering, burned-out, with nothing to give? Are we a blazing bonfire, burning unchecked? We will need that information in order to know how to work with the cycle of creation at hand.

It takes a tremendous amount of energy to channel creation through us. We can approach this process of inspiration and movement in right relationship with ourselves and our bodies when we consider Ace of Wands. Creating with a full tank of fuel is very different from doing so with an empty one. How might we rethink the ways that we embark on a project, collaboration, or dream with the full breadth of that information?

No matter the circumstances that this card shows up in—whether we have a ton of deeply thrilling and externally occurring circumstances that align fully with Ace of Wands' spirit, or are moving through a much more internal, subtle season—that inner check-in is really what this card wants us to focus on.

Ace of Wands is here to help us honor the body, the vessel, that assists us in bringing all these incredibly exciting and inspiring ideas into earthly form. It doesn't want us to go forward into a new venture without bringing our whole selves along for the ride.

Ace of Wands Reversed

Are we pouring from an empty cup? Are we in need of a refueling? Would it be wise to pause and check in about whether something is truly a yes to pursue before proceeding? These are the things that Ace of Wands reversed wants us to verify before we go further into something.

Ace of Cups: A Seed of Self-Love

As a general rule (at least as far as Soul Tarot goes), The Cups suit is not about romantic love or partnership. This is not because I have some big personal case to make. It's simply because, by virtue of automatically assigning The Cups to relationships, romantic love, and/or partnership, we inadvertently put enormous pressure on ourselves as readers to force The Cups into a really limiting categorization, while simultaneously cutting ourselves off from the radiant wellspring of what this suit can bring to our readings. As a gentle reminder: No Tarot card can reliably and consistently tell us when we might meet, connect with, or partner with another person.

What The Cups *do* predictably and reliably bring to our readings is a deep invitation to love ourselves as unconditionally as we possibly can.

When we receive Ace of Cups in a reading, we are being called to plant the seed of a newfound relationship with ourselves, one rooted in respect, compassion, and tenderness. It is a hand on our shoulder, a warm, consenting embrace. It is us turning toward ourselves and saying, *"Dear self, I see you. This is so hard. You're trying so hard. I'm in this with you. I am willing to try to love you as best as I can."*

This card isn't a trumpets-blasting, flowers-blooming kind of experience. We don't have to feel all the feelings or have a rush of euphoric love flow toward ourselves right out of the gate. That's rather unrealistic, and not something we should feel we need to aim for. It is only the first step of many, the sowing of an intention in the soil of our own being.

Ace of Cups is, ultimately, a reparenting. It is the first step of many in the journey of beginning to know ourselves better, and to love ourselves more authentically and completely.

We might begin our relationship with Ace of Cups by sensing into some very simple, baseline questions. Have I eaten enough today? How is my hydration? How is my sleep? What am I needing most at this moment? Sleep, time with friends, a good cry, laughter, or all of the above?

We might zoom out further. Am I treating myself and my body with as much respect and care as is afforded to me? Are there any different choices that I can make for my own well-being, even if they might disappoint someone close to me? Do I truly know how to care for myself? Do I feel safe enough to offer myself a break? What does self-love mean to me personally? What are the systems around me? Do they support me? Do they tend to be more helpful or harmful? Can I be gentle with myself around those realizations?

Ace of Cups isn't a command. We don't ever have to plant the seeds that pour forth from our soul and show up in our hands. We never have to ask these questions. But if we are willing to try, the result of doing so is nothing short of transformative. What would we create, birth into being, or bring to this world if we were willing to stand side by side with ourselves as ally, witness, and—dare I say—friend? How might it change the way we honor our changing, spiral bodies? How might it shift the way we parent, or have a relationship with our children, partners, and beloveds?

Ace of Cups Reversed

Many of us feel that we don't truly know how to love ourselves, or what that means. If you don't feel sure of what you need, or how to offer more unconditional regard to yourself in certain seasons of your life, please know that you are not alone. One beautiful way to show up to ourselves even when we don't know what to do, say, or offer is to simply acknowledge that truth without shame. *"Dear heart, I don't quite know what to do for you. I don't know what you truly need or are asking for. I'm not sure what to do, but I'm here. I won't leave. I'm willing to learn how to love you in a way that will feel truly nourishing for you."*

Ace of Swords: A Seed of Self-Trust

In Soul Tarot, we look to The Swords suit as a deep invitation to befriend and understand the thinking mind, which I understand might be a tall order for some folks to consider. There are numerous beliefs and assumptions about The Swords that loom large for many folks who use the Tarot—namely that The Swords are or seem scary due to their imagery, or they bring or foretell anything from betrayal to loss to death, depending on who is working with the cards, or they are somehow bad and unwelcome.

The Swords cards don't actually bring experiences of betrayal, heartbreak, backstabbing, or nightmares into our lives. They invite us to get curious about our inner stories or beliefs, and gently encourage us to investigate our thinking. Thoughts are not necessarily true, and our feelings, while valid, are not necessarily facts. The scary imagery that is sometimes present in The Swords cards doesn't necessarily yield to scary outcomes or situations. The imagery is a mirror of some of our worst-case-scenario thinking. In Soul Tarot, we go beyond the initial impact of the imagery of the card and center our energy on tending and curiosity: What pain points and beliefs lie under this Sword card, and what do we need in order to greet those experiences with care? When we do this, we not only diffuse some of the contractive charge that shows up around The Swords, but we also give our heart and nervous system necessary care from a spiritual perspective.

When we receive Ace of Swords in a reading, it is a beautiful invitation to simultaneously honor our own brilliance and inspiration *and* remember that we don't have to go about our work alone. We can trust in ourselves and our vision *and* we can ask for support around it. We can do what we can *and* hire help, if need be. We can drop into our own knowing *and* put out a call for guidance. We can trust in ourselves and other people to support the ideas we have. We don't need to isolate, and we don't need to try to muscle through it by ourselves. Creation is never accomplished in a complete vacuum, and Ace of Swords reminds us of this crucial truth.

Both of these notions—that we can trust in ourselves and that it's safe to call upon support—are two of the main topics that The Swords suit is most committed to helping us to explore.

When we work with Ace of Swords, we are not just being called to lean into our Air-element gifts—to communicate, express, write, sing, and connect—but to trust that we are worthy of bringing them forward. It's all too easy to inadvertently get in our own way, to tell ourselves that we don't know enough, that we aren't good enough to put our ideas out there or go for a dream. Ace of Swords calls upon us to screw our courage to the sticking place and try, ideally with support systems around us to help to execute our vision.

Ace of Swords Reversed

Say we want to open a restaurant. We might have beautiful dreams of creating amazing dishes, serving our customers, and perhaps even garnering some praise for our work. But do we know the first thing about opening a restaurant? Do we have a location? Do we have investors, good staff, crucial work experience so we have a sense of what we're getting into? If we answered no to any of these, we might receive Ace of Swords reversed in a reading. Getting this card reversed isn't saying that our dreams aren't viable, just that we might not have enough details, information, and support around us as we embark. Be willing to go back to the drawing board and ensure that you have what you need to execute your vision.

Ace of Pentacles: A Seed of Dreams

The Pentacles help us tend to our earthly bodies while creating and birthing something that feels very meaningful to us. They help us learn the fine and imperfect art of channeling down our soul-led visions into this material, corporeal realm. The Pentacles live in the space that holds both the dream and the paperwork necessary to get it going. This suit is not necessarily about money—in fact, I find that with most of my readings, The Pentacles cards have nothing to do with finances. They have to do with a sense of calling or purpose, and the desire to build something and leave a legacy behind.

Receiving Ace of Pentacles in a reading can be a very vulnerable experience. This card is so deeply rooted in our hopes, dreams, and visions for something great to blossom from something small and humble. Admitting that to ourselves can bring up tender feelings, so it's important to honor that if it shows up in a reading.

The Pentacles gently and persistently remind us that patience will be required for our journey. It can be hard to remember that when we're dreaming about luscious, fragrant, wild gardens and mature fruit trees with a humble seed in our hand. The truth is that Ace of Pentacles is an intention that will require a lot of work, diligence, and commitment. We may make mistakes. We might experience disappointment. We might not ever get what we want. We might veer off the path, or lose hope from time to time. No matter what happens, it is hugely important and valuable that we still plant the seed and give it our all—to understand how it feels to start from scratch.

Ace of Pentacles Reversed

One really important element when working with Ace of Pentacles reversed (and The Fool and The Magician, both right side up and reversed as well, for that matter) is a willingness to collaborate more fully with aligned timing, to surrender to the fact that what we are building is part of something much larger than just our desires. Everything in my life that I have longed for the most and essentially built from scratch (having a baby, forming a business, writing a book, to name a few) came about after years of failure, disappointments, ruptures, and inevitably a belief that what I wanted just wasn't meant for me. Time is a spiral, and sometimes the seeds we plant don't immediately grow, through no fault of our own. It doesn't mean that they cannot or won't eventually grow. Sometimes they grow with additional help, support, or information to guide them along. Ask for what you need, and be gentle with yourself and your heart as you traverse this process.

CHAPTER FIVE

THE MOON WITHIN

Tarot Cards for Intuitive Reclamation

THE HIGH PRIESTESS

THE EMPRESS

THE EMPEROR

THE HIEROPHANT

QUEEN OF WANDS

KNIGHT OF SWORDS

THE TWOS

THE HIGH PRIESTESS

THE EMPRESS

THE EMPEROR

THE HIEROPHANT

QUEEN OF WANDS

KNIGHT OF SWORDS

TWO OF WANDS

TWO OF CUPS

TWO OF SWORDS

TWO OF PENTACLES

In case no one has told you, you are already intuitive. You will always have your own deep, inexorable connection with your inner voice, the channel and cord that tethers and binds you to all things otherworldly.

No one can give you this because you've never been separate from it. There is no certification course, no title, no training, no act of bestowing that can grant you access to what you have a birthright to. Other folks can help us along the way in our lifelong process of reclaiming and trusting this part of ourselves, but they cannot give us a key to unlock the door.

Your intuition—and everything that flows to you from that wellspring—*knows* you. It chooses you, loves you, and witnesses you.

Reclaiming our intuition is a bit like a rewilding process. When we are born, the ecosystem of our intuition is perfectly harmonious and thoroughly wild. And essentially from the day of our birth, most of us are inundated with invitations—however subtle and well-intentioned they might be—to deny our knowing, go against our body's wisdom, push away our feelings, and swallow our truths in place of peacekeeping.

Reclaiming and rewilding our intuition doesn't mean that we must add a lot back into our inner landscape. We don't need a ton of bells and whistles. All we need to do is remove things that are of active detriment to the growth and flourishing of this inner garden, and our intuition will begin to thrive again.

When we want to reclaim our intuition, to call upon and work with the cyclical ocean within each of us, we will inevitably come face to face with the Tarot cards that we will be exploring in this chapter: **The High Priestess, The Empress, The Emperor, The Hierophant, Queen of Wands, Knight of Swords,** and **The Twos.**

INTUITIVE HOMECOMING WITH THE HIGH PRIESTESS

The High Priestess forms the foundation for the lifelong work of intuitive reclamation. This card wants us to understand that we're intuitive by virtue of simply being alive and helps us to know that intuition is allowed to look, feel, and show up in beautifully bespoke ways. We are all intuitive, and intuition is meant to shine through each of us in unique capacities.

This card, despite its reputation, isn't some out-of-reach figure we must journey to find, or a level of infinite wisdom to attain. The High Priestess is as present and within reach as salt, stone, and soil. They can be fabulous and colorful, or deeply subtle, almost invisible. As Mary Oliver wisely expressed in her poem "Praying," meaning can be found in something as simple or seemingly mundane as a weed or small stone.

Intuition doesn't have to be fancy or out of reach, and The High Priestess can be a reminder of that.

It can be helpful to associate The High Priestess (and by extension, our intuition) with the ocean and the Moon because, like The High Priestess, both change wildly through the days and months, but their essence always remains steady and present. The Moon waxes and wanes, ebbs and flows, cycles through phases and astrological signs. There might be times when we cannot see the Moon, but we know it's there. The same is true with our intuition.

The first step to working with The High Priestess is to go into the proverbial cave and deeply sense into your own lunar, psychic landscape: What intuitive inner phase do you feel that you're transiting through right now?

We can and often do experience "winters" with our intuition, times when it doesn't feel like we can perceive anything, or times when we don't want to perceive. We can also experience "summers" with our intuition: wildly creative periods when it can feel like we're practically running to the page, to the canvas, or to a quiet place to channel down whatever it is that's flowing through us before it goes back to the ether. Intuition can drive us to take strong, immediate action, and it can call us into stillness and surrender. Holding a space for the spectrum of what intuition can be is a core aspect of intuitive rewilding.

Intuition is very, very spiralic. It is consistent and steadfast, yet simultaneously ever-changing. It never leaves us and is always available to us, but it isn't necessarily going to present the same way every time we experience it. Receiving intuitive guidance during an emergency, or while we're in the hospital, or when we're in any other unique circumstance, likely won't be the same as a moment when we're at ease and in familiar surroundings. Understanding this can help us make peace with both our intuition and The High Priestess.

When The High Priestess card shows up in a reading, it invites us to remember that we have access to the deep wellspring of wisdom within us (despite how it might often feel), and a warm, loving, spacious coterie of Spirit Helpers who have our back no matter what. Even if we cannot feel or perceive them, they are always with us.

What helps you to feel connected with yourself in this way? What practices help quiet your mind and turn the volume up on your inner voice, the Moon within you?

The High Priestess Reversed

Sometimes when The High Priestess shows up reversed, it can be a gentle nudge to give ourselves a little break around trying to tune in for an answer, especially when it feels like we're straining to receive one. Clarity isn't always available to us for a myriad of reasons, and I have seen it be very helpful to take a break when we hit this kind of wall—go read a book, go out to dinner, etc. Giving ourselves that space is often the very thing we need to come to that desired place of connection with our intuition.

RADICAL RECEIVING WITH THE EMPRESS

If The High Priestess kicks off the journey of our intuitive reclamation, The Empress helps us know that we're worthy of receiving the information that our intuition offers.

The Empress's job is to help us expand our threshold of receiving. It lives in the olfactory song of a wild rose bush; in a gloriously crisp fall day; in the sweet, blood-colored juice of a fresh pomegranate; in the glide of the cool waves of the ocean on our warm bodies; in the drip of honey from the comb.

All of these delicious things exist, and we are worthy of receiving them, drinking from them, seeing ourselves in their beauty. If we feel unworthy of this, uncomfortable with receiving and supping from the pleasures of life, we will be greeted by The Empress.

This card gently (but persistently) helps expand our threshold and capacity for receiving. It zeroes in on where we tend to turn away from or deny desired help, support, kind words, beauty, and pleasure in all its forms. It is here to help us honor and acknowledge the wounds of unworthiness that so many of us have for so many different reasons, in the pursuit of healing and radically shifting those patterns.

Despite its reputation as a beneficial and beautiful card, The Empress can feel pretty challenging to work with for many of us.

My brilliant former teacher Michelle always used to say that she felt that learning to receive was one of the toughest and most daunting lessons that human beings face in our lifetimes. Having our own discomforts around receiving magnified as they tend to be in this card—the way we push away love, the way we might deny ourselves space, the way we might miss moments of beauty or feel ourselves to be unworthy of gifts, time, and friendship—can be devastating to witness and acknowledge.

If you have a hard time taking in sweetness, I want to, perhaps presumptuously, remind you that this is not your fault. The discomfort that you might be experiencing as an individual has a source point in a collective impulse, the same one that tells us to ignore the wisdom of our bodies, deny our gut, keep quiet when it comes to less pleasant topics, and behave in a palatable way that makes other folks more comfortable. Audre Lorde, adrienne marie brown, Tricia Hersey, and others have done immense work around this topic.

The High Priestess and The Empress are strong mirrors and can bring up a lot of big feelings. Did we learn how to trust in our sacred connection to ourselves, or was that bond inadvertently severed or distorted at a young age due to the conditioning of our caretakers; the expectations of the religion or community in which we were raised; the circumstances that we grew up in; our experience with racism, transphobia or homophobia, sexism, a lack of safety, or trauma; and/or any other systemic factors?

The High Priestess and The Empress are the beginning of an important reclamation process, in which we come back home to our capacity to receive and to sense into our deeper rhythms.

When The Empress shows up in a reading for us, it's an invitation to expand our threshold and capacity for receiving.

What is this card illuminating for us? Could we rest way more than what we're allowing for? Could we ask for more help and support? Could we make more space for what delights us?

Pleasure, beauty, and joy are our birthrights. We don't need to do anything special to be worthy of receiving them. How might we take in more of the things that feel lovely to us, allowing our discomforts and any unworthiness we might feel to bubble up in the process, so they can be honored, processed, and acknowledged?

The Empress Reversed

I tend to see The Empress reversed in the presence of a very empty cup, and a nervous system that desperately needs a break, some fun, and a little joy. This card can show up reversed when we've been unable or unwilling to take a little space for ourselves. If this resonates with you, I encourage you to just take an hour, an afternoon, a day for yourself. In the wise words of my former teacher Michelle, "We don't need to have a breakdown to get a break." Start small and build from there.

ROOT AND RISE WITH THE EMPEROR

If The High Priestess invites us to make space, and The Empress calls upon us to be available to receive inside of that space, The Emperor is the one who helps us give back to the world from that wellspring in turn.

The Emperor is, in my humble opinion, one of the most woefully misunderstood and mischaracterized cards in the Tarot. To understand the kind of magic and brilliance that this card brings, let's first unpack what The Emperor *isn't*. It is not, by definition, a cis male or even male-identified figure (as sex and gender in the Tarot are completely flexible and mutable), nor is it necessarily a parental figure. This card doesn't command. It doesn't force. The Emperor isn't necessarily a ruler, or someone with a high degree of power. Like all Tarot cards (from a Soul Tarot perspective), The Emperor is for everyone, including folks who struggle under the weight of oppressive systems, or grapple with finding their strength in a power imbalance. Indeed, when considering those dueling factors, the old paradigm of The Emperor as a dominant conqueror, or a forceful figure who wants to seize as much land, money, power, or attention as it can, really falls flat.

If we divorce The Emperor from these gender-normative, colonialist notions, what do we have? What is the soul, the essence, of The Emperor?

To begin to rewild and form a new relationship with The Emperor—one rooted in trust, repair, and inclusion—we might begin by calling up an image of a vast and mighty old-growth sequoia tree. We might imagine a powerful, ancient, enormous blue whale arcing over a beautiful wave. We might visualize the unending, exquisite night sky. The wingspan of the albatross. The volume of crickets on a summer evening. A field of wildflowers, stretching out as far as we can see. A holy mountain.

The Emperor is anything in nature that takes up aligned, sacred space without apologizing for its existence. It is an invitation to be all that we came here to be—whether that's the enormous pine tree or the humble mushroom growing on a small tuft of moss. We don't need to be huge and loud and unmissable in this card. We just need to be: to trust that we're not here by accident. Each of us is a sacred messenger, a gift to this world, and all of us have something to offer. Whatever you have to offer, The Emperor asks that you be willing to bring it forward. Receiving is a big piece of this. How will we embody what we receive as channels and conduits? How will we bring it forward into the world?

The Emperor might not initially seem like a likely candidate for an intuitive expander, but it's one of the most important ones we have. How can we begin to open our channel to a deeper connection with our Guides, or a more rooted and honest relationship with our own heart, without believing ourselves to be worthy of it? The Emperor, like The Empress, reminds us that we are here on purpose, are innately worthy, and have so much to offer. The Emperor card reminds us that it is possible to bring all that we desire into the world without taking up all the space in the room.

When The Emperor shows up in a reading, it's an invitation to move forward and share our magic, medicine, and gifts with the world in some potent way. This might feel scary, but we have everything we need to do this.

The Emperor Reversed

Are we hiding our light under a basket? Does it feel too scary, too overwhelming, or too intense to imagine bringing our ideas or inspiration into the world? What kind of support, reassurance, and/or resourcing would help bolster you? Or, perhaps, would it feel most supportive to be gentle with yourself and take some pressure off your shoulders? The Emperor reversed is usually a heads-up either that we are camouflaging ourselves or that we need to pause and take the temperature of the spaces we're in. Do the folks around us have space and time to shine, or are we inadvertently taking up more room than is aligned for us to occupy? Pausing and considering all options is wise when this card shows up reversed. Once we know, we can recenter and do better.

BECOMING OUR OWN WISE TEACHER WITH THE HIEROPHANT

There could be no journey of intuitive reclamation or pursuit of a soul-led life without encountering The Hierophant.

The High Priestess helps us begin to acquaint ourselves with the deep quiet necessary for a sense of that inner voice, and the fact that intuition moves as a spiral. The Empress helps us receive guidance within that space, and know that it's safe to dilate enough to open to that wisdom. The Emperor helps us begin to believe that we are worthy of that connection, that we are an integral part of the exchange and delivery, channeling forth intuitive messages onto this earthly plane.

The Hierophant is the card that takes us to the next step of integration—not just around the cards that came before it, but all that comes after it.

The Hierophant card is an invitation to trust in our own intuitive guidance system while holding a space of humility and openness around our own humanness. In other words, this card can help us to live from our intuition while simultaneously acknowledging our own inevitable blocks, biases, and shortcomings. It can and must be both. This card is an invitation to be our own wise teacher while honoring our lineage of learning. It is an invitation to reclaim the power, agency, and autonomy we've given away to others because we didn't trust in ourselves (or because we were manipulated into believing that we couldn't for one reason or another).

In my experience, The Hierophant is not usually a signal that we're about to meet a wise teacher or guide, as it is often described. While excellent and experienced teachers, processors, and Guides are incredibly important and worthy of working with, The Hierophant is a strong call to look in the mirror and understand that a teacher cannot ever be a gatekeeper for our own wisdom. They cannot grant us passage to parts of ourselves that we do not already have access to, nor can they offer us a closer connection to the divine. We already belong to the divine, to the seasons, to nature, and with whatever Spirit, God, or Source might mean to us.

The term *hierophant* comes from ancient Greece. Hierophants were considered deeply wise people who had access to, and were able to interpret, profound spiritual mysteries and arcane texts. While in the most optimistic of situations I have great respect for the good that hierophants were able to bring to their communities and the world at large, I personally feel that transferring that level of power and spiritual gatekeeping into a card in the Tarot is problematic at best, and deeply troubling at worst.

Who checked these people and what they believed? What was to stop them from saying anything they wanted? What prohibited them from allowing political influence, backdoor favors, or nefarious leanings to influence the way they interpreted those arcane spiritual texts and lost mysteries?

The historical context of this card notwithstanding, it is time to break out of the paradigm of spiritual mediaries and come back home to the wild brilliance of our own knowing. Again, it doesn't mean that we won't turn to guides and teachers—I wouldn't be where I am without the range of helpers, healers, and wise ones who have influenced and taught me. We can be guided, supported, and gently (or strongly) called in without giving our power away to someone else, or making them the center of our universe. This is a small but crucial distinction. We are all hierophants, and when this card shows up for us in a reading, we are being invited to reclaim that title for ourselves.

The Hierophant can be an intense initiation, because it also tends to arise at a crucial stage of our intuitive reclamation—a moment when an old, rotted, untrue belief is bumping up against our deeper wisdom in a way that cannot be ignored. It is a crushingly intense experience.

My most significant experience with The Hierophant card came when I knew somewhere within me that I needed to stop talking to my abuser.

This was initially unfathomable, unthinkable. The enabling and gaslighting that went into centering my abuser at enormous cost to my safety, sanity, and well-being had been happening my entire life. I couldn't just pull away, and yet, there was The Hierophant, coming up in my readings again and again and again, tolling a bell that kept getting louder and more urgent with each pull.

No matter how bad I felt, I knew that I could no longer go on living in that dynamic, so I took a leap and cut ties. It was an initiation that both nearly destroyed me and rebirthed me entirely. Working with and saying yes to the repeated presence of The Hierophant enabled me to take this courageous step. It was painful, but it was arguably one of the most important choices I've ever made. Everything in my life that I cherish—my career; this sacred, magical work; a deeper and more present awareness of my intuitive gifts; my relationship with my partner; and my beloved child—sprang forth from that decision.

Not everyone will necessarily make the choices I did; not everyone has the agency, ability, or desire to do so. But I offer this experience to illustrate the intensity and immensity this card is capable of. I believed, so profoundly and unshakably, that I could never break ties with this abusive situation. The Hierophant was the catalyst that helped me to trust in myself despite my conditioning. It was nothing short of a lifesaving act.

When The Hierophant shows up in a reading, it's an invitation to trust in ourselves and our own wise knowing. We can be open to external guidance, but never as a substitute for our inner compass. The Hierophant can also show up as a signal that there is a dissonance between our own wise inner knowing and an outdated, often inherited belief system within us. Working with this card helps us truly unpack and let go of those untrue beliefs, allowing our wisdom to shimmer forth.

The Hierophant Reversed

Are we giving too much of ourselves away, placing all of our trust in others? Does an old belief system feel so true that it's hard to even imagine that there could be anything different that could grow in its place? These are the big questions we ask when we work with The Hierophant reversed. This reversal often emphasizes and zooms in on the work we do when the card is right side up, and usually yields to stronger and more intense work with this card. We have everything we need to untie these knots. Please be gentle with yourself as you do so.

RECLAIMING OUR MAGIC WITH QUEEN OF WANDS

Queen of Wands is known as the witch of the Tarot for good reason.

In Soul Tarot, we consider The Queens our *coves*—a deep place of inner wisdom and sacred retreat that we are called to in significant moments.

Ruled by both Water (Queens) and Fire (Wands), Queen of Wands is the cauldron incarnate, holding space for the alchemical meeting of steady flame and bubbling liquid. The High Priestess and Queen of Wands do very important work together and are arguably our two most important intuitive guides in the Tarot. The High Priestess card does the foundational work: It helps us to understand that we're intuitive in the first place and helps us to know that intuition is allowed to look, feel, and show up in a very bespoke way—in other words, we are all intuitive, and intuition shines beautifully and uniquely through each of us in unique ways. In my experience, Queen of Wands builds upon the work we do with The High Priestess, and goes into some of the more advanced practices of this kind of intuitive homecoming and reclamation.

Queen of Wands tends to show up when we feel like impostors when it comes to our intuition. When we're in comparison, when we feel shame, when we feel so disconnected from ourselves, it is Queen of Wands who shows up and sits by our side, reminding us over and over again in ways both exquisitely fierce and gentle: *You are intuitive, you are magical; these things belong to you and can never be taken away.* When we get pressed into the edges of fear around our intuition and magic; when we fear judgment and misunderstanding, harm and persecution; when we have to hide our tools, or have our Tarot decks and craft work shipped to different addresses for fear of our caretakers finding them; when our bodies, our very DNA remembers burnings and violent deaths for our knowledge of plants, for our witness and help at births and other thresholds, Queen of Wands is there for us. When we watch other people make money for practices that were stolen from our ancestors, Queen of Wands is there for us. Queen of Wands is the old crone, the parent, and the young person.

Queen of Wands has been through it all, remembers it all, and reminds us of the truth. *You are intuitive, you are magical, and nothing can change that.*

Queen of Wands shows up when we're being invited to reclaim our magic in some important and sacred way. Each of us draws from magic that lives within our bones, aspects of our soul expression that are uniquely ours. We might struggle academically for any number of reasons but might be profoundly and naturally gifted at the bedside of folks who are dying. We might not be particularly inclined toward displays of emotion, but we might be very talented at diagnostics. We might be brilliant artists but less skilled at marketing our art. We might, frankly, possess all of these skills, but feel somehow deficient in another area. This gets at the crux of the work we do around intuitive rewilding: We are not supposed to be gifted at everything.

When we work with Queen of Wands, we are being invited to touch down on what we think might be the gift within us (even if it comes so naturally to us that we don't think it's terribly special), and we open to the possibility that this is exactly how God, Spirit, Source, Divine inspiration (or whatever you want to call it) is coming through us. Queen of Wands can help us to come home to this, to feel into the magic that lives within us and hold space for the wounding we have around it. This card can help to set us free.

Queen of Wands Reversed

When I feel contraction around my intuition, when my brain pulls me into comparison, criticism, or self-loathing, I usually see Queen of Wands reversed. This card tends to show up when we're in pain around our intuition in some way, and if it could talk, it might say something like the following: *Your brain, however brilliant, is lying to you about this. You are intuitive because we all are, and it's really wise not to compare yourself to anyone else's gift. It's okay if you don't believe it right now. It can take a long time to cultivate trust in our gifts and our inner voice. Be tender with yourself and take it one step at a time.*

SURPRISING OURSELVES WITH KNIGHT OF SWORDS

In Soul Tarot, we consider The Knights our *currents*. They live within the realm of Air, and all of them help us clarify our relationship to aligned timing and movement through a situation. If we aren't sure whether to slow down or speed up, The Knights can offer a lot of clarity.

Knight of Swords is often thought to be the "fastest," or "speediest," of The Knights—hell, I've even taught and characterized this card that way in my past Tarot courses. With more years of practice and teaching under my belt, however, I'm not so sure. I don't think this energy has anything to do with being quick as a rule, nor do I think it necessarily encourages us to step on the gas. I do think that Knight of Swords helps us move past our mental blocks in transformative ways and assists us in detangling the stories our brain tells us from the actual lived truth of things. I think the reason it has a reputation as a card that speeds things up is because it tends to arise in our readings when our inner narrative is something along the lines of how *brutal* a situation is going to be, how *long* it's going to take us, how *protracted* it all is, and how much we're *dreading* it. As it often goes with life (though not always, of course), the reality is a little kinder than the stories we tell ourselves.

These kinds of situations sometimes wind up being not quite as rough as we might have imagined. So working with Knight of Swords can feel like things are moving faster, but in reality I think this card simply helps us start doing the thing instead of anticipating it. *Don't try to think your way out of blocks and resistance*, it seems to say. Just try and see where you wind up.

This is very helpful (if not unexpected) medicine around the theme of intuitive rewilding and reclamation. Remember: We are creatures with nervous systems that are designed to seek the familiar and the perception of safety. Intuition, and making space for intuition, completely flies in the face of that. Most of us don't grow up tuning in with Source or our own inner wisdom, making space for that kind of quiet presence within ourselves. Most of us grow up with the assumption that living from our intuition is either (a) for fools, (b) totally unattainable, or (c) only for folks who have the privilege of still minds and quiet hearts, those who can seemingly perfectly perceive their intuition. None of that is true. Everyone builds up to a sense of proficiency and comfort with their own channel through a lot of sitting around in silence, wondering whether they're doing this right. Even those of us who came into this world with major intuitive gifts still have to work on them and check in around biases (among other things). In other words, you have everything you need to begin to tune in and expand your channel, even if it doesn't necessarily feel like it.

Knight of Swords helps us to surprise ourselves. When we decide to just do something, try something, or dive into something without letting ourselves get caught up in the story, or in trying to make it all perfect, we wind up soaring. We wind up learning, stumbling, discovering new things. We become the peregrine falcon, diving through the air and realizing that the story that we told ourselves about what this was going to be is not entirely true. We've told ourselves that we cannot fly, and yet here we are, gliding through the sky.

When this card shows up in a reading for us, we can work with it best by gently getting out of our own head, out of our own way, and just flying forward at whatever speed is most appropriate for us. It can be an incredibly transformative thing when we apply this to our willingness to tune in with our own intuition. What would it be like to take a deep breath, check in with yourself, and see what arises?

Knight of Swords Reversed

When we receive Knight of Swords reversed, it can indicate that we might benefit from stopping, pausing, and coming home to our bodies in some important and much-needed way. Sometimes this card shows up reversed after a huge push or deadline, giving way to an organic season of rest to compensate for that big flight.

HEEDING THE CALL WITH THE TWOS

When we work with The Aces, we plant a sacred seed of intention. By the time we get to The Twos of the Tarot, there is the tiniest, most tender seedling peeking its way out of the soil, reaching out toward the sun and sky. Those seedlings need time to grow and flourish without being rushed. They also benefit from conscientious attunement—a watchful and supportive eye, offering whatever might be needed: weeding, more water, more shade.

In most cases, we are both the seedlings and the guardians.

The Twos are about sacred balance and equilibrium. They invite us to engage in radical acts of self-tending, and typically show up when we are in important and significant seasons of *becoming*, times that might require a higher degree of attention from ourselves than usual.

These "seasons of becoming" might yield to us blossoming into a new iteration, evolution, or phase of ourselves. This might be a more expansive, wild, delicious phase of life—perhaps we've shucked off some of the knots that were slowing us down or holding us back, and now we long to fly free. It might be a more focused period of time, one marked by deep study, deep research, or deep seeking. These seasons can also be about our role in the world and the legacy we want to leave. They can be wholly personal and internal, about our growth as a person and a continued discovery of ourselves. Or it could be all of the above. What we need to know is that these seasons—and by extension, our work with The Twos of the Tarot—are *tender* and will ask for us to be our own gentle gardeners.

When we're beginning a brand-new job; when we've just quit our job or gone on a leave of absence to write, create, or birth a new project or venture; when we've just had a baby; when we're on a deadline of any kind; when we're beginning a garden; if we've gone back to school; if we're deep in research, we will likely be orbiting around the energy of The Twos in the Tarot.

The Twos are deeply intuitive energies—we must be willing to get quiet, clear, and attuned to respond to what they are asking of us when they arise in our readings. Our work with them also helps us deepen into our intuition and trust in that aspect of ourselves in a fuller and richer way. The Twos of the Tarot are invitations to come home to ourselves and pour our attention, energy, and effort into what really matters in this season of life.

Beginning the Journey with Two of Wands

Receiving Two of Wands in a reading is an indication that a journey of some kind has already begun. We've shoved off from the shore and are making tracks, whether we're aware of it or not. It is imperative, however, that we acknowledge and remember that we are only a few steps, a few moments, into this adventure that we've embarked upon. We must allow ourselves to be at the beginning of our journey, trusting in the timing and honoring the medicine of what it is to be at the start of something.

Two of Wands is an important anchor for intuitive reclamation because it touches on so many places that can feel tender and tricky when we're just starting to be more present with those deeper aspects of the self. It is incredibly challenging for any human being to be in the unknown. Two of Wands, and an intuitively led life by extension, will ask us to be in the moment, trusting in what's right in front of us, letting each step build on the next.

Paradoxically, the deeper we dive into our intuition and inner knowing, the less we tend to know. We start to realize that it's fruitless to ask for clear visions of what's to come, as the future is not fixed, and life tends to bloom open from the moment we find ourselves in. This card can help us honor the beauty, wisdom, and magic in those places. And if we can't quite get there, Two of Wands can at least help us trust that nothing is permanent: Life is change.

When this card shows up for us, it is an invitation to fully root ourselves into the start of a journey, and to trust in where we're meant to be on that journey. What helps to tether and ground us when we want to be further than where we are, or when we long for more information than we are currently receiving?

Two of Wands Reversed

Are we attempting to rush the moment, to be somewhere other than right here? Are we pushing through something, possibly exhausting and overwhelming ourselves in the process? When Two of Wands shows up reversed, it is especially important not to sprint over to the next thing before the present moment is fully baked. Trust in the timing and where you are.

Loving the Broken Pieces with Two of Cups

Recall that Ace of Cups offers us the opportunity to connect with an intention: to begin to love ourselves more unconditionally, regard ourselves with more compassion, and reparent ourselves in ways that are likely both needed and desired. Two of Cups is a strong response to that initial spell. This card invites us to open our arms to all parts of ourselves, *especially* the parts that feel most challenging to love.

Every one of us has aspects of ourselves that we wish we could change, stuff away, or eliminate entirely. We might find ourselves thinking, *"If that part of me was different, if I was different, I could have ____, I could be ____, I would be more ____."*

Two of Cups invites us to hold those stories with the utmost gentleness and care. Those narratives and beliefs can be there—they don't have to change or go away. We don't, however, have to take them at face value. What might it be like to wrap our arms around the parts of us that are experiencing pain, separation, and self-flagellation? What would it mean to remind ourselves that we are lovable as we are, even (and especially) the broken, flawed parts of us? Who profits or benefits from us being divided against ourselves? These are the questions that Two of Cups asks of us.

This card doesn't excuse harmful, abusive, or problematic behavior. In fact, I have found that the opposite is true. It takes a profound degree of self-tending to be willing to repair past harms from a place of true remorse. It takes all the courage imaginable to make our lives a living amends, to seek out help, support, or recovery. It takes everything we have to break cycles of abuse and harm. We don't have to adore and rejoice in all aspects of ourselves; we only need to be somewhat willing to consider that we might benefit from opening to all parts of our being, both the beloved and the challenging.

When Two of Cups shows up in our readings, we're being invited to embrace all aspects of ourselves, especially the broken, tricky, tougher aspects of our personalities. This card is a huge element of intuitive reclamation. A deep part of that process, at least in my experience, is sitting with what challenges us without shying away, which can be very transformative. Two of Cups can help us root into this process.

Two of Cups Reversed

When Two of Cups shows up reversed, it can be an indication that we might be identifying with the idea that we're unlovable, or that an aspect of us needs to radically change in order for us to be worthy of love. This card's reversal is a gentle but persistent reminder of the truth: Our feelings about ourselves are just that—feelings. Wholly valid, but not necessarily true. How might we come back to an observer role when it comes to these feelings, to be the witness that holds it all, even the parts that feel deeply spiky and challenging?

Taking Sacred Space with Two of Swords

Imagine yourself in a brightly lit house, full of people. Folks are laughing, shouting, engaging in lively conversation. You get pulled into a chat with a few folks. It's nice enough, but you're getting hot and overstimulated. Then, without anyone noticing or following you, you steal out the back door and go outside. It is cold: heaven after the heat and crowding of the party. There is snow on the ground. The Moon is out. You can perceive the music and the jovial conversation going on inside of the house, but, for the most part, you are in peace and stillness. You hear the crunch of the snow under your feet, see your breath in the air. You sit for a while and look up at the night sky. You breathe, ground, and come back to yourself. No one has noticed that you are gone. Suddenly, after just a few minutes, you feel restored and renewed, ready to go back inside and rejoin the celebration.

That is Two of Swords from a Soul Tarot perspective.

When you need to check in, tune in, meditate, clear some feelings, come back to your body and your breath, Two of Swords is your ally. When you need to take a break, to call your sponsor, or to say your prayers, Two of Swords is your champion. Two of Swords is the ultimate invitation to take time for ourselves without apology or explanation. It is a card of sacred boundaries, and of sacred space.

Two of Swords has had an interesting and slightly misunderstood reputation as a card of isolation—that we're somehow pushing loved ones and community away when we engage with the card. I feel that this take on Two of Swords speaks volumes about our culture's general discomfort with boundaries and self-preservation. We're not pushing anyone away when we work with this card, we're just getting closer to ourselves.

We need Two of Swords in all situations, but especially when it comes to matters of intuitive reclamation. We really need space and quiet to fully feel into our bodies and the wisdom that flows through our channel, even if it's just for a few minutes. We engage with helpful energetic boundaries and psychic hygiene when we give ourselves the gift of that kind of deep pause. It allows us to be in right relationship with our needs, to be integral about our "no" and our "yes" to the best of our abilities. In an ideal world, this kind of space-taking would be promoted, encouraged, and championed across the board.

When Two of Swords shows up in a reading, we're being invited to take some space for ourselves without apology or explanation. We might meditate, ground, breathe deeply, listen deeply, or touch in with some important anchor or resource. No matter what you're called to do, Two of Swords wants to support you in taking the time you need.

Two of Swords Reversed

Are we neglecting our needs in service of others? Have we checked in with ourselves lately? Two of Swords reversed can be an indication of a past-due notice from the heart and soul—that we need a break, some time, some space, and we need it yesterday. How can we take even three minutes to pause, drop in, and greet ourselves as we are?

Devotional Discernment with Two of Pentacles

There are moments in life that have a certain charge and magic to them that require more of our energy and attention than other times do. Some examples include the harvest coming in, when we're pregnant *and* when we're freshly postpartum, when we're building our new business, when we have a major deadline, when we're writing our book. Certain periods of life max our energetic capacity more than others. In these full seasons of creation, we want to first acknowledge that our head, hands, and heart are fuller than they might usually be. We might not be as available to certain people, or as able to provide certain services in our usual way. We might not be able to play, concentrate, or perform as we usually do. This is not a failing on our part, but a miraculous sense of internal alignment that helps us to devote everything we have to these projects, cycles, and seasons, and all that they are asking of us.

Two of Pentacles is the epitome of this kind of devotional discernment.

This card usually shows up when we're embarking on or in the midst of something very fruitful and exciting: something that we will need all of our energy and concentration for. Two of Pentacles will strongly invite us to get clear on the things that drain our limited energy and have us dropping balls in ways that could be avoided. This is all the more crucial if our attention and energy are naturally split and in demand. There are certain responsibilities in life that cannot be avoided. Anything else, Two of Pentacles reminds us, can be shelved, put aside in favor of creating and birthing whatever is demanding to come through at this time.

This is a strong part of intuitive reclamation as well—honoring our creation seasons and allowing ourselves to be wholly and unapologetically devoted to them. There are times when that will be asked of us. Trusting in and honoring what stays and what flows away in these seasons is part of the twofold medicine of Two of Pentacles. Don't apologize for devoting yourself to what's calling you to the page, the books, the rocking chair, the worktable again and again. With each visit and each deep offering of concentration and creation, we grow, change, and evolve. How could we not?

Two of Pentacles Reversed

When Two of Pentacles shows up reversed in a reading, it is usually a gentle signal that we are over-giving in a particular area, and would benefit from pausing and recentering. Again, there are particular seasons of life when we just don't have as much to offer others. You're not a bad, mean, or selfish person for placing a boundary on your time. You don't need to clarify, defend, or explain the boundary. Lay it down, and let other people react however they will.

CHAPTER SIX

WHEN YOU'RE ON A JOURNEY

Tarot Cards for Transitions

THE LOVERS

THE CHARIOT

PAGE OF CUPS

KING OF WANDS

THE THREES

THE LOVERS

THE CHARIOT

PAGE OF CUPS

KING OF WANDS

THREE OF WANDS

THREE OF CUPS

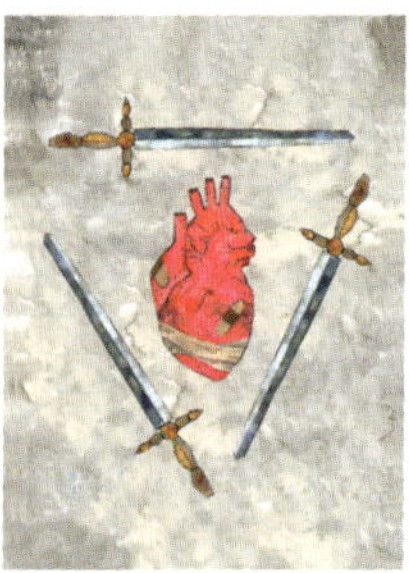

THREE OF SWORDS

THREE OF PENTACLES

The *Oxford Learner's Dictionary* defines *transition* as "the process or a period of changing from one state or condition to another." That process is one of the most powerful, and dare I say mystical, parts of life, isn't it? Change happens all the time. Transition is very much about change, but its true focus is less about who we are becoming and more on the *process of our becoming*. I am interested not just in this process, but in unpacking how we care for ourselves within that process.

How do we hold ourselves in seasons of life when we are literally shedding our skin, changing our name, moving, transforming physically in some way, becoming a parent, choosing not to be a parent, losing someone we love deeply? What kind of resources can we call upon for moments when we are crossing the bridges of life? How do we open to the possibility of rebirth when we've never had a model for it? How do we bow to the grit, the terror, the euphoria, and the hope for something better all in one breath?

How do we root into groundlessness, and find our true north in moments when everything we've known is changing, affecting us mentally, emotionally, and spiritually?

In seasons that involve a transition of any kind, we will likely come into connection with **The Lovers**, **The Chariot**, **Page of Cups**, **King of Wands**, and **The Threes.**

These cards don't necessarily make transitions any easier or less intense, but they can provide a spiritual scaffold to bolster us. These cards in particular can remind us of the profound gifts of transitions, and the equally profound need to tend to ourselves in their midst.

LOOKING INTO THE MIRROR WITH THE LOVERS

At its essence, The Lovers is a gentle, quiet awakening that often shows up at the beginning of transitional seasons, acting as a jumping-off point for the process.

Transitions often get sparked off as a result of an awareness that the current state of things can no longer continue. For better or for worse (although ideally for better!), we have come as far as we can go with what is presently here. We must be willing and able to let go so something new can form.

This awakening, if you will, is what gets the ball rolling for big, soul-level transitions. The Lovers card creates the conditions for this kind of awakening and offers a helpful road map for how we might respond to what it is that we're discovering within it.

The Lovers is depicted as a mirror in so many wonderful Tarot decks (Cristy C. Road's brilliant *Next World Tarot* and Chase Voorhees's equally brilliant *Tarot of the Holy Spectrum*, to name just two) for a good reason: The card acts as a kind of cosmic looking glass, one that has the power to help us see the gaps between who we truly are and our current state of being.

The Lovers card invites us to look into that mirror and witness ourselves, to consider that we are innately worthy and deserving of love, time, generosity, compliments (if that's our thing), and the nurturing that we long for.

For many of us, it's generally much easier to shower those things onto other people than to take them in for ourselves. We can see the beauty, splendor, and goodness in others when they might not be able to see it in themselves—in that way, we become a mirror of The Lovers card, shining other folks' brilliance back to them.

Sometimes people come into our lives for a few moments or a season, purely to be a sacred mirror that reflects this to us. This can get confusing, especially when there is no clear or aligned path for us to pursue a romantic relationship with someone (if that's even something we're available for in the first place). In The Lovers card, we can mistake what can potentially be limerence or transference as true love, when nine times out of ten, we're really meant to receive the reflection and infuse it into our own lives, rather than continuing to chase after the mirror itself.

This is part of why it is so important to begin to divest from The Lovers card as a signal of romantic love, or a connection with a potential lover. It's not that it *can't* be a card of romance; it's just not a reliable rule, and often distracts us from the core work we're meant to do with this card.

The painful awakening that this card can call us into is the realization of how far away we might be from all that we desire. How did we get here? The Lovers card starts to call us into that reckoning.

The first step of this reckoning is awareness. If the love of our caretakers or family of origin was based in conditional means, or if we believe that our receiving love is contingent upon our maintaining a particular kind of appearance or standing in life, then of course we will reach for schools, courses of study, partners, careers, and life choices that hopefully keep us in the good graces of those around us, but aren't necessarily what we want. When we begin to realize this, it can be monumental. If any of it starts to overwhelm your capacity to cope, it's best to have the steady presence of a great therapist or helping professional with you to sort through everything.

The second step of this reckoning is curiosity. If what's here isn't what we are truly longing for, then what is? What work do we yearn to do in the world? How do we long to be in relationship with ourselves?

The third step is transition—the beginning of the shedding process, the release of that too-tight snakeskin. The transition will look however it is meant to look and will take place in whatever way makes sense for us, but there's almost no escaping, denying, or subverting it once The Lovers card arises. That's the main job of The Lovers card—to be a strong, clear, transformative signal that we are meant for more than we might believe, and that we have everything within us to reach for a life that is reflective of that.

This card doesn't promise the arrival of riches or a soulmate. It speaks of a life lived from a sense of purpose, fully rooted in what matters. It means loving ourselves enthusiastically, and allowing ourselves to be loved, witnessed, and wildly adored by the entirety of life. The Lovers card essentially presents us with a cosmic mirror, one that is unconditionally loving and trustworthy. To embody those reflections, we have to be willing to transition away from what no longer aligns.

When The Lovers card shows up in a reading, it is helping us awaken to any points of misalignment in our lives or our relationship with ourselves. As a result of looking into this mirror, we might realize there are certain external factors in our lives that no longer match who we have become. This card can gently and gradually guide us to our next steps, to a world beyond these outdated beliefs that we're beginning to shed.

The Lovers Reversed

Are we giving away too much of our power, or looking for love from an empty source? Are we giving other folks too much credit for our hard work? Is it noticeably more challenging to take in compliments, love, and desired touch? If so, why? The Lovers reversed is usually an indication that it's important to reflect on some of these questions.

PERPETUAL REBIRTH WITH THE CHARIOT

I remember waiting in line at the Seven Dwarfs Mine Train ride at Disney World in 2019 with my little niece and nephew when the essence of The Chariot card truly landed in my soul. It wasn't the line itself that did it, but rather the parade of baby strollers parked outside the ride as folks waited their turn. I remember thinking to myself at that moment, *"We outgrow it all."* We outgrow the womb, our first home. We outgrow our teeth, our baby shoes, our strollers, carriers, cribs, bassinets, swaddles, our parents' arms. We outgrow marriages, titles, identities, and eventually, inevitably, these bodies. This card is truly our most present companion through the cycles and spirals of the life/death/rebirth process.

If you were born, or have watched someone be born, you know what The Chariot is. If you've watched as a chick pecked and hatched its way out of an egg, you know what The Chariot is. If you've ever survived the immense process of leaving a vessel, a home, a place, a space, a way of existing, you know The Chariot card intimately. It is the hard work of perpetual growing and shedding, dying and rebirthing. It is the inescapable reality of death and birth living and breathing as one thing, the inevitable reality of perpetual release and outgrowth that we have all experienced and will all continue to experience. The Chariot is *the* card of transition, transformation, and letting go.

The Chariot card centers our vessel and vehicle, the thing that holds, cradles, and drives us forward, rather than focusing on the charioteer. It does this for a very good reason. The Chariot tends to arise in our readings as a signal that we have outgrown a particular container—that the vehicle we are driving through life in will not be suitable for the terrain that we are about to embark on. This is, of course, terrifying, and often brings up so much resistance and discomfort—we don't want to let go of our chariot. It might be way too tight and something we've really outgrown, but at least it's familiar.

This card is truly a midwife, an attendant at the threshold gates, gently witnessing us as we squeeze through this birth canal into another phase of our lives.

The essence of our existence and the drumbeat that drives us forward is our evolution, both microcosmically and macrocosmically. We are always growing, always rebirthing. It is in our nature to spiral forward and let go of the wombs, the names, the identities, the spaces, the teachers, and the personas that no longer serve us. We—that is to say the soul essence of us—remain, even as we say goodbye to the vehicle that helped us get as far as we did.

The Chariot card can be a gentle meditation on the nature of life, death, and love. With each microprocess of shedding, releasing, and rebirthing that we experience in our lives, we prepare to eventually say goodbye to the people we love, and to this body. Our work with this card can help us embrace the unknown—in fact, one of The Chariot card's key signatures is knowing that what we're in isn't quite working, but not being completely sure of what lies ahead. We must be willing to let go of the other side of the rope, of what has already died, in order to rebirth. To transition is to practice the gentle art of letting go, of knowing that nothing is guaranteed, and that nothing is certain.

When The Chariot card shows up in a reading for us, it is a gentle and clear heads-up that we have outgrown something—an identity, a persona, an aspect of life—and we must move through the intense process of shedding this container in the service of our continued growth. Like a full-term fetus leaving the uterus or a baby chick hatching out of an egg, we are taking a magnificent and terrifying leap of faith—all we know is this too-tight container, and we have very little context for what lies beyond it. Why would we leave? Typically, the answer is that the chariot in question has become too small, too tight, or unsuitable for the journey we're about to embark on, so it must be released for us to continue to evolve on our path.

The Chariot Reversed

When The Chariot shows up reversed in a reading, more often than not it is acknowledging our potential frustration and impatience around this deep shedding process. It might be helpful to be reminded of the fact that you are actively birthing, hatching, and transforming, and The Chariot showing up reversed doesn't change any of that. It instead asks us to tend to ourselves and our feelings around the process taking longer than we might want or exhausting us more than we thought it would. What nourishment do you need to support you through this season?

TENDING TO OUR INNER CHILD WITH PAGE OF CUPS

In Soul Tarot, we look to The Pages as our *compasses*—the roots, tethers, and roads that lead us back home to ourselves. No matter how off the mark we might land, or how lost we might feel, The Pages are always there as shining, glorious, quiet polestars, steadily pointing us back to our true north.

When we're moving through highly transitional times, moments when we're deeply in the process of changing, transforming, and becoming someone new, we can feel tender and vulnerable. It can be challenging to remember who we are, and whether we're actually on our way to somewhere better. The Pages can help us here—specifically, Page of Cups.

Page of Cups is an invitation to connect with our inner child, to embrace the medicine of play, awe, and magic.

This can feel like a bridge too far for lots of folks for reasons that I fully understand and am sympathetic to. Many of us struggle to embrace our inner children, and the idea of connecting with that part of us might seem impossible, or even frivolous. Why might it be important to do so?

One of the most profound things about becoming a parent is seeing how utterly *herself* my child has been from the moment they were born. It's been a wonder and a privilege to witness that. As I write this sentence, she is nearly three years old, and is such a beautiful, immensely wise, observant, funny soul. I feel like one of my biggest invitations as her parent is to *unconditionally* love and nurture her, as opposed to subtly or overtly trying to mold, shape, or guilt her into someone she's not. Most of us were not parented this way, and were subjected to immense pressures, expectations, judgments, and conditional love as a form of punishment when we didn't do what our caretakers wanted of us.

I always felt like my younger self, Little Linds, was a burden until I understood that I was made to feel that way. I absorbed that as a kid and projected it onto my own inner child. Page of Cups can help to gently pave the path for a healing around this kind of core pain.

This card isn't necessarily an invitation to drop into our deepest trauma or wounding around our childhood. It's not encouraging us to rip out our stitches if we aren't ready.

In my experience, Page of Cups does help us to reparent ourselves, to shift our relationship to play. We get to be the parents that our inner kids have always dreamed of. If we can create more safety for those younger, more tender parts of ourselves, play can feel safer and more available to us across the board.

Page of Cups can also connect us back to the medicine of wonder, which is another thing my child has brought back into my life. Their conversations with the Moon, their delight at seeing Venus in the sky, their questions about how twilight is different from sunset, and their excitement about listening to the crickets and the frog song in the summer months are a balm beyond words. I had, at some point, stopped playing, singing, wondering, and dancing, and they brought that back into my life. Page of Cups will help us lean back into those things, too.

In times of great personal transition, when we're in a deep process of change, this kind of connection to play is of the utmost importance. How do we discharge the fear and tension we might feel around the unknown through our willingness to be present with wonder? How can we create a structure of safety around our inner little one who might be feeling more frightened than we are about the current situation? How do we engage with play? Page of Cups can help us get back to that place of magic within, to hold a tender space for ourselves through anything that might be arising.

Page of Cups Reversed

When we see Page of Cups reversed, we can be certain that we're long overdue for some playtime. What feels accessible for you today in terms of play? How might you make even 10 percent more space for wonder, beauty, joy, and fun to flow through you?

BLAZING A TRAIL WITH KING OF WANDS

In Soul Tarot, we consider The Kings of the Tarot to be our *contributors*—the leaders, tenders, and Guides within each of us. We don't need to have a big interpersonal reach to touch base with our inner King; they help us remember that we all have the capacity to be a positive influence and leave a legacy of good, even with the barest of daily interactions.

King of Wands is a trailblazer. They know that they have something special within them that they want to share with the world, and they have just enough gumption and willingness to bring it forward.

King of Wands folks usually see things a little differently than others do and are asked to lean into that for the benefit of all. That is the essence of what it means to blaze a trail, as far as this card goes.

Sometimes our inner King of Wands shines because we are novices and can see potential solutions and failures that seasoned folks sometimes cannot. Sometimes it's the other way around, and we're persistently going to bat to defend changes that would be detrimental to an established system by folks who are not familiar with the ins and outs of the subject at hand. Sometimes we can trace our inner King of Wands, our inner trailblazer, to our rocky and traumatic past, to a loss we experienced at an impressionable age, or to an aspect of our identity that shapes the way we move through and experience the world. No matter where that pull might come from within us and how afraid or nervous we might be, we want to follow it.

It can be scary to blaze a trail. It is nerve-wracking to give something your all, knowing that you might experience ridicule, rejection, or even mockery. You might not get the respect of your peers. You might experience envy. It might be a lonely place for a while.

When I say that King of Wands is about trailblazing, I mean in every capacity. Breaking away from abusive dynamics within ourselves and others, choosing a life of love and peace, and being brave enough to bring ourselves and our own great work forward are all strong examples of how to live from this card's energy. King of Wands is a huge catalyst for change and transition, because it's impossible to work with this card and not be and feel altered by it. It's impossible to blaze a trail and follow our heart without it shifting the course of our lives, even in a very small way. It is the process of this work that powers our continual growth and willingness to be changed by how we're evolving.

King of Wands Reversed

When King of Wands shows up in our readings reversed, we want to pause and inquire: Are we trying to bring something forward before it's fully ready, or before it's time to do so? If that's the case, how might we trust in the medicine of a pause? Can we get curious about why we might be rushing something before it's a full yes? It also could be that we're feeling really shaky and scared at the prospect of trying something new or doing something different from what is expected. How might we hold ourselves through that, and reach out to others to hold us in it as well?

MEDICINE FOR THE PROCESS WITH THE THREES

We plant our seeds with The Aces, and we move through a process of deep and responsive self-tending with The Twos. The Threes of the Tarot usually show up when we are undergoing a deep time of change and transition, essentially serving as the spiritual equivalent of a canteen of fresh, cold water, an energy bar, and an apple in your backpack. The Threes offer deep sustenance and nourishment during some great shift or passage.

When a Three shows up in a reading, we want to consider the process we are in, or undergoing, or moving through. How are we growing or changing in this season of life? Transitional seasons can be very disruptive and, at times, destabilizing. We crave structure, familiarity, and comfort. Those are typically in short supply when we're making our way from one state of being to another.

What's showing up for us right now, and what do we need for this particular journey? The change we're moving through might be big and obvious, or very subtle and more internal in nature—no matter how it presents itself, it is still valid and worthy of our attention.

Change is a process. Crossing a symbolic bridge is a process. In working with The Threes, we learn to responsively tend to ourselves within that process. They point us toward what might be needed in the middle of this kind of season.

Crossing the Bridge with Three of Wands

When Three of Wands shows up for us, we are typically in the middle of an immense transition. We can't quite return to what we've left behind, and our next steps are not yet fully illuminated. If we can't go back and we're not certain about what we're making our way toward, then our work lies in how we tend to ourselves in the middle of this unfinished cosmic bridge of change that we are constructing as we cross it—quite literally forming the ground underneath us as we travel through this card.

Three of Wands doesn't really help us to know what lies ahead, how long we will be on the bridge, or how long it will take to form the rest of the bridge that will carry us to the next season of our lives. That's one of the trickiest things about this card: It shows up when we most want clarity, and it cannot offer that to us. Instead, it offers a beautiful reminder that we are on a "bridge" and a journey of transition to begin with—now that we're willing to be present with that fact, what do we need? What is helpful, accessible, and practically useful to us in seasons like this?

When Three of Wands shows up in a reading, it is a gentle signal that we are in need of sustenance that meets us in the middle of an unfinished bridge. We want to consider our stamina—do we have what we need in our well to finish this bridge? Could something be set aside for a while? Might we leave construction standing for a bit while we take a long weekend? We might consider our nervous systems, and how comfortable we feel in the midst of unknowns. What feels nourishing to you when things are unclear, or uncertain? I like reaching for certain books, TV shows, helping tools (like my Tarot deck!), cozy meals, and more sessions with my therapist, coach, and support systems in those seasons. I need reminders that this time is not permanent, and that I am actually on my way to something. You might need that in your Three of Wands seasons, too.

Three of Wands Reversed

When Three of Wands is reversed, it's a gentle reminder not to get ahead of yourself. You're not really able to go back and you're not really able to go forward. It's okay to feel contracted and possibly frustrated by that. Just be where you are right now—it's safe and okay to be in the middle of this bridge, to be changing, to be creating something new. Would you consider placing a hand on your heart and reminding yourself of this?

Multidimensional Belonging with Three of Cups

In moments of big change, transition, and processing, we need community connection and deep, loving support around us. Three of Cups is always here to aid in that process.

Three of Cups often arises in relatively short-lived, of-the-moment experiences: a group of folks who come together for a special moment, a unique season or experience. To this end, think camp, retreat, or troop friends; the deep bonds we make with cast members of theatrical productions; the team of family members, doulas, and supportive pals who might show up for us in the postpartum haze. When this card arises in a reading, it's a call to reach out to the sweet, beloved kinfolk, soul family, friends, or extended community we might have, or to lean in with a beautiful braid of people who are co-creating something together.

What if we don't have that community, those friends, or that kinfolk? What if that's one of our deepest wounds—our aloneness, or lack of support from other people in our lives? It can be very painful to receive a card like Three of Cups if we don't have anyone to call, text, or connect with. In Soul Tarot, we honor Three of Cups as a deep link to both visible community and invisible community. Indeed, this card is also a profound invitation to open ourselves to the tending and witnessing of our unconditionally loving Guides, ancestors, and beloved dead who are always traveling with us.

There are moments in life, for whatever reason, when we travel solo through the valleys of our experience, when we don't have a human friend in sight. We are, however, never truly alone. In times of huge transitions and transformations, we ideally want to be wrapped in both visible and invisible supports. When Three of Cups shows up in a reading for us, it is a gentle reminder to open to that deep, loving, and nourishing support from our soul's kinfolk, seen and unseen. Reach out to friends, to groups, to beloveds. Reach out to Guides and Spirit Helpers. Pray if you pray. Tune in if you tune in. Take a walk and feel the loving presence of nature all around you. There can be a lot of resistance and vulnerability in these moments, but we can honor those feelings and still extend our hearts to reminders of our deep belonging. Three of Cups wants to help us remember that belonging.

Three of Cups Reversed

Sometimes we just don't want to connect with anyone (humans or beings beyond the veil) for any number of reasons. Not that you need to hear this from me, but that's absolutely okay! I wholeheartedly encourage you to honor and trust that.

Sometimes we don't know how to connect, or we're worried about doing it wrong, or we believe that our connection with other people or with Spirit should feel different than it does. Those feelings are wholly valid, but I gently encourage you to thoroughly investigate them. There's no one right way to connect with our

Spirit Helpers. There's no way you could get it wrong. Sometimes connecting with other people feels challenging and messy, and it's okay to feel unsure about all of it.

How might you honor and begin to untangle whatever is coming up for you around this?

Tending to the Heart with Three of Swords

Many years ago, I was in a lifestyle store in Los Angeles and noticed that they sold a Tarot book written by one of my students at the time. I hadn't realized that this sweet student had written a book, and I excitedly picked it up to give it a quick read. My stomach turned as I saw my own words about the Tarot written in my student's book word for word. I had been blatantly plagiarized. Without even thinking about it, I whipped out my phone, took photos, and went to email this student, immediately ready to call them out and blast them for this transgression. For some reason, mid-draft, I paused. I took a breath, went back to my car, and pulled a Tarot card for clarity: Three of Swords. I took another breath, angry tears welling in my eyes, knowing what that meant. Before I sent a scorched-earth email to this student, I needed to tend to my heart first. In this particular instance, I had to pause before I reacted.

Despite its reputation (and the anecdote I shared above), Three of Swords doesn't often arise in situations where we experience betrayal or backstabbing. No matter the situation, the weather, or the issue at hand, Three of Swords arises in moments when we're in pain. And, as a protective response to that pain, our mind calls us into a back-and-forth process of blaming ourselves and others.

This back-and-forth usually makes us want to take immediate action, believing that our reaction will quell our discomfort. Sometimes that's true, and sometimes an immediate response or confrontation is appropriate. But for the most part, Three of Swords will call upon us to *first* center our wounded heart, to offer witness, compassion, and tender care to ourselves around something that's feeling painful and challenging. Centering our heart doesn't erase our righteous disappointment, anger, or feelings of injustice. It isn't meant to. It just wants us to remember that we're in pain, and that those parts need attention, too.

I eventually emailed that student. I was lucky that they admitted wrongdoing and made things right. I was able to communicate with them from a centered place, after fully processing my grief, fear, rage, betrayal, and disgust around the situation with my support systems. Those disappointed feelings were still present, but I was not reacting from them.

Three of Swords can offer profound sustenance around our emotional transitions. It is a critical stopping point, a "magic quarter-second," as Tara Bennett-Goleman puts it, before responding to a charged situation.

Three of Swords Reversed

Are we rushing ahead before we're ready? Are we pressuring ourselves to respond when things are still too fresh, or too volatile? It's possible that we're feeling great and rooted about our next steps, but when Three of Swords shows up reversed, it's usually worth it to pause and check in about the questions above.

The Half-Baked Cake with Three of Pentacles

Three of Pentacles is often described as a card of sacred collaboration, of like-minded folks working together within their individual zones of genius to create something new. This is a beautiful treatment of this card, but I cannot say that I personally see it show up that way very often in the readings that I've received and given.

What I see more consistently is Three of Pentacles showing up for:

- Someone who is in a period of deep transition and is typically experiencing slow turnover around their pursuits, work, career, or another area of life
- Someone who is being asked to honor exactly where they are in this process, even if it is not particularly exciting or enjoyable

Three of Pentacles is a half-baked cake, a beautiful batter not yet ready to come out of the oven. In this card, we are that cake, and we are asked to honor ourselves in our own half-baked state. This is a beautiful, mystical, and precious place to be. Anything is possible here, and nothing is necessarily wrong. We just need more time in the proverbial oven to become what it is that we're becoming.

When we work with Three of Pentacles, we might feel ready to move onto something new or make a change, but it just doesn't seem like it's time yet. There's usually something to that, hence the need to let the cake fully bake in the oven. When we work with this card, we're being invited to take heart, to trust and know that we're right on the verge of a shift or up-leveling.

The sustenance that we glean from this card is to trust where we are—in this in-between place that we're likely not jazzed about being in. Something new and different is on its way, but it's not quite time to leave or make a change. How can we support ourselves through this tension, allowing ourselves to fully bake through this process?

Three of Pentacles Reversed

What happens when we take a cake out of the oven too early? We won't be able to enjoy it, and we will have to circle back and bake it for longer. This turns out to be a messy, protracted, and longer journey than it would be to trust the timing and know that eventually, our cake will be baked. Three of Pentacles reversed holds the same sentiment.

CHAPTER SEVEN

REST AFTER THE JOURNEY

Tarot Cards for Integration Seasons

STRENGTH

QUEEN OF SWORDS

THE FOURS

STRENGTH

QUEEN OF SWORDS

FOUR OF WANDS

FOUR OF CUPS

FOUR OF SWORDS

FOUR OF PENTACLES

One of my favorite childhood movies was *The Secret of NIMH*. In it, we follow Mrs. Brisby, a shy and quiet mouse who, in the wake of tragically losing her husband, must venture through hell and back to save her home and her children, one of whom is gravely ill. She is asked to blow past her edges again and again through multiple initiatory experiences until, ultimately, she discovers a luminous ocean of mystical courage within her that allows her to save her family. After this climactic finale (seriously consider watching it—it's great), Mrs. Brisby collapses down to the earth, exhausted, and immediately falls asleep.

Isn't that a beautiful depiction of the ideal outcome of this kind of scenario? We move through hell, then we rest. We complete a pilgrimage, then we rest.

Ideally, after enduring a long and arduous journey, one that has required everything from us—all of the courage and willingness that our heart, mind, body, and soul have to offer—we would automatically be given the gift of time: time to process, sleep, cry, or just *be*. Most of us, however, don't get the kind of integration period we long for, desire, or crave, for a myriad of reasons. Those reasons can be systemic, societal, or personal in nature, rooted in a lack of access or ability to take the time and space we need. There are also times when we might have the access and the ability, but we don't feel comfortable taking the space. It might bring up feelings in us that we are somehow selfish or asking for too much.

We don't need to have physically or literally given birth to feel into the postpartum periods of our lives—times when we have symbolically (or literally) climbed up a mountain and need to lay our bodies down for longer periods of time. In seasons when we've been asked to cross bridges, shed old skins, stand in our knowing, defend ourselves, be vulnerable—when we're potentially drained clear of our life force, energy, and momentum—how can we feel into the possibility of refilling our well? How might we reach for the holy medicine of integration seasons in whatever way is most accessible to us?

In seasons that involve an invitation to engage with a necessary period of rest after a courageous journey of the heart and soul, we will likely come into connection with **Strength, Queen of Swords**, and **The Fours** of the Tarot. These cards cannot automatically give us the gift of rest, or afford us the spaciousness that we might not be able to access. They can, however, help us rest in ways that are within our reach. They can also assist us in fine-tuning our boundaries (especially important in times like this), and help us honor our own needs clearly and unapologetically.

HEEDING THE CALL WITH A COURAGEOUS HEART WITH STRENGTH

In the Smith-Rider-Waite image of the Strength card, we see a person placing their hands on a lion. The person in the image seems calm and serene, and the lion seems open and available to their embrace. There are some other strong and significant visuals in this card. The person in the image is wearing white, with a crown of flowers on their head in lieu of protective gear—they are seemingly defenseless. There is also an infinity loop above the person's head, which is important in the Smith-Rider-Waite Tarot. Only The Magician and the person on Two of Pentacles share this visual with the person on the Strength card. It is a clue that lets us know that some kind of spiritually significant process is taking place, or that the figure is connected to and working alongside the divine. It is a creation process. In the case of the Strength card, this creation process is rooted in the medicine of heart-led courage—of facing down a potentially frightful, overwhelming thing and making our way to the other side of it. Just the simple act of being willing to do this is transformative. We open to the possibility of facing our fear, and are profoundly, alchemically shifted in the process of doing so—regardless of the outcome.

There are too many movies, books, TV shows, poems, songs, and pieces of art made about this theme to count or to name. There are so many of these experiences we carry within us. For some of us, it might be giving birth, or making it through a procedure or test, or having that brutally difficult conversation with someone, or opting out of a conversation with a person that we know will lead nowhere. Strength card work can lie in the choice to face something *and* in the choice to say no thank you to something. Strength can follow us anywhere, and doesn't ask us to traumatize ourselves or suffer. It does ask us to touch in with the heart and proceed bravely from that place. It is a rite of passage and, often, an act of spiritual courage that we can draw upon for the rest of our lives. We move past the bounds of our comfort when working with this card and tend to evolve through our experience with it.

Strength often shows up when we're asked to be present with our own inner "lion"—to bring aspects of ourselves into oneness that often don't want to come together.

As a trauma survivor who gains a tremendous amount of benefit from doing internal family systems work, I tend to encounter Strength most often when I'm being asked to turn toward the parts of me that feel the most jagged, overwhelming, and uncomfortable—the voice of my OCD, or my lizard brain, or my inner kid. They are a part of me, but they don't always align with the deepest, most solid truth of my inner knowing. All of us have the capacity to experience duality within ourselves, and mine has the tendency to sometimes be very intense and extreme.

I have found that when I speak directly to these parts, recognizing and honoring them, they soften and ebb back. When I turn toward my scared inner kid and remind them that I have them, there's an even deeper softening process. If you've ever experienced pelvic floor pain and/or dysfunction, doing your physical therapy exercises and breathing directly into the heart of the discomfort can feel counterintuitive. And yet, doing so is precisely what relaxes the muscles and helps to calm a flare. It is a bringing together of two things that don't always make sense, a powerful moment of our inner owl and inner mouse coming together in a moment of undefended alignment, or heightened oneness, seeing and witnessing one another in their value and beauty.

The owl within us has to be willing to be seen, has to be willing to come out of the darkness and into the light. The mouse within us must be brave and willing to show up and bear witness to this fearful thing.

When Strength shows up in a reading, we're being invited to show up to a tricky or uncomfortable internal or external situation with an open, willing, and undefended heart. By showing up this way, we invite the other people we are engaging with or internal aspects of ourselves to drop their defenses as well.

Strength Reversed

Whenever I get Strength reversed, I notice that things might be a little too overwhelming or uncomfortable for me to face on my own. Once I have that information, I can proceed accordingly. If it's something I have no option but to face, I can draw upon more support from various sources. If I absolutely do not have to face it, I might choose not to out of respect for my nervous system. That might be what you feel called to do, too.

THE WILD ROSE BUSH WITH QUEEN OF SWORDS

I was in the middle of a session with my brilliant therapist, Jen, when she invited me into the following visualization:

> Imagine yourself as a wild rosebush, alight and aflame with luscious, pink, fragrant petals. You are open, inviting, and available, welcoming bees, wasps, butterflies, hummingbirds, ants, and beetles to all come to aid in the pollination process. But when you are not available, when grasped without respect, you can trust in your thorns to clarify your boundaries.

It was a very powerful visualization, and a beautiful encapsulation of Queen of Swords from a Soul Tarot perspective.

Queen of Swords is nettle, poison oak, a wild rosebush. It is the sacred act of setting, strengthening, embodying, and/or recentering a boundary for ourselves (to the extent that we're able to) without apology or explanation, drawing a line within the forest of our being with the sword of our heart. Like the rosebush, this card is open and inviting but exists with its partitions clearly defined. It is a potent reminder that we can do the same for ourselves and our own lives—again, to the extent that we're able to.

This card can also show up in moments when we're being invited to take time and space to sort something through for ourselves—specifically seasons when our thoughts and emotions might be too loud or cacophonous for us to tease them apart and sense into what's true. We can use those prickles, that nettle, that sword, to slice through the confusion and sense into the deeper knowing underneath it.

The key to being able to engage with Queen of Swords on any of these levels is *space*: psychic space, emotional space, physical space. The same is needed for deep Strength card–level journeys, and the same is needed for our work with The Fours. Being able to give ourselves the open air we need to listen and get clear on something without rushing is one of the most crucial methods for clarifying our wants, needs, and preferences. We don't always have the option or the privilege to take our time, but when we do, Queen of Swords can help us clarify our next move.

Queen of Swords Reversed

When we pull Queen of Swords reversed, we want to check in and make sure that we aren't needlessly rushing ourselves into a decision. Are we encroaching on our own boundaries? Feeling unsafe or insecure despite trying to convince ourselves that we're fine? Give yourself permission to pause and check in with yourself and your body. You are always allowed to change your mind.

ROOT, REPLENISH, AND RESOURCE WITH THE FOURS

We plant our seeds with The Aces, we move through a process of deep and responsive self-tending with The Twos, and we reach for sustenance and support in the midst of transition with The Threes. With The Fours, we arrive at our destination, slide our backpacks off our exhausted bodies, jump into a cool shower, and crash into bed. We sleep, rest, eat, nourish, refortify ourselves, and consider that to be our most important job. The Fours are about rooting back into ourselves, and replenishing our resources.

We can think of each Four in the Tarot as a sweet, childlike fort—a special contained place with blankets, cozy pillows, and all our creature comforts. We feel held and safe in this fort, and it provides us with the crucially needed space and ability to process, recenter, and come back to ourselves.

This kind of medicine is so important in big rite-of-passage moments, similar to the ones we experience in cards like Strength. We have to be able to process and digest those initiations, have to allow the transformations we've experienced to settle into our bones. The Fours can be of great assistance to us in seasons like this.

Restorative Joy with Four of Wands

I recently gave my partner a slushy machine for their fortieth birthday. They were so excited about it that they opened it a month early and are currently enjoying a frozen margarita as I write these words.

"You know," they remarked after taking a sip, "this is the first birthday gift I've asked for in at least ten years that is purely for pleasure. It has nothing to do with work, just enjoyment."

That, in essence, is Four of Wands.

Four of Wands is a very special and unique energy. The Fours themselves are like little pockets of deep restoration and renewal. When we receive a Four in the Tarot, it is a call to curl up into a metaphorical nest with all of our coziest resources and sink in, allowing ourselves to be refueled in some much-needed ways.

Four of Wands is exceptional because it is an appeal to have fun for fun's sake as an act of deep fortification. It's your version of that slushy machine, and it shows up around whatever form of pleasure is within reach and accessible for you. It reminds us that fun, laughter, and joy are medicine. They make life worth living and help us prioritize delight in our lives wherever possible.

After hugely transformative events and courageous feats, moments when we face down those internal or external sources of fear, we need levity. We need enjoyment, satisfaction, laughter, felicity. It is one of the toughest things to give ourselves in seasons of replenishment after intense periods of soul evolution, but one of the most crucial.

When Four of Wands shows up in our readings, we're being invited to make space for deeper joy in our lives. This doesn't bypass any of the challenges, difficulties, or tricky things you or the world might be going through. It makes them more bearable. One way to begin to work with Four of Wands is to make a list of things that bring you comfort and delight and are completely within reach. How might you make more space for these things in your life?

Four of Wands Reversed

As I sit here writing on an early autumn morning, I hear the sound of the migrating geese through my open window and it fills my heart with luminous joy. It reminds me that Four of Wands moments can be so simple, so accessible. Is there some resistance coming up for you around deepening into available joy, fun, and play right now? If so, what might be at the heart of that? I encourage you to be gentle in your exploration of this question. Sometimes current situations are too spiky for us to come to laughter. Sometimes we feel too overwhelmed to play, and sometimes we can feel so daunted by the idea of playing that we can't quite make our way into this card. Is there something you can reach for that might help you to get even 10 percent closer to a Four of Wands invitation?

Declining the Invitation with Four of Cups

There is a Tarot meme about Four of Cups that has been floating around on social media for a while. In this meme, we see the Smith-Rider-Waite version of the Four of Cups, which is an image of a person leaning on a tree with three cups scattered around them, and a fourth cup floating toward them that they don't seem to be aware of. The text on the image reads, "Just take the fucking cup, dude."

This humorous sentiment is perfectly pitched toward the old paradigm narrative about Four of Cups, namely that we're missing a sign or a signal (possibly because we're being moody or gloomy or deep in our feelings), and that we need to wake up and grasp this opportunity before it slips away from us. While certainly a valid and arguably more mainstream take on Four of Cups, it's never really resonated with me, and there are a few reasons for this.

For starters, just as a baseline, if we see that the person in the Smith-Rider-Waite Tarot card has consumed three cups worth of something, they might be full, complete, or even a little sick. Do they have room for what the fourth cup is offering?

Secondly, when we peek ahead in The Cups suit, we see that that fourth cup doesn't go anywhere, even if we say no to it. It shows up (with an additional fifth cup) in the Five of Cups card. In light of that, we might consider Four of Cups to be an overarching invitation to trust in ourselves and our timing, which is the deepest medicine of The Cups suit. There are other cards in the Tarot (Nine of Wands and Knight of Swords, for example) that show up when we're in a situation where it might be beneficial to edge past our comfort zone. With Four of Cups, if we don't have room for something, we don't have to push it.

Lastly, I am wary of any narrative that cajoles or pushes someone to take *more* of anything when we don't necessarily have room for it, especially as it relates to our body, our boundaries, or our emotional experience. I'm wary of it from a framework that acknowledges the insidiousness of colonialism, systemic oppression, and white supremacy, and how easy it is to want more and more of something, even when we're already full. I'm wary of it as I continually shuck off the unending harms of an ableist culture that tells me that I'm lazy for resting. I'm wary of it as someone who survived abuse; who lives with PTSD, multiple autoimmune diseases, and chronic pain; and who has strong people-pleasing tendencies that will run rampant and leave me withered if left unchecked.

Who benefits when we push past our limits and take more of something, even when we don't have room for it? Who wins when we ignore our digestion—whether emotional or literal—and pile on top of something that doesn't have room to be processed?

Within a Soul Tarot framework, Four of Cups invites us to consider the exact opposite sentiment of what we see in that meme (as delightful as it is). It is an invitation *not* to take the cup, because we likely don't have room for whatever it is offering, and because we're being invited to trust in the time and space we need to emotionally digest and process something. Sometimes Four of Cups shows up in a moment when we're being invited to not even touch something; it's just a no, and we want to honor that empowered awareness that we can pass on something without regrets.

When we receive this card in a reading, we're being encouraged to go slowly, to follow our body and heart's lead. It's safe for us to say no thank you to something when and if it really is a no. It's okay to feel worried about that. It's okay to move through some contraction about that choice—will we feel that we've missed out? Most of the time (because that fourth cup pops back up in Five of Cups), whatever it is that we haven't had room for cycles back around to us at a time when we have space for it.

Four of Cups Reversed

Have you said yes to something you'd rather not do, or overcommitted yourself? Four of Cups reversed wants to remind you that you're allowed to change your mind at any time.

Powering Off with Four of Swords

Four of Swords invites us to take a mental break in whatever ways suit us best. For some of us, that might mean a nap, turning off the phone, and/or going on an impromptu trip. Sometimes Four of Swords is a top-to-bottom pause, especially if we are burned-out and need to broadly shift the way we're approaching our lives to heal from how exhausted and overloaded we've become. Sometimes Four of Swords is very light and subtle, and all we need is a little space to come back to our center. Regardless of how it shows up for us, we want to be sure to embrace it as much as we possibly can.

Many aspects of the Tarot involve a reparenting of sorts. We can really see that reflected in the Minor Arcana, especially with The Cups and The Swords. Four of Swords is an act of tending, wrapping the fried, exhausted, overloaded parts of ourselves up in love. It is a reminder that rest is safe. We don't need to earn rest, or space, or a break. We can remodel for ourselves that times of repose, relaxation, or inactivity are deeply healing to all aspects of us.

It is an act of profound care to nurture ourselves and reach for the things that we know will mitigate and soothe that frenzy, rather than leaning even deeper into our continually losing steam. When we receive this card in a reading, we want to think about the parent, caretaker, and witness in us, as well as the parts of us that need to be cared for. We want to ideally reach for things that don't further the cycle of burnout and exhaustion and that help us get the break we deserve.

In Four of Swords, we aren't opting out, bypassing, or dissociating. In fact, the opposite is true. A vehicle cannot run for long without power or gas. It needs to be regularly charged and refueled. With this card, we are merely honoring that we deserve space and rest. Engaging with these things is a radical reclamation of softness, ease, and support as a birthright.

Four of Swords Reversed

Are we pushing past our limits repeatedly? Four of Swords wants us to check in about that. Sometimes Four of Swords can show up reversed when we've actually gotten all the fuel we need, and we're ready to come back into the world with a charged sense of energy, but it is always helpful to check in with ourselves to make sure that we're getting what we need in the first place.

Sacred Boundaries with Four of Pentacles

Four of Pentacles is not a card of stinginess, greediness, or miserliness. It doesn't signify that we're holding on to anything too tightly, as many definitions on the card would suggest. It is a card of boundaries and sacred protection, specifically around our physical bodies and our energy.

I have strong memories of pulling Four of Pentacles as a thirteen-year-old (with no money of my own) when I was learning how to read Tarot and feeling shame and confusion when confronted with the more classical interpretations. Could the Tarot know something about me that I didn't know about myself? Was I a selfish, greedy person?

The answer to all of this, of course, is no. It also calls up a very important question: Why has a card that is so clearly about leaning into the agency and permission to unapologetically take space for ourselves been relegated to a description about monetary rapacity? Karen Vogel and Vicki Noble's *Motherpeace Tarot* and Cristy C. Road's *Next World Tarot* saw this about Four of Pentacles, too, and have offered up similar sentiments about this card in their respective decks. Who profits when we eschew deep bodily replenishment for fear of looking standoffish, cold, or antisocial?

The Pentacles as a suit are not exclusively rooted in the topics of money and finance. They can (like all of the cards in the Tarot) be inclusive of money and finances, but it's not the rule. The Pentacles help us act as cosmic gardeners, so we might bring our soul's dreams and visions into form on this planet. A great deal of that process comes from our having a willingness to be in touch with our bodies. We don't have to be jazzed or passionate about our bodies. We just have to be willing to remember that every great creative act, every birth, every leap, every expansion, every great learning that we undergo happens because we are in a body, and as such, our bodies need periods of rest after seasons of creation.

Four of Pentacles is a reclaiming of those seasons of essential physical replenishment. It is a mini postpartum period, one where we might be drawn only to see certain people or have certain energies closer to us than others for a time. This is deep wisdom. Honor it without apology and take your space.

Four of Pentacles Reversed

Are you pushing past the limits of your boundaries, your yes, or your internal permissions? Four of Pentacles reversed often suggests that we're in a much more intensified version of the right-side-up meaning of the card. If you're able to, I highly recommend that you make a shift. You can say no at any point. You can take space for yourself. You can rescind an invitation at any time. Honor your body and what it needs as you can.

CHAPTER EIGHT

THE WAITING ROOM

Tarot Cards for Liminal Seasons and Unclear Times

THE HERMIT

WHEEL OF FORTUNE

JUSTICE

THE TETHERED ONE

KNIGHT OF PENTACLES

THE FIVES

THE HERMIT

WHEEL OF FORTUNE

JUSTICE

THE TETHERED ONE

KNIGHT OF PENTACLES

FIVE OF WANDS

FIVE OF CUPS

FIVE OF SWORDS

FIVE OF PENTACLES

There are moments in life when it can feel like we are in a waiting room. We flip through magazine after magazine, watch as other people's names are called, and quietly wonder if we've been forgotten.

Most of us have been through big transitions in our lives, which are absolutely a rite of passage. Transitional seasons are very much a process of becoming something and someone new over time. But what happens when there's no sense of movement at all? How do we respond when *everything* is void-like, unknown, and unclear? I refer to these times as liminal seasons, times when we're floating in the unknown, encased in a kind of chrysalis, with no sense of how we got there or how long we might be there. There is a brutality to liminal seasons, because they are unyielding in their stretch. These seasons can bring us to our breaking point, and we can find ourselves demanding a shred of clarity, a signal to guide us, but we encounter only silence as a response.

I believe that liminal seasons are initiations. Moving through them is often a kind of a death cycle in our lives, a process of surrender, of clearing, and of deepened trust. Liminal seasons are a preparatory time, even though we might not necessarily know what we're preparing for. We know we're in a liminal time when we feel like nothing is going on, and we cannot get a clear answer about what is next in our lives. It can feel like we're trying to get comfortable on a pincushion. We're in the hallway, in the waiting room, sitting and sitting, seemingly doing nothing, until all of a sudden we've emerged from a cocoon that we didn't even know we were in, with wings that we didn't even know were forming.

The Hermit, **Wheel of Fortune**, **Justice**, and **The Tethered One*** are our Tarot cards for liminal seasons. They show up for us when we're moving through this dark, deep, void-like time, when we are undergoing profound transformation

* I prefer referring to this card as The Tethered One, rather than The Hanged One, so in this book and for our purposes, I'll be using that term throughout. I gratefully acknowledge Chase Voorhees, who originated the term The Tethered One for their wonderful deck, *Tarot of the Holy Spectrum*.

and change that happens just outside of our conscious awareness. As a departure from our work with the Tarot cards in chapter 2, where they all flow together and build upon one another, we are exploring these cards as independent anchors for whatever kind of liminal season we might happen to be in. We can absolutely experience them in tandem, or in a linear order, but that's not always the case.

In either scenario, these are our teachers when we're sealed inside of the chrysalis. When we consider supportive anchors that can hold us while we're going through this kind of season, we can lean into the medicine of **The Fives** of the Tarot, as well as **Knight of Pentacles**, all of which we will discuss in this chapter.

THE HOLY LANTERN WITH THE HERMIT

It is befitting that our journey into liminality begins with the flickering light of a lantern.

The spotlights, flashlights, and high-watt bulbs all get left at home in these seasons. In liminal cycles, we travel by candlelight, moonlight, and lantern light.

The Hermit is never really alone, nor are they necessarily a loner. Sometimes folks who are seeking a beloved or another kind of relationship will gulp at the sight of this card, believing that it might be guiding them into a more monastic phase of life, but that's not often the case.

The Hermit is a seeker, a wanderer on their way to some new destination. That is an important piece of counsel for those of us who are working deeply with The Hermit right now, and who might be in that kind of deep liminality: We *are* moving in this card, even if it doesn't necessarily feel like it. Our pace might be slower, and the path wilder and less familiar, but there is movement.

The Hermit usually travels in the dark, hence the lantern. This piece of information is also helpful because it offers us a huge clue about how Hermit seasons tend to feel: like we're in the dark, moving through the unknown, unclear about our next steps. As discomfiting as this might be to our ego and nervous system, which are designed to seek out and stick to what's known and familiar, our soul is very intimate with this experience. The soul thrives and expands in the presence of mystery and springs forth from a place between worlds. The Hermit card is a slow, gentle, but persistent call to come back home to that pace and tempo, to start to surrender and open to the gifts that can come from a walk on a dark path, lit only by a lantern. The Hermit is the initiation into a space of numinousness.

The lantern that The Hermit carries is not particularly good at illuminating anything other than a patch of light around our feet, and maybe a larger circle that encompasses our next immediate step. Other than that small area, things will likely be shrouded in mystery, which is part of its design.

The Hermit card can be experienced as a kind of sacred pause, but we're only ever really pausing our engagement with mindless habits or patterns rooted in escapism. The pause allows us to come home to ourselves and gently work through what's asking to be witnessed and processed at this time—and indeed, when The Hermit card shows up for us in our readings, we want to heed its call however we can.

When we're moving through a Hermit season or cycle, we're being directed away from focusing on the future or what might be next. Instead, that energy gets redirected back to ourselves. The Hermit's lantern cannot illuminate the bigger picture of our lives right now, so we have no choice but to shine that lantern within, looking closely and intimately at what wants attention right now. This deep inner exploration—as well as our tacit willingness to flow through life in a very different, more hermetic rhythm—is the first step to the kind of deep transformation that happens in liminal seasons. It is what kicks off this process, our slow journey into the chrysalis, a portal of radical change and self-discovery.

The Hermit Reversed

There are certain journeys with The Hermit where we can feel like we're losing it. We want to get in a car, get the hell off this wild path, and just make some kind of solid plan in our lives. We are always empowered to do this, but in Hermit seasons, these plans usually fall flat. When The Hermit shows up reversed, we're usually working through impatience, resistance, and discomfort with the energy of the card and what it's asking us to do. We want to be as compassionate with ourselves as humanly possible in these moments. It's completely valid that we would feel frustrated and over it. What might help us feel more resourced and supported as we travel through our Hermit season?

THE CENTER OF THE WHEEL WITH WHEEL OF FORTUNE

Wheel of Fortune has a big and storied reputation. Often seen as an epic, swirling, cosmic card of fate and destiny, it can be challenging to assume that this card would be anything but a big mover and shaker in the presence of our readings. While I wholeheartedly respect the history and lore that is threaded through the bedrock of this card, I've never personally experienced much pomp and circumstance when it shows up in a reading for myself or a client. Make no mistake—when Wheel of Fortune shows up in a reading, it's always bringing something big to the table, but it might not always *feel* that way to us in the moment we receive it, which is a crucial distinction.

Wheel of Fortune usually shows up in our readings when major change is afoot or underway. The cosmic wheel is turning, and something is getting reworked, reshaped, or ushered in when this card is present with us (usually something that is outside of our purview or awareness).

That shroud is a part of the medicine of the card. There is a curtain over the wheel as it turns, and trying to peek behind it is like attempting to cup water in our hands: It just slips away. Part of the reason for this is typically because whatever is getting woven behind that curtain is not fully formed or written. Another part of it might be that it isn't our business to know just yet. To offer a gentle refresher, Wheel of Fortune is a part of Line Two of the Major Arcana, a cluster of seven cards that pivots us from the ego driving the car of our lives to the soul sitting in the driver's seat. It is truly with Wheel of Fortune that we start to sense the scope of what's in our highest interest to know and what's not. It is also a deep and beautiful continuation of the work we do in The Hermit. It widens the lens and brings the liminality into sharper focus.

We can expect to see Wheel of Fortune anytime we are waiting on an answer, when something is as of now unclear, or when we find ourselves trying to grasp for any clarity around a situation that is totally obscured. Indeed, that desire to know, to get a sense of why and how that outer wheel is turning, is so real and so valid, and yet there's really no way to get to the bottom of it. Trying to get a sense of what's happening around that outer wheel is like gripping the tread of a tire while a car is in motion. We're going to feel every single pothole and bump in the road. We're going to exhaust ourselves and get dinged up in the process.

The only way to move through a Wheel of Fortune experience is to position ourselves at the *center* of the wheel. It doesn't change much about the ride itself, but it sure can make the process much more graceful and less bumpy.

What does it feel like or look like to stay rooted at the center of the wheel in a Wheel of Fortune season, when things are typically very liminal and rife with unknowns?

Staying close to the center in Wheel of Fortune means that we plant ourselves firmly in the realm of the accessible, the present, and, often, the mundane. We're chopping wood and carrying water in this card, busying ourselves with what's in our control, and shifting away from what's outside of our control. In other words, what is right in front of you that needs your attention?

In spite of how grand and epic this card seems to be on paper, embodying and moving through Wheel of Fortune largely feels like showing up to the stuff that's in front of us while more macrocosmic unknowns swirl around us, just outside of our awareness. It is good practice for life, and good medicine for transiting through liminal seasons.

We wonder when we will hear back from that person, and then notice that there's a teacup on the nightstand that needs to be washed, so we take it downstairs and wash it. We worry about what our test results will say, and we put the laundry away. We fret about our due date, and we take the tape measure back downstairs. This is the deal we strike in Wheel of Fortune and, really, in any liminal season: We rest in the medicine of the accessible and the tangible, showing up to what's here with us, and trust that the wheel will continue to turn. No matter what, we will eventually receive an answer to the wondering and worry on our heart. We will eventually get clarity on what was getting formed on the other side of that curtain. For now, we close the window. We walk the dog. We blow out the candles. We go to that meeting. The center of the wheel will be here to hold us through it all.

Wheel of Fortune Reversed

In my experience, Wheel of Fortune reversed is not remarkably different from Wheel of Fortune right side up—both positions essentially bring the same invitations and medicine to our door. We might notice a bit more frustration, resistance, or impatience with our situation when Wheel of Fortune shows up reversed, but not always. I encourage you to stay open and curious about whether or not there's anything more for you to know as you travel through the reversal of this card.

BEING WITH WHAT IS WITH JUSTICE

The perfectly understandable hope, assumption, and expectation that many of us carry about the Justice card is that it will bring a moral or situational correction to an unfair or unjust situation. It can indeed show up amid legal battles, at court cases that we're favored to win, or in a situation where we're deeply engaged in a restorative justice model of repair with another person or group. However, it's just not necessarily the most consistent way that the Justice card presents itself.

Justice is an invitation to be with what is, rather than what we feel should or shouldn't be. It doesn't call upon us to cast aside our devastation, outrage, or displeasure about the present circumstances. It doesn't negate the reality of unfairness, injustice, and systemic oppression in our lives and the world around us. It holds a passionate, acknowledging space for all of that and more. Justice also doesn't encourage us to choose inaction, or to bypass the totality of our experience around whatever it is we're moving through. On the contrary: The more we're able to be with what's *here*, the more available we will be to reach for recovery, for necessary change, for time to heal and grieve, and, ultimately, for justice.

About ten years ago, I had the honor of serving a client who had just experienced a devastating loss. We were doing a reading about how they might begin to support themselves amid this grief, how they might start to heal. Justice was the first card that showed up for them, planting itself squarely in the heart of the reading. I remember staring at it, honestly a little rattled. I was a much newer professional reader, and I wasn't initially sure what it was doing there, or how I could respectfully work with it in conjunction with this client's situation. I knew that Justice wasn't saying that this loss was somehow meant to be, and there wasn't much in the way of "justice" to be found within this brutal, unfair, and agonizing situation. It was this experience, the honor of holding space for this person, that taught me a great deal about the Justice card, and how it can be a bedfellow to us when we're traveling through liminal seasons.

This was what came to me when I was reading for this sweet client who had received Justice within the context of a deep loss:

> You didn't do anything wrong, and you don't deserve this. I'm so sorry for all that you're going through. Justice is an invitation to just be here, in whatever way feels accessible and safe for you, with all that is arising. Be willing to be with it all: all of the avoidance, all of the feelings of collapse, all of the feelings of grief, of rage, of fear, and of loss. Be with it all, as gently as you can, as tenderly as you can. Take it one moment at a time. That is, ultimately, all you can do today.

The Justice card has shown up for me amid so many heart-wrenching, world-altering health events that I've experienced, many of them unforeseen and rife with complications. To reach for our decks in search of a warm, soft, and gentle anchor of support and to receive Justice can be really challenging, depending on the season we are in and our emotional state. Despite how it feels, this card *does* bring medicine—medicine that can help us when we're floating in the void in vast ways.

Justice can also show up in moments when things are not so extreme, not so dire. It can sometimes arise in moments when *we* feel like things need to change, to be different, or to shift in a particular way, but there's nothing truly wrong, emergent, or in need of adjustment in our current circumstances. In these moments, we're invited to check in around what's driving that desire for change. Is it boredom? Hypervigilance that has us wanting to escape a situation before the rug gets ripped out from under us? Justice showing up around these kinds of situations will help us tend to the root of what's driving us and relax a little more fully into the moment.

When we're in liminal seasons, times when we cannot feel earth under our feet, moments when we're in free fall and cannot feel the edges of the container around us, we want someone to tell us that we're okay. We might want something to fix us in place, to make it better, to rescue us. I want that, too. I think we all do. Justice cannot give us that, but it will encourage us to be with everything that arises within the moment we find ourselves in. Being with it all allows for us to, paradoxically, be the most direct agent and advocate for change in our lives.

Justice Reversed

When Justice shows up reversed in a reading, we might be really struggling with the idea of "being with what is." It might not feel like enough for us in our current circumstances, which is wholeheartedly understandable. It can be useful to pull some clarifying cards in the presence of Justice reversed and those feelings of frustration. Some questions that we might consider asking are: How can I support myself best in this challenging season of my life? Is there an aligned action, if any, to take right now? When Justice reversed shows up in a reading, it can also be useful to reflect on whether it is even in alignment for us to be with what's arising on our own. We might need to process what's here with a great and skilled therapist, chaplain, death doula, or supportive friend. If you need or desire help, please know that you are wholly worthy of reaching for it.

THE LAST LEAF ON THE TREE WITH THE TETHERED ONE

The Tethered One is an initiation, a portal, a threshold, and the apex of what it means to live from the heart of liminality.

This card *is* the chrysalis, the last threadbare leaf on a bare winter branch.

This card is an experience of hanging out in the unknown, in the void, in the unseen, so that incomplete or unprocessed material in our lives has the space to bubble up and be witnessed. This card gently fixes us in place so we can be free, but while we're in it, it might just feel like we're in the dark without a single clue as to what's happening around us.

This is a very normal and common experience in The Tethered One and is part of a process of stages when it comes to this card. We often feel a rotating mixture of confusion, resistance, frustration, and desperation when we work with The Tethered One, longing to get out of the emotional and psychic suspension we find ourselves in. If we are able to come to even the barest flicker of acceptance or surrender in our work with this card, we can make space for the transformation that comes hand in hand with this energy.

We are rarely in a situation where we sit still for so long that we allow for layers upon layers of emotional material to be processed, cleared, and burned off, but this is precisely what can happen when we work with The Tethered One.

The Tethered One is, quite literally, the dying process. It is the dying of an old aspect of ourselves in order to rebirth into a new form.

The Tethered One is the midwife that ushers us through the doors of transformation, holding us while we complete the shift from caterpillar to butterfly. It is a potent and moving reminder that we can die with all our beloveds surrounding us, held in warmth and familiarity, and still not be able to avoid the liminality of the situation. We're not supposed to. The Death card (which follows The Tethered One in the Golden Dawn ordering of the Tarot) isn't really about the death process so much as it is about what happens on the other side of the threshold. The Tethered One is the hard work of the actual dying process, a soul death/rebirth experience. When we're able to surrender to this card and its energy, so much magic and change can begin to occur in our lives.

When we receive The Tethered One in a reading, we're being invited to surrender to the unknown, to give in to the fact that we're the last leaf on a tree that's ready to get blown off the branch that we've been hanging on to for so long. It might not feel that way. It might just feel like we're in a state of discomfort and suspension, without much clarity on what we're in or what we're moving through. The potential feelings of anger, frustration, desperation, sadness, and confusion that can come up around this card are wholly valid. They are a natural response to what really happens when we're in The Tethered One, which is nothing less than a full death/rebirth process, guiding us to another stage and season of our lives.

Giving over to the medicine of The Tethered One enables us to move through our grief, to be fully steeped in our process, greeting anything that wants to bubble up during this season—namely, anything that is not meant to come forward with us into this new cycle. How can we bow to the fact that we're in a chrysalis, that we're in the process of getting blown off the tree that we've known for so long, and that nothing is wrong with that? It's okay that we might feel contracted around it, and it's also safe. This is what we're being invited to hold when we move through this card.

The Tethered One Reversed

When The Tethered One shows up reversed for us, it usually indicates that there's a very high level of contraction, resistance, and impatience with this card's energy and what it's bringing to us.

When I was going through a very memorable and intense Tethered One season in 2019, it was so uncomfortable that I needed some good distractions, which led me to Stephen King novels. I hadn't read much of his work prior to this time, and while the novels were great, I haven't returned to them since. This taught me that it can be very useful to bring good material into the cocoon with us. We are heartily encouraged to engage with things that feel interesting, entertaining, comforting, and enlivening for us during these seasons. This can be especially useful when we're in Tethered One reversed.

TRUSTING IN THE TIMING WITH KNIGHT OF PENTACLES

I always think of trillium flowers when I think of Knight of Pentacles.

Trilliums grow very slowly. It can take almost two years for trilliums to germinate, and then up to *ten* more years for the plant to be robust enough to bloom.

Trilliums don't get self-conscious about that. Once they finally get going, trilliums bloom each year. When they are established, they also become very hardy. How might we envision ourselves as that sacred trillium flower, letting ourselves take the necessary time to bloom, and trusting that going at our pace ensures the strength of our roots?

We consider The Knights of The Court Cards to be our *currents*, representing and holding a space for the various ways that we work with timing in our lives. The Knights help us to get a better sense of our pace, tempo, rhythm, and way of moving through the world. Like the wind itself, all of The Knights flow a little differently from one another.

At first glance, Knight of Pentacles might seem to be our slowest Knight. It is the Knight that seems to be really comfortable with the idea of taking their time, and when we spend a lot of time in Knight of Pentacles energy, we can feel held in place, like we've been waiting for the light to turn green for a little too long.

It can be useful to consider Knight of Pentacles as more preparatory than slow. It can seem like they're aiming their arrow at the target longer than anyone else in the competition, but when they finally release the arrow from the bow, they are more likely than anyone else to hit a perfect bullseye. This Knight helps us to trust in the flow of our timing, and is an incredibly supportive ally in liminal, more void-like seasons of life. It reminds us that we aren't just sitting still—we are growing, evolving, blooming in place. We are waiting for that light to turn green and trusting in the medicine of what it means to be in a state of sacred pause at the red light. Knight of Pentacles will encourage us to pack the best snacks, to have a great podcast, audiobook, or playlist on while we're waiting. It wants us to embrace the flow and enjoy the ride as much as possible, because once that light turns green, we're off!

Knight of Pentacles Reversed

When Knight of Pentacles shows up reversed, it can sometimes affirm or acknowledge our impatience with the pace of this energy, or it can have us feeling like we might miss out on something because of how suspended we are. This is a gentle reminder that we can trust in the timing, and that it's also perfectly okay to be over it. It's perfectly okay to feel impatient *and* to trust that we are still moving at an aligned pace.

TURNING TOWARD OURSELVES WITH THE FIVES

The Fives are contractive energies, and usually show up when things feel prickly, tricky, squeezed, or thorny. The feelings that typically coexist when we pull or work with a Five of the Tarot are absolutely real and valid, but—given the nature of contraction—they might not always be *true*, which is an important thing to remember when working with The Fives and, by extension, with contraction.

We move through contractive seasons for a variety of reasons. We say the wrong thing. We mess up. We are misunderstood. We forget our beloved's birthday. We send an email that we really regret. Maybe we're worried about something, are experiencing financial stress, or are feeling ashamed and sad about the way an interaction went down with another person. Whatever the cause or the reason, contraction can be so, so painful. It narrows our view of the world, making things around us feel squeezed.

My former teacher Michelle used to say that it is never a good idea to make any big decisions while in contraction, and if the option to refrain is available to us, it is in our best interest to pause. In these tight, thorny moments, we're not always able to see the whole picture around us. We don't have all of the information. We cannot always feel or remember the love around us, or our basic goodness, or the temporary nature of things—even the toughest of things—in contractive moments.

In terms of the Tarot, there is no greater medicine for contractive seasons than The Fives.

We might feel like everything is going to shit when we're in a Five, or that things are falling apart, or that we will never be okay again. That might absolutely be true, but it's in our best interest to check in about that and stay open to the possibility that we might not have all the information at the present moment. That said, we don't need fixing in The Fives—we need nurturance, love, and support, remembering that whatever it is that we're moving through is likely to shift, ebb, and change shape with time.

It is very common to run into The Fives of the Tarot during liminal seasons, times when we're in the waiting rooms of life, because of how activating and tender those times can feel. Our inner protection system wants things to be predictable and familiar. When we're swimming in the void, or in the unknown in any capacity, things are anything but familiar. Alarm bells in our system can go off, even when we're perfectly safe. The mind can turn on itself, churning us up even further in the wake of majorly contractive feelings.

How can we hold ourselves amid these feelings? How can we bear witness to them and assist ourselves in crossing over to the other side of them? The Fives are here to be a source of immense support to us in that process.

Medicinal Messiness with Five of Wands

Five of Wands is messy as hell, and that's exactly what it's supposed to be. The energy of this card is akin to being at the halfway point of a massive home renovation, or huge clutter clearing, and everything is chaos. When we feel creatively blocked or stuck, when nothing seems to be flowing—when we're so completely not where we want to be (or where we thought we would be)—it is likely that we will see Five of Wands show up in our readings.

This doesn't mean that we're headed for a big old mess whenever we pull this card, or that the only thing we can expect from Five of Wands is a frustrating ball of loose ends. It actually indicates that we're well on our way to a time of organization, flow, and expansion. Five of Wands is a tricky stopping-over point in the middle of our journey.

I don't know if it's possible to organize without mess. I don't know if it's realistic to renovate, improve, or restructure without first tearing down that which doesn't work. That process usually involves some measure of dead ends, shitty contractors, and wrong turns. Having now written a book, I don't know if it's possible to avoid times when you feel that everything you write is shit, or *not* experience temporary blocks around the process of your work. The blocks, the tear-downs, the dead ends, and the mess are essential to creation, to renewal, and to moving toward an expansive and delightful time of satisfaction and completion. Five of Wands doesn't predict mess, per se, but it does help us wisely respond to these kinds of situations.

When Five of Wands shows up for us in our readings, we want to turn toward ourselves and be our best, most compassionate ally. We can remind ourselves that there's no creation, no improvement, no reorganization, without mess, and that it's not our job to judge how a project looks when it's in the middle of forming itself. It is crucial that we not forget that whatever it is we're working on right now—a project, a book, a home, our life—is still in process, still in progress. When contraction inevitably arises about that, and we find ourselves getting swept up in stories that we'll never finish it, or that everything's going to suck, we want to do our best to acknowledge those invitations, but not take them on. When we're in the chrysalis, a gooey mess between caterpillar and butterfly, we don't want to judge ourselves. The goo is gold, and we are growing from that place.

Five of Wands Reversed

When Five of Wands shows up in our readings reversed, it usually indicates that this period of necessarily medicinal messiness is coming to a close, or that we've been in this contractive state for long enough and it is now beginning to recede, making way for movement and expansion to cycle in.

Making Space for Our Grief with Five of Cups

Five of Cups is an invitation to make space at the table for our grief. It is a call to deeply digest and move through big emotions that need to be felt and experienced. It is a gentle invitation not to push those feelings away, but to let them be and give ourselves unapologetic space to experience them.

In the image of Five of Cups on the Smith-Rider-Waite Tarot deck, we see someone in deep mourning, standing over three spilled and empty cups. Behind them, just out of sight, are two full cups. The two full cups that lie just out of sight represent a beautiful beacon of hope and faith for us to root into in challenging and heartbreaking times, but it's not usually where we find ourselves resting our gaze in this card.

This card is a strong call to center and pay attention to whatever those three spilled and empty cups are for you. To give your grief, disappointment, concern, or point of contraction your full presence, while simultaneously honoring that there is something waiting for you beyond the pain of this experience that you haven't yet seen, felt, or touched. We aren't done with this life and this situation yet. There will still be joy, love, and things to welcome and celebrate, as impossible as that might feel. But right now, none of that matters. There are only these three cups—and our feelings about them—to be with. How can we be as present as possible with our grief, centering it at the heart of the current situation?

A few years ago, my husband Chase and I went for a weeklong stay at a vacation home in the Outer Banks of North Carolina that my grandparents had rented every summer since I was a baby. It was so meaningful to me that I had gotten married there in 2014. We hadn't been back since that time, and we decided to treat ourselves to one last visit with some pals before we moved to the West Coast in a few months.

When we unlocked the door and let ourselves in for that particular trip, I was surprised to find myself overcome with grief. I could feel my departed grandfather everywhere, as well as younger versions of myself who had laughed, cried, pined, bled, and grown up in that home over the summers of my life. I pushed away my tears at first. But after a while, I finally let loose and wept deeply. Once I had finished, we went for a gentle walk on the beach and I felt different—shifted. My grief still stayed very close to me for the entirety of our visit, but I was able to be more fully present with the joys and delights of our trip now that my feelings had been honored, and space had been made for them.

This specific example does not encompass the full range of Five of Cups, but it does illustrate both the importance of our willingness to honor our grief and the kind of transformative inner process that can happen when we do so. Even when we're not explicitly in an experience of grief when working with Five of

Cups, we want to be fully present in our honoring of whatever is coming up for us—because it not only is a beautiful thing to be able to offer to ourselves, but it actually brings us closer to the two full cups behind us.

How might we honor the contractive feelings that are showing up, giving ourselves permission to be present with whatever might be arising?

Five of Cups Reversed

When Five of Cups shows up reversed, it usually indicates that we might feel a little more space around our feelings than usual—perhaps like we're a little closer to the two full cups. Honor and trust whatever might be showing up and (as a gentle note) be willing to hold a space for it changing again.

Fucking Up and Forgiving Ourselves with Five of Swords

Despite the title of this section, Five of Swords isn't necessarily about us making mistakes or fucking up. This card *does* tend to arise when we *feel* like we've fucked up, missed something crucial, or made a mistake. Sometimes that's true; other times it isn't. Sensing into that truth is a big part of this card, but perhaps the most important work we do with Five of Swords is offering ourselves tenderness and compassion amid some incredibly spiky emotions and internal experiences.

If we truly have hurt someone's feelings, messed up, or caused harm in some way, Five of Swords will show up as a call to witness and repair to the best of our ability. It reminds us that we can apologize, acknowledge what we've done, and make our lives a living amends, especially if the transgression was big. Five of Swords calls upon us to feel the regret and the pain of what we've done, but not to the point where it overshadows our ability to stand in the light of accountability. When I've been called in by one of my students or podcast listeners about something I've said that inadvertently caused harm, I first center them and their experience, doing whatever I can to make immediate repair, and privately tend to my own feelings. Of course, like all humans, I experience defensiveness, as well as tremendous guilt and shame when I've messed up. Those experiences, however, are mine to be responsible for and to process with my therapist and helping team.

They have nothing to do with the student or listener who deserves full-hearted acknowledgments and apologies. Five of Swords can help us hold both of those experiences, caring for ourselves and responding appropriately in one motion.

With all of that said, nine times out of ten, Five of Swords shows up when we haven't actually messed up or done anything wrong; we just *feel* that we have. We're consumed with grief or guilt, beating ourselves up for something that we couldn't have foreseen, making something our fault or responsibility when it actually has nothing to do with us. We might feel swept up in regrets, feeling like we've made every shitty choice imaginable and it's ruined our lives. It can be oddly comforting to blame ourselves for a hard season of life that's fully out of our control. It is easy for the mind to divert us into this space of "you fucked up" when we're in a liminal, and often contractive space, too. Liminality—being in a void space, or ensconced in a chrysalis of sorts—can be very activating. It can draw us into some heavy stories, that everything we've done was wrong, and those wrong choices led us here. In these moments, it is crucial to remember that our thoughts are not necessarily true, and we don't have to believe them.

When Five of Swords shows up in a reading, don't take the bait. Don't let the contraction swirl you out and drag you under the waves for too long. Feel the feelings—weep, rage, vent, and process—but then respond as wisely as you can. Get a second opinion if needed, especially if you can't see the forest for the trees. If you tend to blame yourself for everything, even when it's not warranted, it's important to have that scaffolding around you to reflect to you that this isn't for you to take on. If you historically tend to get extremely defensive, it's just as important (if not more so) to have those loving and honest witnesses around you. Believe them if they tell you that you messed up and need to repair.

Whether we've fucked up or just believe we did, Five of Swords is about being tender with ourselves when things feel tremendously spiky, and forgiving ourselves if and when we've messed up, which we're all going to do. Either way, we are invited to be gentle with ourselves.

Five of Swords Reversed

When Five of Swords shows up reversed in our readings, some of the bite and sting of the card is typically blighted or softened. Perhaps we've been in a more contractive season, and that's starting to ebb a bit. Either way, Five of Swords reversed is usually a much less intense experience than when we receive this card right side up.

Tending to Ourselves in the Squeeze with Five of Pentacles

Five of Pentacles is a card that typically shows up when we're afraid or worried that we're not going to have what we need when we need it. We might see no clear proof that we will be okay, or that our needs will be met. We might be so scared that we won't be okay that it feels like the truth. Five of Pentacles affirms our feelings, but it in no way indicates that we won't actually have what we need when we need it. In fact, I have found that the opposite is usually true.

Just like The Lovers card cannot ever predict our meeting a lover, and The Cups suit is not explicitly about romantic love, The Pentacles does not hinge on our financial situation as a part of its core interpretation. Of course, financial stress is a reality for many, and this isn't an attempt to bypass or negate that. However, The Pentacles, and by extension Five of Pentacles, are not strong representatives of those experiences as a rule, or as a given.

Five of Pentacles often shows up in liminal times, or seasons when it feels like we're in the waiting room. It also shows up in any moment when we are afraid or unsure about whether we will have what we want or need. It can be challenging in those moments to believe that we will ever make our way out of that chrysalis. The truth is that we might not have what we need today, but our journey is not over. Five of Pentacles is the drought that is about to be nourished by the sweetness of rain, ushering in a lush blanket of wildflowers that live just under the surface. "The rain is just around the corner," this card whispers to us, "even if it doesn't feel like it is."

When we receive this card in our readings, we want to try to remember that whatever we're experiencing at this moment in our lives is temporary. The tightness, the squeeze, the crunch is so valid, but it's not here to stay. How might we stay rooted and grounded in the midst of the potential discomfort of this moment? If we're in a liminal, unclear space, that kind of tethering is even more crucial.

Five of Pentacles Reversed

When Five of Pentacles shows up reversed in our readings, it usually signals that a season of tightness, worry, and squeezing is coming to a gentle close, or that we're moving into a more expansive season. It can also indicate that we're still experiencing that contraction, but it might be to a lesser degree than if the card was right side up.

CHAPTER NINE

WHEN WE'RE BLOSSOMING

Tarot Cards for Creation Seasons

DEATH

TEMPERANCE

KING OF CUPS

THE SIXES

DEATH

TEMPERANCE

KING OF CUPS

SIX OF WANDS

SIX OF CUPS

SIX OF SWORDS

SIX OF PENTACLES

When we are moving through a creation season, a time of deep blossoming in our personal, artistic, and/or professional life, it is much like a full harvest for a gardener or farmer. We're often up before dawn or working much later than usual; we might have dreams about our work and are often awakened from a deep sleep to feverishly write down a sudden inspiration. We're often working harder in those seasons, attempting to keep up with the level and degree of exquisite growth that is ready to be harvested from the trees and bushes and soil of our own soul. In creation seasons, the current of our creative life becomes so swollen and full that the only thing we can do is surrender to where it guides us.

Many of us desire and long for these blossoming seasons to come into our lives. Who doesn't want to feel like an overflowing fount for the muses, steeped in that sense of rooted oneness with creation? Very few of us account for (or remember, if this isn't our first creation season rodeo) how *absolutely intense* these seasons can be, how unromantic and scary they can feel when you're in them, and how mind-bogglingly exhausted and fatigued we can become. Channeling and creating is hard work and requires a high degree of rest.

Many of us also don't account for all that might need to be cleared out, released, or recentered in order for us to engage with these kinds of creation seasons. Anytime we are called into a big harvest season, there will naturally be a deep audit or reckoning around our lives. Is there enough room, time, or space for us to lean into these seasons as they're asking us to? Is this blossoming illuminating what we're complete with, or what no longer serves us? How might we respectfully ritualize the release of these things?

When we're in a deep creation season and in a process of birthing something new, we will likely come into connection with the energy of **Death, Temperance, King of Cups**, and **The Sixes**. These cards can help us to ride out the cycles of death/rebirth and can assist us in reaching for support as we hold space for a creation season to flower open within us.

SACRED COMPOST WITH DEATH

The other week, while laid up with a bad migraine, I staggered into bed with some ice packs and dropped into a BBC show called *Tales from the Green Valley*, which was highly recommended by the great Phoebe Wahl on her Substack.

In it, a few hand-selected historians and archaeologists attempt to live on and operate a seventeenth-century farm in Wales for an entire year. For a few episodes of this show, the men on the farm toil through the backbreaking work of clearing out the thick mass of bracken roots that have completely taken over a field that they want to reclaim to plant their crop of peas. Of all the things that these folks do over the year that they live on this farm—building cowsheds and stone walls, plowing fields, living through a freezing winter—the task of uprooting the bracken is reflected upon by the farmers as the absolute toughest job, both mentally and physically.

It takes *tremendous* work to clear the space for new growth and new life to come through. It requires patience, willingness, discipline, fortitude, softness, and presence. It requires immense courage. Everything in our nervous systems is primed to reach for familiarity. To do the opposite—to dare to clear out those pesky but familiar roots in the pursuit of making space for new growth—can bring up so much contraction. Whether the clearing is welcome (like the one illustrated in *Tales from the Green Valley*) or fraught, rife with grief, indecision, and toil, there is no way to a creation season without our willingness to move through an uprooting phase of our lives. We must make space, and there's no real way to do that without a reckoning or an audit of what is no longer of service to us in the garden of our hearts. This is where the Death card comes in.

Death is about transformation. It can accompany literal death and loss, but it is much more common for it to show up in our readings amid deep soul-level personal shifts. We see the Death card in moments when we are being called to uproot something in the garden of our heart and soul that is no longer serving us, or that has already died, or that is threatening the health of the garden on a whole. When we work with this card, we go into that garden and uproot those plants, placing them on the compost pile of our soul so that they can become the sacred fertilizer that helps new things in our lives to grow forth. Nothing ever truly dies in the Death card. It lives on the axis of release and reclaiming, where something must be shifted and transformed not only for it to exist in a new and necessary form, but also for us to continue to grow and evolve on our path.

When the Death card shows up in a reading, it's an invitation to honor and move through an ending, allowing whatever we're releasing to become cosmic compost and sacred fertilizer that nourishes the next chapter of our lives. Nothing is ever lost in this card—it only changes form. What kind of ritual or ceremony might we engage with to mark this shift in form?

Whether we feel devastated or joyful, it is important to be gentle with ourselves when we work with this card. Either way, we can take heart in knowing for sure that we are on the verge of a rebirth, and a new and welcome cycle in our lives. The Death card is a consistent reminder that there is no birth (or rebirth) without death, and no death without rebirth.

Death Reversed

When we receive Death reversed in a reading, we might be experiencing some resistance or contraction around our work with this card. How could we not? It is immense work to let go and release all that doesn't serve us, and our ego and inner protectors can kick up a lot of valid dust around that process. How might you offer yourself some much-deserved additional compassion around how tough this work is, and how much it is asking of you?

COSMIC COLLABORATION WITH TEMPERANCE

After a cycle of deep release and transition, we organically make our way to a more creatively led season—a time when there is space for new inspiration and ideas to crack out of their pods and begin to sprout. Now that all the dead plants, thick roots, and brambles have been cleared from the fields of our soul, there is room for the new, the fresh, and the welcome. This is where Temperance comes in, a card that is both the epitome of what it is to move through expansion and an energy that is a deep and true anchor for these big blossoming seasons of life.

Temperance can be tough to sense into, partially because of how slowly this card moves (which is a part of its function and medicine) and partially, frankly, because of its name. Temperance has nothing to do with abstinence or self-restraint but is rather about deepening our capacity to co-create with Source, or Spirit, or the muses through a gradual, soul-led tempering process of our very being.

In working with Temperance, we create a kind of a cosmic aurora borealis through collaboration with our Spirit Helpers and wise inner knowing. Auroras occur when charged particles from the Sun launched along Earth's magnetic field collide with gases in Earth's upper atmosphere, creating glorious bands of color in the night sky. The same kind of process can happen when we form a beautiful and expansive alliance with our Spirit Helpers.

Temperance is also a gentle reminder that there's only so much we can control. We have to be willing to ask for help when we need it, and acknowledge that there are certain things we simply cannot figure out or make happen on our own. *"Spirit/Higher Self, I have tried to do everything I can think of here, but it's still not happening. Please help me, show me, guide me. I want to work with you."* The ego must melt away as we become more willing to collaborate with the muses, and the spirit of whatever we are trying to create. This is the first part of the tempering process.

We cultivate more strength and stability in our work with the Temperance card, too. Like a piece of metal that has been heated and then cooled over time, we clear out some of the volatility of the ego and become even more reinforced and less fragile around matters of creation.

What does any of this have to do with big blossoming seasons? When it comes to any great creative act, we are often in a larger conversation with the muses and the Divine. We are of service to the music, the writing, the harvest, not the other way around. In the Temperance card, we stop attempting to force what our ego wants to do and begin to be open to what we're *invited* to do. We begin to work more fully in service of the soul and, by extension, Source, in this card—collaborating in a beautiful and meaningful way.

Generally speaking, Temperance wants us to take the longer route to our destination, ideally with good sightseeing and delicious food along the way. We often want to get to places as quickly and cleanly as possible, but Temperance values the gifts of unexpected detours and delightfully unplanned divergences. The point of this card is to live out the fullness of life's experiences, to become as wise and as traveled as possible. It wants to make us richer in practical, lived wisdom—it just doesn't want us to feel like we have to do it alone.

Working with Temperance slowly transforms us, softening, humbling, and opening us fully to a larger conversation with the Universe and the inspirations that live within us. It expands us profoundly while leaving our free will, autonomy, and agency intact. It is a big turning point in the journey of the Major Arcana, where we pivot from an egoic way of existing to a more soul-led life. It is through our work with Temperance that creation seasons can truly begin to spark and flow from within us. Once our inner brambles and roots are uprooted, leaving space for us to rebirth in a new way, a bigger vision often starts to come into shape. That creative river starts to become rich and full, carrying us to a new stage of our lives.

Temperance Reversed

Temperance can be a challenging card to root into. It can sometimes feel tricky to open to what it is asking of us, to soften and surrender to a collaborative process with Spirit. If we're feeling resistance around that, or like we want things to move faster or to have more to show for the work we're doing, Temperance might show up reversed. That's okay. Those feelings are so deserving of witness and sweet tending. Even if it's not necessarily how you feel, Temperance reversed is an invitation to check in with ourselves about how this larger process feels. No matter what we feel, we're deserving of tenderness around it.

FILLING THE WELL WITH KING OF CUPS

In Soul Tarot, we look to The Kings as our *contributors*—offering something to the world of themselves, longing to leave a legacy of good. King of Cups is a deep symbol of the spirit of healership, or helpership, in the world. This card holds space, listens, gives of themselves, and has that deep calling to service that cannot ultimately be taught or enforced; it exudes from their very heart and soul.

King of Cups qualities exist in all of us and take form in an infinite number of ways. We might feel centered in our King of Cups-ness when we parent our children, hold space for our clients, patients, or students, or show up as a caretaker in some way. In fact, the presence of King of Cups in a reading isn't really an indication that we're being awakened to healing gifts that may exist within us. It can be, but it isn't a consistent reason that this card shows up. In my experience, King of Cups tends to affirm that the fact of our helpership is undeniable, a given. Its main point of concern is how we're caring for ourselves as we continue to be of service or be present for others.

When King of Cups shows up in a reading, it is an invitation to refill the proverbial well, to ideally drink from our own cup for each one we offer to another person. When that well starts to get a little low, this card will present itself in our lives in some way.

It is impossible to move through cycles with the Death and Temperance cards without making contact with King of Cups, even if it never physically shows up in a reading for us. Laying things down on the compost pile, moving through spiritual rebirths, and engaging in creation seasons will all draw from our inner reserves. To channel inspiration and creation through us, we need fuel in the tank—that's what King of Cups focuses on when it shows up in a reading.

King of Cups Reversed

When we receive King of Cups reversed, that inner well might be a little past low and into the realm of nearly dry. We have likely received lots of invitations to refill it prior to this moment, but we've been either unable or unwilling to do so. Whatever got you here, I encourage you to be patient and gentle with yourself. Each moment presents us with a new opportunity to shift the way we approach care for ourselves—we can try something new right now.

NOURISHING THE VESSEL WITH THE SIXES

After moving through the contractive squeeze of The Fives, we flow into the buoyant realm of The Sixes.

We don't ever move through creation seasons alone, or in a vacuum. Even if we reside in a tiny cottage by ourselves where we never see another living soul, we are never truly solitary. The Sixes help us to understand and embody that on a deeper level and, by extension, widen our capacity for support and nourishment, encouraging us to ask for more guidance, loving witnesses, or helping hands.

The Sixes are also highly expansive. They signal longed-for movement—the perfect medicine for big periods of release, of rebirth, and of channeling inspiration for new projects in our lives. It's very difficult to be available for creation and channeling seasons when we are closed off and locked down. The Sixes help to crack open the door to our heart again.

When we're embarking on any kind of big harvest season in our lives (or moving through Death and/or Temperance card seasons), we want to be focusing on nourishing our vessel—this heart, body, soul, and being. We can do this by opening to both visible and invisible supports, in the form of friends, community, and even our Spirit Helpers. The Sixes can help with all of this.

The Art of Celebration with Six of Wands

Six of Wands is an invitation to celebrate ourselves (and allow others to cheer us on) around all that we have accomplished in this season of our lives, even if we haven't necessarily achieved our ultimate goals or reached the "finish line" of a particular situation.

It can feel very challenging to properly honor our personal victories, to meet ourselves in this moment of our lives and offer ourselves acknowledgment and grace without comparisons. Taking a shower for one person might seem completely rote, but if we're moving through an illness that has us feeling weak, or we have a disability or condition that makes showering challenging, getting in that shower can be a mighty victory. It deserves to be cause for celebration, but we rarely, if ever, honor it that way.

Six of Wands invites us to greet ourselves, and allow others to greet us, where we *are* and drop any stories around where we think we "should" be, catching ourselves in painful comparisons about what we used to be able to do, or what others can seemingly or truly do with ease. How can we allow ourselves and other people to really celebrate us? How can we let others in more, and allow our beloveds to witness us?

The work we do with Six of Wands is crucial for any big creation season. If we're in a kind of "soul labor" where we're slowly birthing something, or we're attempting to create something under challenging conditions, or keep up with a huge harvest when we have tons of other tasks and responsibilities, or channel something down when our bodies are exhausted, we might not be able to keep the pace we hoped or imagined we would. This card can help us make peace with that disappointment and cultivate a new way forward. How can we hold a space of loving regard for all that we're doing and all that we've achieved, even if we're still in the middle of our journey, or moving down the path differently than we might have envisioned?

Six of Wands Reversed

Are we putting too much pressure on ourselves, or driving ourselves too hard? If we find ourselves in a place where there's no witness, no support, no honoring, no celebration, we might get Six of Wands reversed. It's not here to admonish us; it's here to be a loving reminder of the benefit and gift of self-acknowledgment. You're doing a great job, even if it feels challenging to admit that to yourself.

An Overflowing Heart with Six of Cups

Six of Cups is an invitation to truly share what's on our heart, holding nothing back, allowing ourselves to be witnessed in an embrace of true intimacy.

There is a reason that the Smith-Rider-Waite Six of Cups card has two children on it, looking at one another and sharing a flower that has grown out of one of the cups: Children are born into this world with hearts wide open, spirits shining.

We need to spend only a small amount of time with a child to see an incredible capacity for emotional depth, along with a complete willingness to share their love in their own unique way. This existed in us, too, before we might have had reason to clamp our heart shut in self-protection. If we've ever been told that we're unlovable, too much, or too loud, Six of Cups is a balm for our most tender wounds. It places a hand on our guarded heart and gently encourages us to share who we are with the people who matter to us, to offer our soul to this world without hiding it.

The process of hope is very fraught, especially when we've experienced tremendous pain. The act of clearing out a field that's been overtaken by weeds to plant something new, or writing a book, or expanding (or not expanding) our family, or going for our dreams, is incredibly vulnerable stuff. We could fail, have our dreams dashed, be misunderstood. Why do it if we might get hurt or experience that kind of pain? As corny as it might sound, the only true regret we could ever encounter is never reaching for a dream at all, never telling someone we love how we feel about them or remaining closed when our heart aches to expand and come into glorious connection with this world and other human beings.

When we get this card in a reading, it's an invitation to not only share what's on our heart, but to really allow ourselves to be witnessed in that vulnerable sharing. So much can flow open from that place.

Six of Cups Reversed

We might feel like it's unsafe to share something that's on our heart for any number of (likely) very good reasons. How might we hold a space of compassion for that protective part of us, and simultaneously feel our way into a willingness to crack open the door to our hearts by even a small degree?

Inviting in Another Perspective with Six of Swords

Six of Swords is an invitation to allow ourselves to be cared for in highly specific and bespoke ways. During difficult or impossible times, we need sturdy, capable systems of support to hold space for us. Not everyone has access to this kind of loving witness, but for those of us who do, it can be challenging to call upon it and ask for help when we need it. It can be easy to withdraw and isolate during heavy times, believing that no one wants to help us, that we are a burden, or that we are beyond help. That internal story can feel incredibly real, but it's not true. We are all worthy of support, no matter what we're moving through. Six of Swords can help us pierce through that tough and tender membrane of resistance and hold our arms out to community care.

Let's look at this card in a more granular way. The Sixes in the Tarot all have community care and interpersonal witnessing at their core. The Swords suit is ruled by the element of Air, and generally invites us to find balance in the imbalances, comfort in the discomforts—to engage with our communication, our actions, and our thinking in radically new ways. This suit can offer transformative spaciousness to our toughest places. It can serve to validate our feelings. It can assist us in tending to anything that comes up in our emotional field. The Swords call us to befriend and become curious about our mental stories, as opposed to identifying with them, so that we can move forward into the world from a place of truth, openness, and personal responsibility.

Just by virtue of its existence, Six of Swords presents us with a radical opportunity: Can we bear witness to the belief that we don't deserve to ask for help and support—and *ask for help and support anyway?* Can we consider doing this as an act of reparenting ourselves, and as an act of defiance toward the aspects of society that tell us to suffer in silence, get over things quickly and quietly, handle everything by ourselves? We won't always feel able or willing to do this, and that's absolutely okay and understandable. This card can hold a place of gentle possibility for us when we feel ready for it—if we ever do.

Six of Swords Reversed

When Six of Swords shows up reversed, it invites us to ask for help and explore the roots of our resistance to widening our circle of support. If we literally have no one to call upon, is there a hotline, online community, or other resource that might give us a glimpse of what we're looking for as a starting point?

Sacred Reciprocity with Six of Pentacles

Six of Pentacles wants us to think about our needs. It wants us to be held and tended to by the community and kin that adore us and have our back. It would like us to refrain from pouring from an empty cup. This is a card that seeks to give us what we're truly crying out for.

Six of Pentacles is a call to action that ideally leads to greater equity, reciprocity, and reparations for all. It is concerned with centering the well-being of the person who needs it most, and pouring back into their well. It acknowledges our labor, time, and service and wants to create better conditions for us within those paradigms.

If you are always teaching, holding space, or giving of yourself, Six of Pentacles will—respectfully but persistently—get in your face and encourage you to take back your time and energy. If we're consistently in a position of being supported, served, and witnessed, we might want to reflect on whether it might actually be appropriate to spread that energetic overflow around, and give from that surplus.

Death/rebirth cycles and creation seasons are both extremely physical experiences, something that my former mentor Michelle used to remind me of all the time. It's exciting to think about channeling down our inspirations or uprooting what doesn't serve to clear the way for something new to take form, but we don't often account for how utterly *exhausting* this process is. It requires a lot more energy, stamina, and capacity than we give ourselves credit for. Lucky for us, we have Six of Pentacles, who is always here to remind us of how important it is not only to regularly check in around our unique needs for these kinds of bigger soul seasons of life, but also to take active steps to nourish ourselves around them.

Six of Pentacles Reversed

Six of Pentacles usually shows up reversed when we're somewhat burned-out or in deep need of a break. There's no other way to work with this card than to heed its urgent call to attend to ourselves as soon as we're able.

CHAPTER TEN

THE CENTER OF THE CYCLONE

Tarot Cards for Self-Doubt and Contraction

THE DEVIL

PAGE OF PENTACLES

PAGE OF SWORDS

THE SEVENS

THE DEVIL

PAGE OF PENTACLES

PAGE OF SWORDS

SEVEN OF WANDS

SEVEN OF CUPS

SEVEN OF SWORDS

SEVEN OF PENTACLES

CHAPTER TEN: THE CENTER OF THE CYCLONE

This chapter is dedicated to Michelle, who taught me everything I know about cycles of expansion and contraction, and to Jen, who helped me to befriend my mind and come home to my heart.

I don't know whether this is because I'm an abuse survivor living with complex PTSD, but every one of the greatest, most exciting, *exactly right* things I've had the privilege of experiencing in my life so far has been steeped in an internal experience of anxiety, fear, and worry.

My brain/inner protector, at least, is consistent: *"This will hurt you, you will be devastated, it'll ruin your life, you'll fuck it up."* Interestingly enough, my brain never seems to do this around things that are genuinely harmful for me. For those, the door is wide open and the lights are all green. It is only the sweet, hopeful, delightful, and expansive things that cause my mind to go buck wild and make my life hell.

My abuse and trauma were profound, so exhilarating things (that most folks might feel delighted about) sometimes feel terrifying for me. It would seem that the state of chaos and harm that I grew up in inadvertently created an internal setting for me that chaos = familiar and that peaceful = unfamiliar and, therefore, a potential threat.

But honestly, I think that this is something we all share, regardless of our upbringing. Any expansive experience is going to come hand in hand with contraction.

When we experience contractions in labor, the muscles of the uterus tighten and then relax over hours or even many days in order to dilate the cervix and move the baby down. The same process happens to us on a soul-led level when we encounter expansive life experiences. Because the mind is deeply committed to protecting us at all costs (even when its perspective on protection feels more harmful than helpful), it can be very alarmed by the presence of unknowns, which expansion often falls under. As miserable as it can often be to experience contractions, or discomfort in the face of expansions, it is also, often, an initiatory experience of sorts, one that can help us continue to grow, evolve, and uplevel through our experiences.

If you're on the verge of some kind of huge expansion in your life, **The Devil, Page of Pentacles, Page of Swords,** and **The Sevens** can help. They can provide context, nourishment, and a reminder of the impermanence, the ebb and flow, of these kinds of experiences.

CUTTING THE CHAINS THAT BIND US WITH THE DEVIL

As I often say to the students in my courses, we only ever see The Devil card when we're on the right track in some way. I acknowledge that that might initially sound very unusual, to put it mildly, especially when considering this card's reputation.

The Devil card has historically been associated with everything from the presence of evil, malevolence, or bad people in our lives, to an addictive process that we may or may not be engaged with, to societal "vices" that we may need to purify ourselves of and from. I'm not taking anything away from anyone who has a strong and possibly even beneficial connection with this card that is related to one of these situational examples. If The Devil card has helped you to break cycles around addictive processes or has been an important heads-up about a toxic person in your life, I think that's genuinely wonderful and empowering. Even while holding that space of possibility, however, I would be remiss if I didn't remind everyone that it's not likely that the above qualities (addiction, challenging people, vices) can be present *every* time we pull this, or any, card in the Tarot. And even if these qualities are indeed present every time you pull The Devil card, it's also important to remember that that might not be present for the person you are reading for. It is always in our best interest to expand our capacity for curiosity around cards that we have very strong relationships with, and The Devil might be among the most important of this lot.

The Devil card is not, at its core, a red flag for questionable relationships, "sinful" behavior, or addictive patterning. It *can* be, but it is not always the case. Regardless of the external situations in our lives, The Devil card almost always shows up when we are in contraction, or when we are getting invited into a contractive process. The reason that I mentioned that this card always tends to show up when we're doing everything right is because it's rare that contraction shows up without there being some kind of expansive process happening in our lives. It's a part of the communication between Death, Temperance, and The Devil in the Golden Dawn ordering of the Major Arcana—we release, we expand, we contract. The Devil is a natural response to the profound openness and gradual change we encounter in Temperance. It's a response born of protection, even if that protection might feel a little warped or painful.

How and under what kinds of circumstances does The Devil card usually present itself to us? As I mentioned above, The Devil card usually shows up when we're moving through some sort of expansive process, which usually calls us into contraction.

We're feeling great about something, then all of a sudden start thinking about an old, seemingly unrelated memory of someone who was unkind to us, or a challenging dynamic we have with someone. We're plowing away at a project, then suddenly get sucked into a time-consuming distraction. This might be more personal to me, but I have previously experienced a pattern of reaching for things that I know make me feel terrible when life is going well because it *slows me down.*

All of these situations pertain to an underlying intention to *slow down expansion*, which is exactly what we encounter when we work with The Devil card. It might feel a little safer for some of us to feel like shit than to be soaring. It might feel a little more familiar to be in the comforting arms of a distraction than to be in the void of a new project.

The Devil card also shows up when we're getting invited into guilt, shame, or stories about how we are "bad," "sinful," "shameful," or "disgraceful," or that our caretakers/society were "right about us." While absolutely holding the depth of pain and validity around those stories, they are just not truth. Every kinky, delicious, wild part of you has medicine to offer. Your experience in your body, and the joy, pleasure, kinship, and euphoria you might feel upon truly rooting into your essence, is your birthright. The rest is just projection.

For many of us, feeling good can feel a little unsafe. It can take a lot of repetitive, conscious repatterning to remind ourselves that it's safe to feel good, even great, in our lives.

What do we do with The Devil when it shows up for us? How can we respond to some of its invitations? *By cutting the chain of reactivity and remembering that we don't have to automatically believe our thoughts.* Feelings, while incredibly important, are not always facts. Thoughts are not always true. We do not have to believe them. The Devil card can facilitate a liberation and transformation process when it arises, because it can help us link patterns together without making anything wrong or bad.

When I get invited into a pattern with The Devil, I try not to take the bait. Or if I do take the bait, I try not to engage with the aftermath of that pattern, which dumps me into shame, guilt, and self-loathing.

BRAIN: **What is wrong with you? Why are you like this? You can never do anything right. You always fail at what you do and let everyone down.**

ME: **Wow, that's really painful. I don't think that's true, even though it might feel that way sometimes. I'm learning and allowed to learn. I'm not supposed to be perfect, and I am allowed to make mistakes. In fact, mistakes have offered me deep lessons. I wonder if maybe you are lashing out like this because we're tired, and L is having a hard time, and you feel under-resourced. I'm going to focus on tending myself, not kicking my own ass.**

Chains cut. Not taking the bait. We get curious and try to compassionately tend to the mechanism and wounding underneath the stories, rather than believe them outright. Noticing the thoughts, the subtle whispers of shitty memories and depressing thoughts about ourselves and saying no thank you to them. Saying no thank you isn't a magical panacea. It doesn't, as Tara Brach says, "take the waves away," but it does shift our relationship to them. When we remain at the center of the cyclone, dropped into our knowing amid swirling, choppy pulls into contraction, we can notice the stories without engaging in our usual ways.

The Devil Reversed

I usually find that The Devil reversed is pretty much the same process as The Devil right side up, with the benefit of the mind's volume being much lower in the reversed position. We are still being called to be gentle with ourselves around a contractive season, but it might feel much more subtle and subconscious.

REACHING OUT FOR SUPPORT WITH PAGE OF PENTACLES

The Pages in the Soul Tarot are our *compasses*, roots that guide us back home to our soul knowing and who we are. Whenever we might feel a little lost, or in need of some deep tethering support, The Pages are the ones to call upon.

Page of Pentacles is our bridge back home to Source, nature, or God. *"Where would you have me go? What would you have me do?"* is the open, vulnerable, prayerful ask of Page of Pentacles. This archetype doesn't want to be whipped around by their whims anymore. They want to be of service. They want to be present, to truly sense into what might be aligned for them to participate in. When we receive this card, we're being invited to tap into the nature of this kind of experience and see how it might feel to open more fully to it.

Page of Pentacles is immensely helpful in all seasons, especially in contractive ones. When we're floating through a Devil season, or working with The Sevens of the Tarot, when the mind is spiky and screaming, we can close our eyes and tune in.

> Spirit, I am so contracted, so overwhelmed, so caught in my own painful thoughts. I don't want to be alone in this moment and I am asking for help and guidance. I ask for the courage to move through this moment, to remember that nothing is permanent. May I be held in love as I navigate it. What, if anything, would you have me know about this?

We don't need to believe in spirits or a god or a higher power to connect with this card. Walking through nature and speaking aloud to whatever witness is present in those ancient oaks or poppy fields or birdsong will do it. Closing our eyes and feeling into this will be just as sacred on the subway, or at our desk, or during a bathroom break. Spirit is with us wherever we are, always reminding us that we're not alone and we don't need to move through these things alone. This is the deepest reminder of Page of Pentacles.

Page of Pentacles Reversed

Sometimes Page of Pentacles can show up when we resist the practices, rituals, and actions that support us or when we avoid tuning in with our Guides or checking in with our decks. Page of Pentacles reversed doesn't signify that we have to do anything differently. It's here to remind us that we are surrounded with beautiful help, witnessing, and support from our Spirit Guides, and that they would always welcome an audience with us, should we elect to grant it.

ALLOWING OURSELVES TO BE STUDENTS WITH PAGE OF SWORDS

Page of Swords is one of those cards that most of us know without knowing it. If you've gone through vigorous training, schooling, or residency and then started on the first day of your official job feeling like you know nothing, you know Page of Swords. If you've ever had a baby and then brought them home and thought, *"Oh my god, now what?"* you know Page of Swords.

Page of Swords is the soul-led epitome of someone who has moved through something that has enhanced their knowledge and lived awareness—be it schooling, training, a birth, or a mentorship—who is now moving into real-world, on-the-"job" experience. This transition, as most of us know, can be nerve-wracking, even harrowing. We can feel so green, so new, so completely unprepared in all aspects to transition from knowing and practicing the thing to actually *doing* the thing.

Page of Swords is here to help us hold both of these situations, to acknowledge the pressure, responsibility, and nerves that come with being a kind of beginner in our own way, and to consider that we have so much to offer as beginners, not in spite of our newness, but because of it.

It is a beautiful thing to be the newest, least practically experienced person in the room. We have the chance to listen, to observe, to be humble, to get it wrong and recover. It is also a beautiful thing to come into an established cohort, job, or container with fresh eyes. There's a lot to be gained from a novel perspective if we're willing to make space for it. Page of Swords invites us to occupy both zones—we're open and available to learn, and we're seeing what we see, making observations based on that.

We're learning and allowed to learn. We're allowed to be like the newborn colt, wobbly on our feet, gaining wisdom through lived, felt experience. This kind of reminder can be so helpful when we're trudging through a contractive moment or experience. In seasons where we're wrestling with The Devil card themes, struggling with Seven of Cups, or moving through a completely different kind of situation, unrelated to the presence of a Tarot card, it can be really nurturing and healing to remind ourselves that it's okay to be learning. It's okay to not know. It's okay to be unsure, and to feel a little nervous and insecure, or like we don't know enough. If we can hold those stormier feelings and continue to show up with all that we are, and all that we have to offer today, we will evolve through the experience.

Page of Swords Reversed

Page of Swords reversed usually shows up when we're not able to be a reliable narrator about our experience. We might feel like we suck and are failing horribly, but it's simply not the case. Even if it was the case, we can always improve and learn. Is it possible for you to chat through some of the feelings you're having, or ask for more support around your trickier spots? Either way, you still have so much to offer. Hang in there!

INTERNAL RECENTERING WITH THE SEVENS

When it comes to moving through contraction, we have immense supports and bolsters in both The Fives and The Sevens of the Tarot.

As we explored in chapter 5, The Fives are balm cards that assist in contractive seasons, helping us to tend to our painful beliefs and feelings as we experience them. The Sevens offer some of the same medicine but with a slightly different twist, a twist that is especially useful when working with a card like The Devil, or when we're in a season of life where we're trying hard to stay at the center of that cyclone.

The Sevens usually show up in our readings when some part of us might be wanting or seeking some kind of external validation or confirmation. What's the next step? When will that person call? Should I say yes or no? Sometimes we ask those questions and the answer becomes clear, or the road opens and we are able to discern and take action on our next steps or get the aligned answers we want around something.

When The Sevens show up, however, it is usually a signal that there really are no aligned answers and no clarity on next steps right now. These cards call on us to get curious and inquire about why we want that external validation and clarity so badly. What will that offer us? Will it assuage some belief, story, or anxiety to receive that confirmation, to have that person call or not call? Sometimes, the answer to that question is a resounding yes. There are many times in life when we concretely know that getting that approval, that phone call, that email, that test result will give us something that we wouldn't be able to get otherwise:

closure, relief, grief, etc. In those cases, we likely won't see a Seven card. When we do, we can be assured that there is likely more to know, more to glean from wisely and sensitively exploring why we want or feel we need something in the external realm.

This kind of internal inquiry and investigation is so important in contractive seasons, especially ones where we're in a Devil-like period: a contraction that precedes or accompanies an expansion.

Amid big unknowns, or seasons in which we are transforming or growing in some way (and even in seasons when we aren't doing any of those things), it can be tremendously difficult to trust in ourselves and the timing of things. It's so easy to believe that things are going too slowly or too quickly, or to believe that if we don't act fast or find someone or something now, we will miss out, lose out, be alone. So, we understandably try to rush things before they are ready or clear yeses, halt things before they are quite finished, or occupy ourselves with shiny, distracting, or seemingly affirming things, only to realize that they didn't really fill the well we wanted them to. This is all part of the intricate (and predictable) web of distraction the mind creates during contractive seasons, but when this particular brand of obfuscation is looming in our lives, we can be sure of seeing a Seven somewhere in our readings.

If a Seven card shows up, we can drop in, pause, and get curious. Are we uncomfortable with some kind of unknown or unclear situation and thus are trying to rush, or pump the brakes unnecessarily? Is there a way for us to more fully trust in the timing and unfolding of things?

Tending to Wise Vigilance with Seven of Wands

I've had the privilege of leading a few Soul Tarot retreats over the last ten years, and in every one of the retreats, our discussion on Seven of Wands always brings forward tears, deep shares, and acknowledgment of inner wounds on the part of the participants. It has taught me so much about the wells of tender pain that this card can brush up against, something that I think is important to acknowledge and hold space for as we explore this card.

Seven of Wands usually shows up when we're in a state of hypervigilance. Sometimes that vigilance is absolutely warranted. We might be in an active state of defense, of scanning the environment for legitimate danger, threats, or problems. Other times our vigilance is not necessarily connected to something tangible and present but is likely corded to some past experience that lives in our bones and blood. If we or our ancestors have experienced the trauma of land theft, of forced removal from our home; if we have experienced abuse or harm at the hands of someone known or unknown to us; or if we have had our work and art stolen, lifted, or ripped off, we know this feeling. If we have been through a shock or if the rug got ripped out from under us, we are likely (and perhaps wisely) going to experience vigilance. Whether real or imagined, presently happening or in the past, our body and nervous system remember and hold the traumas and devastations of those events. They will do whatever they can to protect us, even if we don't necessarily need that protection at the present moment.

Seven of Wands is a challenging card to work with and bear witness to, and it can arise in contractive moments when we are in an active and appropriate state of defense around something in our lives, and in moments when we are not sure whether there's anything to be defended against. We might feel pain and confusion and recognize the desire to come out of that space of protection, to soften, but we are not sure if it is safe to do so.

Our work with Seven of Wands is dependent on the situation. If we are engaged in a circumstance where we are appropriately defended or defending, then we want to call upon our village, our support systems, to wrap around us as we move through this time. We don't need to do this alone.

If we aren't quite sure if we need to occupy this space of inner vigilance, this card encourages us to pause and check in. This is a situation in which checking in with trusted loved ones, colleagues, a therapist, and/or a coach is all potentially helpful. We want to be very gentle with ourselves and get a sense of whether that armoring is truly needed right now, or if we can put it down. To put that wand down, we have to feel supported. What kind of warm tethering might we call upon to be able to do this?

Seven of Wands Reversed

When this card shows up reversed, it sometimes signals that a longer and more protracted dynamic—one that we usually need to be in a state of defense for—is coming to a natural close. Seven of Wands reversed can also double down on the need to call in different outside perspectives around a situation. It is possible that we might be armored without any true "threats" around us. Check in with folks that you trust to get a sense of whether that might be true, while honoring the parts of your nervous system that are just trying to keep you safe.

Pausing and Dreaming with Seven of Cups

Seven of Cups tends to show up in our readings when we have several possible next steps in front of us, but none of them are exactly right. We might not want to admit this to ourselves. We catch ourselves weighing these options, as misaligned as they likely are, trying to convince ourselves that it wouldn't be so bad to make a move on one of them. This is a common experience, especially in contractive and/or liminal moments.

One of the best ways to work with Seven of Cups is to shift our focus from trying to figure out our next move to a space of surrendered dreaming. The next aligned thing likely isn't quite ready to be birthed into reality yet; it may be still forming itself. By prematurely rushing into something to alleviate ourselves from the discomforts of the unknown, we run the risk of (1) creating more complications for ourselves by getting ourselves mixed up in something that is truly a no for us, and (2) potentially missing or delaying the thing that *is* a yes for us but just isn't here yet. If you feel a bit grumpy about this, or if some part of you is insistent that you cannot just sit around and do nothing, Seven of Cups will help you to hold space for those feelings but not necessarily make choices from them. It's true that there are times when we must make a choice from a multitude of terrible options, and we try to pick the least terrible one. Usually when Seven of Cups shows up, there's a bit more spaciousness available to us for curiosity and inquiry. Are we really being pressured to act, or are we just uncomfortable?

These things are all wise medicine: letting things take the time they take, not rushing into things that aren't a yes for us, and tempering our egoic discomfort by honoring the soul knowing underneath it. The gift of dreaming is a much-needed slowdown in a moment when we might want to press the gas pedal—it allows us to practice simply being in a moment when we want something to do. Dreaming allows us to tend to the richness of the inner self, our inner lives, to imagine something even better flowing into our lives. When we lean into this during a contractive time, we can make better sense of why we might want to rush into something before it's ready and understand the gifts of pausing and dreaming in a liminal space.

Seven of Cups Reversed

When Seven of Cups shows up reversed, we really, really want to take care to not rush into something that isn't a yes for us. Sometimes we have no choice but to lean into something. When this card shows up, especially reversed, we want to gently inquire as to whether there's any urgency to our situation. Do we have more agency and ability to wait than we think we do? It is sometimes useful to check in with a loving, supportive, objective outside eye in these moments as well.

Trusting in What's Here with Seven of Swords

Imagine for a moment you are holding five swords in your arms. It's a lot to hold and, for obvious reasons (see: five swords in arms), what you're carrying is asking for a great deal of your attention and care. The only way to move with these five swords is forward, but there are two additional swords behind you. There is no room for these swords in your arms right now, but you find yourself ssplit, strategizing, wondering, worrying: How can I get those other two swords? In that moment with Seven of Swords where our attention is torn, or broken, we're not really with the five swords in our hands *or* with the two behind us.

This is the visual tapestry that the Smith-Rider-Waite Seven of Swords card weaves, and it truly strikes at the heart of such a relatable experience. How can we be with what's here when we're distracted by what's over there?

Seven of Swords has a thoroughly undeserved reputation as a card of sneakiness and trickery. In all the years that I've given readings to folks, I've never seen it come up around those themes. What I have seen to an almost universal degree is that Seven of Swords shows up when we're struggling (for one reason or another) to be present with what's here with us. Instead of being totally present with whatever our version of the five swords is, we're a little more focused on the two swords behind us—the things just out of our reach—that we either don't have room for or that aren't totally available yet. This card isn't here to call us out; it's here to help us check in about why it might be happening.

In Soul Tarot, we view the Seven of Swords as a balm around the myth of not-enoughness, an experience that many of us can identify with. We can get so worried or scared about missing out on what we're longing for that we can inadvertently (and even subtly) check out of what's here in our lives right now. This can show up around time anxiety ("I have only x years of fertility left," "My parent were married at my age and I'm not even dating anyone yet," "I need more followers in order to ______"), distractions (endless scrolling, checking relevant apps compulsively), or even whipping up drama to sweep us away from the lonely, pressing, and anxious voice within that is clamoring for our attention: *"Will those two swords ever come into my life? What if I miss my chance at grabbing them?"*

Seven of Swords is a card that shows up when someone is in pain, believing that it's not safe for them to be present with what's here for fear that they'll miss out on what they are longing for. When this card shows up in a reading, we're being invited to gently pause and check in about this. It's never too late to shift our perspective—to literally turn our head and turn our attention back to the five swords in our hands. We can trust in the timing. We can trust that the things in our hands, in our life, taking up the space that they do, are nourishing, deserving, and worthy of our time, energy, and presence. When there's more room and bandwidth in your life, those two swords will likely find their way to you. Until then, recognize the attempts to pivot you away from what wants your attention most, and come home to what's already here.

Seven of Swords Reversed

When Seven of Swords shows up reversed, we can think of a teakettle boiling, getting louder and louder as it shrieks on the stove. There is nothing that can come from seeking out the two swords behind us right now, and the five swords in our hands are crying out for our attention. What support might we need to show up more fully to what's present in our lives right now?

Aligned Ripening with Seven of Pentacles

Seven of Pentacles is gloriously simple in its invitation (and often maddeningly challenging in its practical application): Don't pick the green strawberries. Allow them to ripen to their full, sweet glory, then harvest them.

Again: conceptually simple, often practically challenging.

When fruits ripen, they become sweeter, softer, and less green. A berry that's ready to be picked will practically fall off the vine, bush, or plant when we attempt to harvest it. On the contrary, when fruit isn't yet ripe, it's generally sour and less palatable, not to mention nearly impossible to harvest without force. (Are you starting to see where this is going?)

Seven of Pentacles comes to us when we might be tempted to try to figure out how to harvest something in our lives that is still ripening. Usually in the case of Seven of Pentacles (as opposed to Seven of Cups, which tends to come to us in a moment when we have a few options in front of us, but none of them are quite right), we are somewhat aware of our next steps. We know we want to expand our family, or leave our job, or start writing, or begin a remodel, or get a tattoo, or start a garden. That desire is likely aligned, maybe even a full yes. It just might not be the right timing to begin now.

We're called upon to lean into the medicine of patience in Seven of Pentacles, and to trust in the unfolding of how and when it happens—that, possibly, Source's timeline, or the timeline of the event in question, might differ from our preference. It's okay if that feels uncomfortable or frustrating. It's okay to not like that, to even mourn that. After all, this is a chapter about contractive seasons—it's normal to experience this feeling inside a Seven of Pentacles season.

What we're called upon to consider, for even the briefest and barest of moments, is that the waiting might allow whatever it is that we're longing for and calling in to become even more ripe, even more sweet, and even more soft. The waiting might help to clarify certain things. It might help us to get organized, to research further, to gain the skills, wisdom, or confidence necessary for the journey we're longing to embark on.

In Seven of Pentacles, we're not waiting or cultivating patience just for the hell of it. We're coming into a space of deeper and richer trust around aligned timing, and we're practicing what it means to surrender to the possibility of something ripening to its fullest point of sweetness.

Seven of Pentacles Reversed

When Seven of Pentacles shows up reversed, it usually means that we're working through some enhanced impatience with regard to the matter at hand. We might be having a truly difficult time waiting for this sweet fruit on our vine to ripen, which is completely understandable. What kind of compassionate support would be most useful as we navigate this situation?

CHAPTER ELEVEN

WHEN YOU'RE IN HELL

Tarot Cards for Impossible Seasons

THE TOWER

THE STAR

THE MOON

THE SUN

QUEEN OF PENTACLES

KNIGHT OF CUPS

THE EIGHTS

THE TOWER

THE STAR

THE MOON

THE SUN

QUEEN OF PENTACLES

KNIGHT OF CUPS

EIGHT OF WANDS

EIGHT OF CUPS

EIGHT OF SWORDS

EIGHT OF PENTACLES

There are times in life when things are impossible to contend with. We are on a different planet in those times, in a different time zone, moving at a different speed of life than other people around us. It can feel like we will never recover, never be the same, never come back from what we've experienced. Some of us don't. Some of us survive and are forever scarred—a vein of gold running through our hearts, formed by one of life's inevitable earthquakes.

Sometimes these situations are an initiation. We may feel like Persephone or Vasalisa, descending into the Underworld or into the deep forest. In those seasons, we recover and discover things we could never have imagined, going far beyond what we ever thought we were capable of. Other times, there is no rhyme, no reason, no perceivable rose within all of those thorns. It's just pain, grief, horror, and loss. How do we hold ourselves in seasons like these?

For these seasons, whether we're moving through a soul led initiation or we're in the wild throes of grief, or both, we will greet and experience unique growth and evolution that comes through the journey from **The Tower** to **The Star** to **The Moon** to **The Sun.** The cards that can assist us amid that journey and process are **Queen of Pentacles, Knight of Cups,** and **The Eights.**

Moving from The Tower to The Star to The Moon to The Sun is the wildest, deepest, most transformative path of healing in the Tarot. It is the road map that helps us to find our way from devastation to rebirth, holding us as we slowly crawl our way from night to day.

WHEN THINGS FALL APART WITH THE TOWER

My barn having burned down, I can now see the moon.

—MIZUTA MASAHIDE

The Tower is a profound energy of transformation and regeneration, one that can show up in a dazzling and remarkable array of situations, ranging from gentle to ferocious. It upends the ground under our feet, shifting the tectonic plates within our foundation. If we've built a structure on top of a broken, uneven, or unsustainable foundation, The Tower will help to level those structures as a service to us, drawing our attention to the wound or imbalance that was festering underneath.

The Tower, despite its reputation, wants to help us. It wants us to be free of something that was out of alignment to begin with, or that we've outgrown. This card can be a deep gift—albeit often a spiky one.

Every one of us has moved through a Tower experience, or a season with The Tower card in the Tarot. Some of us have lived a life marked by Tower cycles or have gone through Tower experiences so profound we weren't sure we would make it to the other side.

Some of us are unwitting members of what I affectionately call "Tower club," which describes a life marked by immense challenges, trials, and pain in varying degrees.

Clarissa Pinkola Estés, author of *Women Who Run with the Wolves*, coined the term *scar clan*. Estés says that members of the scar clan were "that timeless tribe of women of all colors, all nations, all languages, who down through the ages have lived through a great something, and yet who stood proud."

"It is a good idea," Estés writes, "for women to count their ages, not by years, but by battle scars. 'How old are you?' people sometimes ask me. 'I am seventeen battle scars old,' I say."

Most of us can apply this powerful sentiment to our experience in and with The Tower card. There are many levels and layers to The Tower, each of them bringing their own lessons, gifts, and challenges.

Sometimes just the roof of our Tower gets struck by symbolic lightning. These are moments when The Tower can also skew neutral, even gentle. If we've always believed that we were ugly or unattractive, and all of a sudden there's someone that we're attracted to who totally desires us as we are, that can be a Tower-like experience. If we've always been told that we're bad or worthless, and we manage to cultivate a beautiful life for ourselves, that can be a huge Tower experience.

But then, on occasion, we will pull The Tower card amid experiences that have no discernible benefit or reason and are just deeply painful. These are rites of passage, or experiences where the entire structure is ripped out of its socket, leaving us with a gaping hole in the foundation of ourselves, ground smoking, devastation everywhere.

It is so important to remember that The Tower card is not bringing this devastation to us. It is merely an acknowledgment and symbolic representation of these kinds of soul-shattering experiences, ones that come for all of us at some point in life. When our lives are blown apart, when the ground beneath us shatters, when we've lost everything, we are usually traveling through a Tower experience.

How do we survive and endure such a thing? And perhaps, even more unthinkably, how do we grapple with the possibility of healing, and potentially rebuilding an even more supportive structure in its wake?

We take it one moment at a time. We show up for ourselves as we are, where we are. We reach out for help, support, and nurturing where we can. We remember that we have teachers all around us to remind us that healing after the unimaginable is possible: the burn scars and new growth from land scorched by wildfire, the miracle of seeing bunnies and birds coming back to what seemed like ruined landscape. The song of the mourning doves at dawn after a deep night. Nothing is forever, and The Tower can help us see that.

The Tower Reversed

Often The Tower reversed is a less intense presence than The Tower right side up. The reversal of this card is a little more subterranean and is more likely to be an internally felt experience, as opposed to one that is external. We still want to take care to be gentle with ourselves as we move through it.

HEALING THE HEART WITH THE STAR

After the fires of The Tower, we pray for cooling, soothing, healing rain. After we fall into hell, we pray for help and support. The Star is the answer to that prayer.

The Star is a deep and profoundly healing energy. They sweep in during the night, carafe of hot tea, thermos of warming soup, and suitcase in hand. They make themselves comfortable in our spare room or on our couch. They know that they will be here for a while. The Star washes our feet and oils our hair. The Star feeds us, listens to us, cradles us, and witnesses us as we weep, scream, sleep, and slowly, slowly heal. *Slow* is the key word with The Star. It reminds us that healing is a journey, a spiral path, and that we cannot rush our way through it.

This card can be fierce with us sometimes. It doesn't give up on us, even when we might want to give up on ourselves. It cools the inflamed earth of our soul and nourishes our whole being. In time, we might even be shocked to see that there are shoots coming up from that charred earth within us—small slips of hope, joy, and wonder forming in our heart again. It travels with us, side by side, as we slowly transition out of hell and back to this planet.

I remember visiting Windy Ridge, the site of the 1980 eruption at Mount Saint Helens in Washington State. I was taken there by my friend Erin, as it was a very special place for her. It was a profound experience for me, too. I remember thinking that there was no finer embodiment of The Star card than that land. The charred, black trees from the volcanic eruption were still present, while all around, vibrant wildflowers, grasses, and trees grew. I saw myself in that landscape.

The devastation from the eruptions of our lives doesn't vanish. It remains, and new life grows up around it. Nature illustrates this more elegantly than any other teacher. We cannot ever go back to where or who we were before that inciting event, and The Star doesn't expect us to. Working with this card gets us more accustomed to the idea that we can only go forward. It holds the possibility of a future for us when that might seem impossible.

How can we anchor and open to The Star? If we've gone through any kind of trauma, rupture, loss, or heartbreak, we can expect to hear from this card. There's nothing we need to do to call on it, as it is already here with us.

The key is to surrender to this energy and open to the sweet medicine it has to offer. It often will ask us to go slowly and move at a different pace than what we're used to. This pace is not permanent, but for the time that it is with us, it will be important to respect it. It will invite us to be patient with ourselves as we traverse this landscape of our healing. It will ask us to be so, so gentle with ourselves, to call upon softness, ease, and care as we journey through this spiral of healing.

The Star Reversed

When we get The Star reversed in a reading, it might be useful to pause and check in with ourselves. Are we rushing ourselves out of this space of healing? Are we trying to move on too quickly? If we're receiving The Star reversed, it might be the case that we're feeling or experiencing some resistance around this energy. If so, what resources can you call upon for support in slowing down and trusting the pace of your healing?

RESTING IN THE VOID WITH THE MOON

Once we move through the scorch of The Tower and the cooling rain of The Star, we enter a kind of void-like space, ruled over by The Moon card.

The Moon is mystery, the unknowable, the unseeable. It is the epitome of an end point, the deepest darkness right before the horizon begins to shift on its route toward dawn. The biggest asset to working with The Moon card seasons is our mindset.

Being in a Moon card season is like floating in the ocean in the middle of the night, illuminated only by lunar light. It is easy to experience illusion in The Moon card because everything is somewhat blurred and in shadow. Nothing is particularly clear.

There's a lot to potentially fear in that situation. There's nothing perceptible under our feet. It is everything that our nervous system is trained to get us the fuck away from. But when we feel safe and resourced enough to surrender to the waves and engage with them, it can utterly transform us. We begin to embrace the medicine of the unknown, to be cradled and rocked by it. We can begin to travel under the waves in a safe and measured way, simultaneously recovering long-buried treasure that hasn't been cherished in a long time and releasing old material to the depths. We can move from the mind to a more psychic, subconscious space, opening to the gifts that this card holds for us. It helps us face our fears, and alchemically shift in the process. This is one of the reasons that The Moon card is such a crucial part of any deep healing season—we can't ever move through the full spiral of healing without greeting this card, even if it's for the briefest of moments.

Perhaps none of that cathartic stuff happens for us in a Moon card season that we travel through. Maybe we're just in the void, in a middle space, with no clarity on when or how things will ever begin to change. Moving through a Moon card season like this can give us the gift of truly knowing that nothing lasts forever, nothing is permanent. No matter how endless the night might seem, the light is always around the corner. As Rilke says, "Just keep going; no feeling is final." We can apply this same prayer, this same spell, to our Moon card experiences. This is temporary, like all things. This is not forever.

The Moon card helps us to rest in the void, to embrace mystery. It helps us stay rooted and grounded in moments when we feel like our every thought and emotion is swirling us out, when we're not sure what's real and what's not. In these seasons, we want to reach for every available resource and helpful reflector we possibly can to remind us of what's true. What are some of those deep truths that we can tether to in times of unknowing and uncertainty? The night and the dark bring gifts to be cherished and embraced. With the sound of birdsong, the heralding of the dawn is right around the corner. We don't have to be afraid.

The Moon Reversed

Can you ask for more support right now? Sometimes when The Moon card shows up reversed, it can intensify the depths of the void we're in. This reversal doesn't predict that intensity will arise, but it does suggest that more reinforcements are likely a benefit to us right now. It is usually helpful to have kin around us or, at the very least, a loving ear. You are being invited to gently resist the pull of isolation and to fiercely reject the idea that you need to do this on your own. We deserve to move through void seasons in community, and if you have to build and reach for your own, do so.

A NEW DAWN WITH THE SUN

I traveled through hell and back after the birth of my daughter. My birth was lovely, and the bond I had with my child was profound, but I was completely upended by unforeseen medical events after the birth, including two hospital stays and emergency surgeries less than four months after my C-section. I was wracked with postpartum anxiety, depression, and rage. I was traumatized and felt devastated about the way my postpartum had gone, despite all of my best efforts. I remember so much time in the dark during that first year, literally and metaphorically.

I would rock and rock my daughter in our rocking chair, day and night, overwhelmed with love for her while immensely painful thoughts raced through my head. I barely went to my Tarot deck in those days because I knew I was traveling the long path from The Tower to The Sun. I kept reminding myself of that, and it helped profoundly. So much of those first nine to twelve months postpartum was a carousel of Tower to Star to Moon and back to Tower to Star to Moon. The Sun never came. The Moon persisted. The Tower came roaring back. The Star felt fleeting.

And then one day it was different, or at least I realized it was different. The "different" had come to me gradually. I slowly started noticing that I was less charged, more even, more joyful. The immense drop in mood that I'd had around sunset for months and months like clockwork wasn't there anymore. My body was healing. I was slowly but surely starting to feel better. The Sun had arrived at my doorstep, heralding not a parade of joyful and orgasmic exaltations or showers of flower petals, but a gentle, gradual awareness that things had shifted. The night had gone, and the light was back.

I wish The Sun card were all it is chalked up to be. I wish it provided half of the things that are attributed to it—that it was a luminous and expansive rebirth, that it would help us concretely feel amazing and new. The truth is that this card offers none of these things as a rule, at least not in a linear way. The Sun card is simply a dawning after a period of night. Nighttime isn't necessarily a problem, and daylight isn't necessarily a balm for all that ails us, but in this case, it is usually a seismic shift.

The Sun card closes a long chapter with its presence. We travel many nights and days by candlelight, by feel, by moonlight in the journey of the Major Arcana, and The Sun card brings about a ceremonial close to that journey. It brings illumination and the opportunity for reflection and earned perspective on a situation. We might be in a Sun card season if we start to talk about something in the past tense. We can start to see things in ways we haven't before, and this is usually when medicine starts to form around the scar tissue. This is when the writing, the words, the laughter, and even more tears begin to flow. Something, for one reason or another, really is behind us, and our entire body and soul know it. Now that we are here, a whole new layer of healing and regeneration can begin.

One of the trickiest parts of working with The Sun card is that because it is so gradual, it can be difficult to understand when we are even in it. This is also because Sun card seasons tend to come our way after an intense, tumultuous time—after surviving such a time, how on earth can we begin to trust that the warm light of day won't be ripped out from underneath us? We do so over time, with care and compassion for ourselves. We treat ourselves like a bird that has smashed into a window while flying. We lie there as long as is needed, and then we shake and clear and allow ourselves to slowly, slowly, sense into what it might mean for us to consider taking a symbolic step, and then flying. The Sun card is a definitive signal that a challenging chapter is behind us, but it knows that we might need time to trust and believe that.

The Sun Reversed

It's okay if you don't believe that the nightmare is over. It's okay if you still need to hide. It's okay if you're not ready to come out of your thicket. You will when you're ready; the warmth, the light, and the new cycle you're in aren't going anywhere. Take your needed space and cultivate that trust on your own timeline.

TENDING TO THE BODY WITH QUEEN OF PENTACLES

Queen of Pentacles is a call to tend to the body, to nurture the vessel that we move through this life with. This card isn't rooted in fluffy, inaccessible self-care, nor is it centered in a harmful framework of faux body positivity. It is raw, fierce, and highly nourishing, interested only in offering the highest degree of care to us in the precise way we need it most, when we need it most.

Whenever we find ourselves in an impossible or challenging time, we are going to feel that in our body. We will feel it in our exhaustion, or in our inability to sleep. We will feel it in our constant need to eat, or in our complete lack of appetite. We will feel it in our stress levels, our aches and pains, our heart, our bones. Beyond any specific support or care that we might need during a particularly challenging time, very often our bodies simply want to be held. We want to feel cradled and taken care of, and Queen of Pentacles is often a signal to deepen into the resources we have available to us to do just that.

In the midst of a very, very challenging time in my life, I have a memory of swimming in the ocean for the first time in years and floating on my back, weeping from the very depths of my being. I wept for the guilt, grief, and self-hatred I had been experiencing, and wept because I felt so held, so *mothered*—a feeling that was at a profound deficit in my life. The ocean was cradling me, rocking me, nurturing me. It was so much bigger than me, my trauma, my self-loathing, and my pain. It held it all, and all of me.

The ocean gave my body what it needed most at that time: help, support, witnessing, and love. It brought me back to a sense of God at a time when I felt so alone. In that moment, God was the ocean, and the ocean was my mother when I needed a loving mother most. It was so impactful that for years I would call upon the memory of floating in those waves, of being held by something so vast and loving.

I share this story about my experience in the ocean because it is a perfect parallel to the medicine of Queen of Pentacles. Whenever we work with this card, we're gently invited to come back to nature and allow ourselves to be held by something bigger than us and our experience. What is our body whispering and longing for? How can we offer it to ourselves in an accessible way?

Queen of Pentacles Reversed

When we pull Queen of Pentacles reversed, it can be useful to sense into the resistance that we might have around this card's invitation. Has our body been talking to us, and have we been ignoring its calls? What might it be like to simply place a hand on your heart (if that feels good for you) and say, "Hey body. I've been feeling like you've been trying to get my attention, and I haven't had time/space/courage to heed that call. I'm really sorry about that. What can I do for you?"

A STEADY PACE IN UNSTEADY TIMES WITH KNIGHT OF CUPS

In Soul Tarot, The Knights in the Tarot are our *currents*, our movers. Ruled by Air in Soul Tarot, all four of The Knights have their own rhythm, pace, flow, and style. Whenever we feel a little unclear or confused on how to move or whether to take action, if we're stuck or in process, if we're going too fast, we can call upon The Knights for gentle clarity. When we pull a Knight in any given situation, it is a helpful hint on how to approach that situation with regard to how we are physically making our way—how are we greeting it or moving through it?

Knight of Cups is not a card that focuses on quick versus slow, but on *quality* of movement. If we think about the idea of someone carrying a cup or chalice of water over a long distance on a horse, it seems daunting and exhausting—if not impossible—to accomplish. Not for Knight of Cups. Knight of Cups has learned the subtle art of holding the vessel steady, of deftly and elegantly doing so despite the inevitable bumps, bangs, and mishaps along the journey. It is the anchor we can call upon when everything has gone to hell, but we still need to pick up our kids and do the dishes and call the plumber and show up for our clients. It helps us embody the idea of keeping the inner cup steady while the water sloshes and foams, while we rock and weave and grapple with our current situation.

When times are challenging and contractive, it can be helpful to remember that we're not reaching for perfect in our day-to-day life. We're going to make mistakes and feel messy. We're going to have days when everything slips away from us, when we fall behind. This is not only valid but should be normalized. When we're in impossible times, we deserve to have all those other life needs handled, but for so many of us, this is out of reach. Knight of Cups is a small, humble helper with a warm hand on our shoulder. It is the inner wisdom within us that rises up in unsteady times. It is the part of us that doesn't know how we would ever handle something, until it happens to us and, somehow, we endure it. This card can be a lighthouse for graceful, wise, and vulnerable responsiveness in the face of life's inevitable challenges.

Knight of Cups Reversed

When Knight of Cups shows up reversed, it can be a gentle indication that we need a little more support to travel through our current experience. Is that available to us? If so, how can we ask for that support without apology?

SOUL EVOLUTION WITH THE EIGHTS

We evolve when we gradually shift or change from one state of being to another. Evolution is often responsive—we're shifting in collaboration with our circumstances and environment.

The Eights of the Tarot are about transformation, pivoting us from caterpillar to butterfly, but at a digestible pace. There is a gradual nature to the change that is present with these cards, and they often show up when we're on the verge of moving from one place to another from within. In fact, I find that the true point of change that happens in and around an Eight card isn't so much related to the final destination, but to the journey itself.

Mastering a craft helps us evolve and grow more knowledgeable over time.

On that road to mastery, we have to fail many times and be willing to try again and again. The Eights rule over these kinds of change seasons, ones that happen over time, through lived experience and repeated practice. This is also the spiral and process of soul evolution. We cannot read about transformative experiences as a substitute for living them—we must fully embark on and undergo them ourselves.

We can look back at our lives and see where we've grown or evolved. We have literally gotten taller as we've gotten older, and our bodies have changed. We also might have chosen recovery at a certain point in our lives. We might have been raised in a culture of violence or been close to perpetuating a cycle of abuse in our own lives and have made the choice to stop and make our lives a living amends. We might have gone through hell and back in a way that we never asked for, never deserved, or never dreamed that we would experience. These things are all examples of soul evolution: experiences that rock us to our core and gradually change the trajectory of our lives, as well as the legacy of service that we might long to bring to the world. Journeys through hell or through impossible seasons often transform us in ways we didn't ask for and didn't expect, and that are also undeniable. I don't know that I would be drawn to the work that I do—deep soul care, threshold work, and community death care work—without having lived through what I did. When I was in my twenties, I wanted to be a performer. Life had other plans for me, and I evolved to meet them.

This is much of what happens to us when we move through the journey from The Tower to The Sun, and it can be reflected in our work with The Eights as well.

Trusting the Process with Eight of Wands

Eight of Wands usually comes to us in a reading when something is in process, in progress, or already en route. It occupies a very important and specific note on the piano with regard to the Tarot. We don't need to shoot the proverbial arrow when this card arises in a reading; it's already been done. The shooting of the arrow isn't where the medicine of change lies with this card. The font of evolution that is available to us in Eight of Wands can be found in our response and relationship to the overall process of waiting and trusting that something is indeed on its way.

When we've purchased something and we get a notification that it's shipped and headed to our door, some of us might spend every waking moment obsessively updating the tracking info to make sure that it doesn't get lost, but the majority of us will let it be and wait until it comes to our door. There's very little to do about that other than to wait. It is in the act of waiting, surrendering, and trusting in this eventual delivery of this "package" that such change and a soul evolution can occur.

The more I work with The Wands, the more I suspect that they might be the energetic base and foundation for all the work that we do with the Tarot, especially the Minor Arcana cards.

The Wands are most concerned with helping us to experience what it is to trust in the timing and unfolding of things, what it means to wait and not flame ourselves out, and how to ideally create without burning out or becoming exhausted. Eight of Wands is no exception.

When Eight of Wands shows up in a reading, it's a gentle heads-up that something is in progress or process. Now that we know this, we can make the courageous choice not to obsess about the details—the when, where, and how of it, or what this shift might be. Instead, we can leave the cake to bake in the oven and concentrate on making space for what wants to come through. We can allow ourselves to surrender to a timeline that is ever so slightly out of our hands. This is a profoundly brave act, one that has the capacity to be transformative.

Eight of Wands Reversed

When Eight of Wands shows up reversed in a reading or a card pull, it is usually a heads-up that we might need a little reminder that it's safe for things to take the time they take. It can be hard to trust in the flow and timing of life, but this is one situation where you can let go of the controls. What kind of support might be helpful as you navigate this situation?

Saying Goodbye with Eight of Cups

Eight of Cups usually shows up when we're on the verge of a very big change in our lives, often one that involves letting go of something or someone. Eight of Cups can be a deeply emotional card, and a slightly complex one, because its presence can encompass a wide spectrum of potential experiences. In other words, if we're navigating a divorce, the closure of our business, or the death of a beloved, it might be very obvious as to why Eight of Cups is showing up for us. If nothing at all appears to be happening on the surface of our lives, Eight of Cups can be confusing, even a little activating. We might wonder and worry about whether something is going to be rupturing or ending in our lives that's just outside of our lived awareness or purview. With regard to the latter of these two examples, I'd love to offer some gentle support for your nervous system around this. Eight of Cups can show up around processes that are entirely subconscious and internal. This card doesn't have to align with an earthly example of a big transition or point of completion.

Eight of Cups shows up when, in one way, shape, or form, we have outgrown something. It can also show up when we're making our way through a deep audit, deciding whether we're going to continue with a job, a career, a relationship, or a pattern in our lives. Eight of Cups usually moves slowly, and like all Cups cards, holds a space of deep patience for our processes. This card can be so fraught and complex because often what we're considering saying goodbye to (or what is saying goodbye to us) isn't completely a no or a terrible option. It likely isn't meeting all our needs or we have outgrown some or all of it, but we might be talking ourselves into staying with what's familiar because it's, well, familiar. The undercurrent of evolution that is present with Eight of Cups is a small flake of gold within this deep consideration about staying or going, giving up or fighting—a kernel that has us wondering whether our current circumstances could be better, more aligned, and/or more sustainable.

When things aren't completely awful, it can feel like a real contractive point to imagine that we could have something better, or even a little more supportive. *"Who are we to ask for that?"* we might think. *"I should be happy and satisfied with what I have, even if it's not perfect."* Sometimes that's true. Other times—especially in moments when we see Eight of Cups—we might want to rethink that perspective. Are we telling ourselves that we cannot have better? Are we believing that things cannot be easier? If so, why? The process of sensing into these questions, and of potentially saying goodbye to something in our lives, is something that will absolutely provide the ingredients for a soul-led evolution in our lives. If we believe that things can't get better, and we move through the terrifying decision to make changes, *and our circumstances improve*, that will alter us in a profound way.

Eight of Cups doesn't ask that we make any decisions right now, only that we sit with the information that's showing up in our heart and body. From there, a clear choice will emerge.

Eight of Cups Reversed

When Eight of Cups shows up reversed in a reading, we want to pause and get a sense of our timing and how we're approaching a situation. Are we pushing ourselves into a decision, or into being ready for something before we actually are? Or, on the contrary, are we unnecessarily delaying the inevitable because we aren't ready or willing to deal with the truth? Be gentle with yourself as you sense into these inquiries, and why they might be present with you.

Choosing the Open Window with Eight of Swords

Eight of Swords tends to show up in our readings when we are like a trapped bird, desperately trying to break out of the top of our cage, not realizing that the door is wide open. This card comes to us when we believe (likely for good reason) that we are caught, bound, and utterly stuck, when that's not actually the case. It doesn't mean that it doesn't feel true—it likely does. It also doesn't mean that situations where we are truly bound and caught cannot happen. Of course they can, but when Eight of Swords shows up, it's a flag that there's an open window somewhere: an opportunity, another perspective, another way of imagining something.

Because this card belongs to The Swords suit, we're dealing with the realm of the mind. If we've experienced any kind of challenge, setback, or past trauma that has us quickly getting flung into a fatalistic feeling around a tricky moment, it can be incredibly challenging to imagine anything different, or sense into an alternative, even more spacious, way forward. This is especially true in seasons when we're going through hell, where it can be even more impossible to imagine that there's an open door or window somewhere in the situation. And yet, Eight of Swords wants to help us do just that.

To make the choice or even consider that it's an option to turn away from an unyielding door and toward an open window usually takes quite a bit of work. We have to wade and cut through a lot of our conditioning to even understand that there's a window in the space with us. Our ability to understand this and to begin to look for those open windows is work we do over the course of a lifetime, and we are encouraged to be gentle with ourselves in the process.

Eight of Swords Reversed

When Eight of Swords shows up reversed in a reading, it can be an indication that whatever we've felt so bound and trapped about is starting to loosen up. It can also show up when we're feeling even more stuck than we did before. To sense into which might be occurring for us, we can do a gut check: Do we keep trying to knock down that locked door again and again, looking for a different result, or have things begun to change and shift? If that feels unclear, we can also look to the Tarot cards that surround this one to get a better sense of what Eight of Swords reversed might be bringing us.

Transformative Apprenticeship with Eight of Pentacles

Eight of Pentacles usually shows up in our readings when we're slowly gaining skill and mastery in a particular area of our lives. We gain this skill through repetition, lived experience, and slow apprenticeship. This card reminds us that soul evolution and personal growth can't be hastened; they have to move at their own pace. The transformation that comes through working with this card occurs through our willingness to learn over time, to be imperfect, to fuck up often, and to learn from our mistakes.

If we know what it is to study something in school, pursue a degree, or move through a rigorous training for work, we have a good sense of what Eight of Pentacles is about. This is a powerful and important card for Tarot readers, too. I can't tell you how many folks I've had the privilege of teaching who share with me that they've been reading for 10 or even 20 years but don't have the cards totally memorized and/or experience a lack of confidence in reading for others. First and foremost, while memorizing the card meanings helps, it's in no way a prerequisite for furthering our work with the Tarot. I don't, however, believe that there is a shortcut to gaining confidence, experience, or facility as a reader other than to throw yourself in the arena and practice it regularly, which means that you're likely going to flop from time to time. You'll freeze, get nervous or thrown by a client's energy, or forget what a card means, and it will all be immensely and indispensably important experience on the road to making you a strong and beautiful reader. This is the medicine of Eight of Pentacles: our willingness to not know, to make mistakes, and to allow them to help us grow and learn along the way. It's part of what creates mastery.

Sometimes in seasons when we're moving through hell and back, we can get caught up in wanting to do the right and best thing, to take the smoothest and easiest course through a given situation. That is incredibly valid—why shouldn't we want to have the least amount of hassle during such a challenging time? Eight of Pentacles can be an anchor to us in times when it seems like we are taking the long road to healing, resolution, or recovery. Without romanticizing it, how might we consider this longer road as a kind of foundation for our evolution in some way, helping us to gain skill and mastery around anything from navigating hospital visits, to communicating with a care team, to tending to ourselves amid an incredibly challenging time? We often need to do these things in repetition to help us come to a place where there's a large well of wise, lived experience to draw from. This can also be incredibly helpful when holding space or supporting other people moving through a similar situation. When this card shows up for us in a reading, we're being invited to trust in that process—to remember that we're gaining facility through whatever it is that we're repeating right now.

Eight of Pentacles Reversed

When Eight of Pentacles shows up reversed, it usually reflects an impatience on our part regarding this slower, more methodical season of lived experience and practice. We sometimes wish that we knew this stuff already or that we didn't have to climb this mountain step by step. There's ultimately nothing to do about these feelings when this card shows up reversed other than hold the space for our experience.

CHAPTER TWELVE

LIVING ON SPIRAL TIME

Tarot Cards for Soul Pilgrimages and Heart-Led Awakenings

JUDGMENT

QUEEN OF CUPS

KING OF SWORDS

THE NINES

JUDGMENT

QUEEN OF CUPS

KING OF SWORDS

NINE OF WANDS

NINE OF CUPS

NINE OF SWORDS

NINE OF PENTACLES

Living with chronic pain, invisible disabilities, autoimmunity, and complex PTSD often makes me feel like I am on "Spiral Time." This term is used by lots of people in different ways, but to me, it describes a state of being that makes time and our experience in the world uncertain and changeable.

There are certain experiences in life that make us acutely aware that we're living on Spiral Time, in spiral bodies: a brush with our own mortality, or accompanying someone who is close to death; witnessing how our kids have grown, seemingly in the blink of an eye; watching as our caretakers age, and in time becoming their caretakers; seeing aspects of our own caretakers in ourselves, in spite of our best efforts not to emulate them and/or seeing with awe how much further we've gone than the people who raised us, and how many curses we've broken along the way. Spiral Time honors that the past, present, and future are all happening in the same moment.

For someone perpetually living on Spiral Time, these reminders are constant companions. Grief might arise as shockingly and unexpectedly as a sinkhole opening up, or a sense/body memory from long ago that can hurtle us back 20 years in the blink of an eye. You get used to plans changing quickly (often abruptly and devastatingly). A migraine upending your day, a surprise trip to the ER, or a missed bedtime routine with your child because you're in too much pain to get out of bed.

There is a thoroughly unromantic initiation in these experiences, pressing a persistent reminder on those of us who regularly live on Spiral Time—life is full of unexpected turns, and our time on this planet and in these bodies is temporary, which is somehow a fact that many of us forget.

In these moments, it can feel like you are on another planet of one, with everyone else on their own alternate planet, making plans, having dinner, going to the events that they planned to go to that night. It both slows down and speeds up time. It brings you very close to the lonely tenderness and fragility of this life.

It can call you into work that can be equal parts excruciating and awe-inspiring. How do you trust life when you aren't sure if your own body is a safe place to land? What kind of refuge can we build for ourselves in those moments when the veil drops and we remember that this life is fleeting, we will all eventually transition away from these bodies, and nothing is promised to us? How can we befriend ourselves and be our own best allies in these experiences?

In this chapter, we're going to sense into some powerful Tarot Anchors for moments when we feel like we're living on Spiral Time: **Judgment**, **Queen of Cups**, **King of Swords**, and **The Nines.**

REMOVING THE VEIL WITH JUDGMENT

Judgment is an excavator.

It unearths, reveals, opens, and unmasks. It profoundly transforms.

It liberates, clarifies, and occasionally horrifies. It understands and honors that sometimes horror precedes understanding, which can lead to right action, forgiveness, compassion, and repair.

It removes illusion, opens our eyes, and helps us see that we are a part of something larger than our own experience, than this lifetime.

Judgment is profoundly spiralic, stretching and rolling in between space and time. I often associate it with Eclipses, because working with Eclipse energy is exactly what this card feels like, bringing with its presence the opportunity for accelerated growth, awareness, and awakening.

Judgment has been associated with Pluto, which can help us get a strong sense of what this card is made from. Pluto moves very slowly, taking anywhere from 12 to 30 years to move through each astrological sign, and 248 years to make a full rotation. This dwarf planet is associated with secrets, hidden information, power, and generations. When we think about our ancestors, caretakers, and generational lessons and differences, we are in the world of not only Pluto, but of Judgment.

Judgment helps us unburden ourselves from generational curses, family legacies, abusive cycles, and inherited patterning. It is the card that helps us see how we might be continuing those cycles and believing those untrue stories. It hands us a key and wants us to be brave enough to unlock the locked places in our hearts, liberate ourselves from these patterns, and open to a new way.

Our hearts are walking, breathing memory boxes, locked and full with the whispered stories from our kinfolk, the longing for the knowledge of who our ancestors or family of origin were, the longing for ancestral homelands that we were ripped from—languages, traditions, and memories lost with the old ones who went long before us. We live with everything from abuses, family legacies, inherited beliefs, treasured memories, and sweet connections running in our veins. Judgment doesn't try to bypass this or remove it entirely. It wants us to know that that's not our limit. That's not where we start and end.

If we developed a habit of people pleasing and fawning in order to survive and ingratiate ourselves to people (even when those people take advantage of us and treat us like shit), Judgment might open our eyes to this in a flash around a friendship or work colleague. We might see it all in a moment—all the missed signals, and the fullness of the pattern at work. Our awareness around it can help us transform, shift, come into greater awareness, and more importantly, be gentle with ourselves. If we realize that we're unconsciously perpetuating an abusive or harmful cycle within any of our relationships, we can shift and pivot into repair, making our lives a living amends. Most of us will be grappling with some measure of both these things for the rest of our lives. We have to see it to heal it, and that's what Judgment helps us do.

When Judgment shows up in a reading, we are being invited to open our eyes to something that wants our attention, that is ready to be acknowledged. Remember: Judgment is not The Tower. Generally, The Tower which often moves swiftly. Judgment tends to move *slowly*, excavating and revealing over time. It also makes space for deep healing around these patterns. If we are willing to go on the journey, this card will take us back and forward into time and space, into our very blood and bones. Judgment helps us be better ancestors.

Judgment Reversed

When Judgment shows up reversed in a reading, it could be an indication that there's a lack of willingness on our part to see something that's ready to be acknowledged. Perhaps it's simply too painful, or our nervous system might be protecting us from information that we're not ready to digest. We want to respect this resistance, never forcing it, trusting that it will blossom open in its time. It might also be worth mentioning that the work we do with the Judgment card can be profound and life-changing. It can also be very solitary, as work of this nature—awakening work, curse-breaking work—can be. We may want to dive into the work around this card with a trusted attendant—a therapist, coach, or beloved friend—knowing that we don't have to travel through these places alone.

RETRIEVING OUR SEALSKIN WITH QUEEN OF CUPS

In Soul Tarot, The Queens are our *coves*—the deep place of wisdom and replenishment that we retire to in order to reconnect with our own wise energy.

All Queens are a call coming from inside the house, but none more than Queen of Cups. Queen of Cups has a liminal, mysterious, almost mythical quality, and certainly looks the part as a being who resides at the edge of the sea. The truth is that Queen of Cups is an indelible part of all of us, representing the wildness within. It is, frankly, a part of us that might not get a whole lot of attention. Some of us might not understand how we could be wild or even connected to wildness. The truth is that we couldn't be disconnected from this aspect of ourselves if we tried. When Queen of Cups shows up in a reading, it is here to reconnect us with the truth.

Queen of Cups is very much like a selkie. Selkies are mythological creatures that shape-shift from humans to seals by putting on or taking off their sealskins. This idea of belonging to two places, both land and sea, is deeply ingrained in the medicine of Queen of Cups. It reminds us, sometimes very persistently, that we too have a sealskin of sorts—an inner life, a set of our own desires, preferences, wishes, wants, and needs for space and time—that is all our own. We might be someone's partner, parent, or caretaker, but we still have a place within us—the sealskin—that both needs and deserves our attention and time, whether we want to admit that to ourselves or not.

When they lose their sealskin, or when it is taken from them, selkies cannot return to the sea. When we give away our power, get pulled into obligations and expectations, we can lose sight of our sealskin, something Clarissa Pinkola Estés brilliantly illustrates in her book *Women Who Run with the Wolves*. We can lose our very soul in the process.

Queen of Cups doesn't want us to abandon the things or people we love, but it does want us to come closer to ourselves. This card wants us to make time for ourselves and give ourselves space at the edge of our own wild sea—to think, to breathe, to paint, to dream, to watch reality TV, to come back to ourselves by whatever method is necessary. It is nothing less than soul retrieval in its deepest form.

When Queen of Cups shows up in a reading, it is inviting us to take space for ourselves, and to remember that there is more to us than our everyday activities and the expectations (if any) that are placed upon us. We have a date with the wildness within, with our soul, our inner sealskin. We would be wise to RSVP to the invitation.

Queen of Cups Reversed

When Queen of Cups shows up reversed, many different things could be happening. We could be ignoring the call of Queen of Cups. We could desperately want to connect with Queen of Cups, but we don't know how to take the space or time. Maybe we simply have no space and time. It might feel too devastating to connect with this card for fear that we wouldn't be able to commune with it in the way we want. We owe it to ourselves to be honest about what might be keeping us from connecting with Queen of Cups (and, by extension, with ourselves) in this deeper way.

SHARING OUR TRUTH WITH KING OF SWORDS

In Soul Tarot, we consider The Kings of the Tarot to be our *contributors*. King energy puts us in touch with the symbolic fruit of our tree, inviting us to consider what it is that we're bringing here to this planet, and what legacy we'd like to leave behind.

The more we acknowledge that we live in a spiral body moving on Spiral Time, the more we will begin to see things clearly and understand our needs, limitations, and desires in new ways. King of Swords is who we call upon to communicate these needs into form.

We have all seen beautiful and striking examples of King of Swords' embodiment in our lifetimes. Brave leaders who have stood up to evil and opposition despite great risk to themselves. Folks who break a family legacy of abuse, shame, and secrets, coming forward with their lived experience. Naming that we need help, that we want a divorce, that it's not working, that we love it, that we want more of it, that we never want to see it again—all King of Swords.

It is a vocalization, expression, or sharing of a truth in our heart that allows the road in front of us to blossom and open up. This share can be very public, or it can be a whispered acknowledgment to ourselves.

We may not get everything we want by speaking from the heart and sharing a difficult truth, but the act of doing so is its own liberatory and transformative spell. It can help us to clear illusion and delusion. It can allow us to live outside of the mantle of scant hope, prayers, and promises. It can encourage us to advocate for ourselves and live from what feels like alignment to us.

King of Swords isn't a proselytizer. It doesn't share its experience in order to force or move someone to its side. King of Swords acknowledges that some people may not come along with us. Some folks might not agree. But as long as we have some rings of support around us, holding space for us, loving and cheering us along the way, we can lean into the medicine that this card has to offer.

King of Swords Reversed

When King of Swords reversed shows up in a reading, we might feel nervous or afraid to speak out for fear of retribution, harm, or repercussions. How can we call upon the strength and courage of those who have come before us, who have spoken out or expressed themselves despite having everything to lose? We are not alone, and you are not alone as you travel through the terrifying and nerve-wracking experience of sharing your heart's truth to others. How can this card anchor you as you navigate this?

RESPONDING TO THE HEART'S CALL WITH THE NINES

The Nines of the Tarot are a climax before the culmination in The Tens—a crucial moment of reckoning, reconciliation, and acknowledgment before we can fully close out a cycle one way or another. The Nines invite us not only to sense into and admit to ourselves what we really long for, but also to be brave enough to give that to ourselves. All of The Nines are highly solitary and represent those crucial seasons of life where we must go deeply into ourselves and away from kinfolk, responsibilities, and expectations to feel into and respond to the call of the heart and the cry of the soul.

Working with The Nines can be profound in any season of life, but they are particularly potent when we are being called to witness, process, or integrate something that has been holding us back, or doesn't belong to us. Each Nine is a gentle whisper from Spirit to come back home to ourselves, to respond to an unmet inner need and uncover a treasure buried within the garden of our hearts.

Resting Through the Journey with Nine of Wands

In 2017, I embarked on my first teaching tour. I planned to do readings and teaching in Los Angeles, then fly up to Northern California to do a new round of readings and workshops, culminating in a two-week teaching near Mendocino. I was delighted and excited—my first tour!

I remember being on the airplane to California from New York City, where I lived at the time, and pulling a card to represent the most important anchor for me on this trip—the card I could come back to and lean on whenever things got tough or tricky. I pulled Nine of Wands, which gently suggested (at least to me) that my exciting tour would wind up being a lot more draining and exhausting than I bargained for, which it was. But I knew exactly what to do to care for myself through it, thanks to this card.

Nine of Wands usually shows up when we are symbolically running a marathon, ascending a mountain, swimming a long distance. This card acknowledges that this process is taking place without making it a problem, or something to correct. Nine of Wands helps us to embrace rest in the midst of a big push. It is the two-minute nap between contractions, or a tangled attempt at sleep in a hospital chair, anxiously awaiting updates on our loved one. It is the break we sorely need in a moment of frustration around a project. It is a momentary pause and rest in order to pace ourselves.

Nine of Wands is the crucial difference between a huge push that lands us in a crash-landing level of burnout, and a huge push that lands us in considerable and understandable exhaustion, ideally making space for a spell of integration in order to fill up our cups again. It interrupts the ego's desire to have us "just get it over with" or "push through it." Nine of Wands knows there will be moments when we will have to push through our limit. It wants us to honor that and rest when and where we can along the way.

As a person living with multiple autoimmune diseases, PTSD, and chronic pain, I am no stranger to working with Nine of Wands. Living in a body that operates on Spiral Time much of the time gives me no choice but to be in intimate connection with my limits, and what it requires for me to move through big pushes or creation seasons of my own.

It took many, many years of harsh stops in the form of injuries, burnout, and breakdowns to get me to come home to my body and honor what it needs in conjunction with the work, service, and art that I love and long to bring to the world. Nine of Wands wants that for all of us.

When Nine of Wands shows up in a reading, we are being invited to pace ourselves and build in more opportunities for rest during a big undertaking, push, or project. It reminds us that it's okay to move through these big undertakings as long as we know what we're getting into and have a plan in place. This card advocates for accessible, simple, unromantic rest—a catnap here, a podcast break there. It all adds up.

Nine of Wands Reversed

When Nine of Wands shows up reversed, we might be resisting this need for rest. We want to gently inquire as to why that might be. Do we believe that we will rest when it's done, rather than offering ourselves a moment here or there to recharge? Are we in a culture or community where hustling, grinding, and constantly working are celebrated and prized, and/or where there is so much trauma and activation that it doesn't feel safe to rest? If so, it can be challenging to believe that we are worthy of a nap or rest. It can be difficult to cultivate that sense of safety around breaks. We can take it one step at a time with this energy, going at a gentle pace.

Our Heart's Desire with Nine of Cups

I was lying in the dark with my two-and-a-half-year-old daughter, singing her our nightly repertoire of songs before bed. Stroking her hair, we cycled through "The Circle Game" and "Twinkle Twinkle Little Star," then landed on "Gartan Mother's Lullaby," which is one of her favorites.

"Gartan Mother's Lullaby" is one of the songs I most loved listening to before bed as a child. It is an old Irish song and poem, and part of my self-soothing routine before sleep was to play that song on a tape of lullabies, intentionally slowing my breathing, imagining that a gentle and tender mother was singing the same words to me that I was now singing to my child in her bed:

> A leanbhín ó, my child, my joy
> My love and heart's desire.

My daughter stopped me. "What is *heart's desire* mean?"

"It means something that you wish for and want so badly. Your heart is longing for something, and that's the way that mama feels about their baby in the song. You are my heart's desire, too."

Lynx persisted. "But what is heart's desire *mean?*"

I paused and reflected, offering examples of moments when I know my daughter has experienced that deep heart longing in her nearly two and a half years of life on this planet. For a used copy of Elsa Beskow's *The Sun Egg* to come in the mail. For the hope that a particular book would be at the library—and then it being there! (The joy!) For ice cream, or the dream to soak in wild hot springs, or to one day see fireflies.

She took it all in silently, and we continued to snuggle in the dark.

Nine of Cups represents our heart's deepest desires. It is a longing of the soul and a whispered prayer. These desires are so profoundly vulnerable, so tender, so confronting, that it can crack us open to even acknowledge them to *ourselves*, let alone another person. Our most fervent wishes live in the sacred curve of this card's energy.

Nine of Cups is a gentle whisper that it's safe to get our hopes up.

Can we imagine anything so foolhardy? To hope in the face of possible heartbreak, to long for something in the light of potential failure? Why want at all? Why admit or confront our soul's desire, even to our own hearts?

Because the cost of denying these desires is too high a price. It is too high a price to wither away or warp our desires into disdain or even hostility toward those who are courageous enough to take the leap and live from their soul's longing. Because it is terrifying to reach for all that we want, but it is more devastating than we could ever imagine suppressing and denying it.

The longing and desire I had for my child, to be a mother, was something that took me years to admit to myself for a myriad of reasons. The radiant maternal energy that my own younger self was able to draw from—self-soothing with lullabies before bed—sprang up from a place of profound loneliness, despair, and necessity within myself. It was also, oddly, a training ground for the love and tenderness that I am able to offer to my own child. There was no way that I could touch into the wild longing I had for a child without being willing to feel into my own vulnerability and softheartedness, two qualities that I needed to be armored against in order to survive my childhood. The longing was the thing that tore down the scaffolding of my heart, connecting me with parts of myself that were denied and buried. This is part of the spiral of Nine of Cups. It is a card that guides us back home to ourselves.

When Nine of Cups shows up in a reading, we are being invited to acknowledge that we are longing for something; our heart is harboring a deep desire. We are invited and encouraged to be brave enough to explore what these desires might be—whether it's to be a parent, to write a book, to make a new friend, to come out, or all or none of the above. What would it mean to wish and ask for these things, and be open to the possibility of receiving them? What would need to be recovered in order to do this?

Nine of Cups Reversed

Because the soul-led desires we experience in connection with this card are so vulnerable, it can stoke the possibility of our mind doing everything it can to deny them out of a sense of self-protection. Is it possible that those stories are safer to feel than the wildness of your desires? Are there some internalized judgments about how other folks are loving or living with regard to their desires? What might it be like to acknowledge that those judgments are rooted in a wanting that lives within you, too? What would need to be released, confronted, or acknowledged in order to free your soul and reach for this desire—to acknowledge that you long for it, too? Alternatively, if you're grieving a dream that cannot be, or did not happen in the way you'd hoped, Nine of Cups reversed can be the loving witness and affirmation that we need in those seasons. Your grief, anger, and experience matters.

The deeper we go into our work around embracing deep mystery, opening to our heart's wisdom, honoring our desires, and healing the things that may be blocking us from admitting that we have these desires in the first place, the more we are changed. We cannot do deep work with Judgment and The Nines without it pivoting aspects of our lives, opening us to a richer, fuller, more authentic relationship with ourselves.

Radical Self-Parenting with Nine of Swords

I had a very powerful spiritual experience when I was around 16 years old.

I had just been beaten and ran to my room to recover. One of my survival mechanisms after these experiences was to try to stifle and stuff down my tears, but this time they just flowed from me, unbidden. I wept and wept, feeling the full weight of despair, terror, and shame on my shoulders. In that moment, I felt a comforting presence around me and heard whispered words: *"One day, this will be different. You will be away from here, and you will be happier. I am with you and I love you."* After feeling those words bubble up from my soul, I was still devastated, but my heart felt fuller. I believed the words that I heard, and I felt less alone.

I had always assumed that these words were from a Guide or an Angel, sent to protect me. At this stage of my life, I am now certain that those words came from me—an older, wiser part of myself that stretched around the spiral of time to communicate to my younger self who desperately needed them in that moment. I believe this not because I haven't experienced my Guides and Spirit Helpers sharing this kind of comforting information with me, but because the voice I heard matches the kind of gentle, warm witness that I've learned to offer the frightened, traumatized parts of me. Life is a spiral, and in light of that, it makes sense that past or future parts of ourselves might show up in the most unlikely of places.

Nine of Swords represents exactly this kind of experience, inviting us to offer gentle, compassionate, affirming counsel to the parts of us that feel worried or scared.

We don't ever need to fear the presence of Nine of Swords. It doesn't bring in fear, trauma, or spikiness with it. It honors and names that there is likely fear, trauma, and/or spikiness *already here with us.* These feelings are asking for our attention, asking to be acknowledged, named, and bowed to *without us necessarily identifying with them.* We can notice our what-if or worst-case-scenario thinking and not buy into it as gospel. Thoughts are not necessarily true. Feelings are not facts. We don't have to believe them. We can, however, honor and name what is present and tend to those fears, checking in about whether something is absolutely true. This is at the heart of the work we are invited to do with Nine of Swords.

When moving through big-awakening, Judgment card–level experiences, we can be sure that big fears, anxieties, and worries will arise. Our inner kiddos and frightened selves will turn up the volume and make themselves known. Our job is to tend to them with care.

When a child is worried or scared that a monster is under the bed, do we as the parent leap onto the bed in horror with our child, screaming, "There's a monster? I'm so scared!"? Hopefully not. Ideally, we get on our child's level, honor their fear, grab a flashlight, and take a look.

When we work with Nine of Swords, we are often *both* the frightened child and the confident, capable adult who grabs that flashlight and says, *Monsters, huh? Whew, that is a scary thought. Let me get down on the floor and take a good look with my flashlight.* Grabbing the flashlight and looking under the bed is the equivalent of *Huh, you're saying that this person can't stand me? Let me really reflect on whether that's true. I'll even go so far as to ask them whether there's anything to unpack or repair between us.* When we get invited into a scary, worrisome thought (*This is a disaster/I'm fucked/This is forever*, etc.), we want to grab that cosmic flashlight. We want to, as my old teacher Michelle would say, "call the brain out on its bullshit." By doing so, those thoughts tend to lose some of their grip on us.

When Nine of Swords shows up in a reading, we are being invited to pause before we identify with our thinking, check in on the stories, fears, or worries that might be arising, and offer direct reassurance to the parts of us that are scared. It asks us to live in the both/and: in the scared self and nurturer self, in the worried self and the capable self, the child and the parent. It nudges us not toward collapsing in fear but instead toward liberating ourselves from it.

Nine of Swords Reversed

When Nine of Swords shows up reversed, a few things might be happening. We might have cleared out a layer of fear and are emerging on the other side more reassured, our nervous systems more relaxed. Check in with yourself and see if this resonates with you. Sometimes Nine of Swords reversed can encourage us to invite in a helping professional such as a therapist, coach, doula, or healer as an aid to our work with our scared selves. We don't ever have to hold that flashlight alone or shine it on anything that isn't ready to be witnessed yet.

Making Space for Pleasure with Nine of Pentacles

I was doing a reading for a beloved, longtime client who was feeling thoroughly drained. They got emotional as they described how burned-out they were from their bodywork business. "All day long, people get on my heated massage table, and there is never a moment for me to rest, take a break, or lie on my own massage table." It was no surprise to me that Nine of Pentacles showed up as the first card in their reading.

Nine of Pentacles is a clarion call around our relationship to work and pleasure—usually arising in readings when it's been all giving and no receiving. It invites us to reflect on our relationship to pleasure, specifically in connection to our service or what we offer to the world. The image I always see in my mind's eye when I reflect on this card is someone who has an orchard of peach trees, and day after day, they do the hard work of managing and selling those peaches to customers. A Nine of Pentacles moment for that person might be getting up early, heading out to the orchard with a basket, and picking some of those peaches for themselves. This card wants us to think more holistically about saving some of the peaches we grow for ourselves—it wants us to be able to savor the fruits of our labor.

It can be really confronting to think about our relationship to Nine of Pentacles and, by extension, our relationship to breaks, pleasure, and rest for several reasons.

For many of us, it's not a resistance issue as much as it is an accessibility issue with these Nine of Pentacles themes.

Systems of oppression want us broken down, exhausted, and overworked, and many of those systems set folks up to fail—especially folks going through hard times, or folks who have been historically marginalized. If we are a single parent, supporting our kids and running our household and working multiple jobs, we might not be in the season of our lives to be thinking too much about pleasure. Hell, even if we aren't a single parent but are just working our asses off to make ends meet, we may not have the privilege to be thinking about savoring the fruits of our labor. I really believe that Nine of Pentacles honors and holds space for that, so when it comes up in a reading, we are encouraged to sense into accessible, available pleasures—pleasures that are small, simple, freely offered, and/or inexpensive. The scent of a delicious body wash. The lighting of a simple candle. Fresh air. A comfortable and familiar book. Time outside under a tree in a park. What is both accessible and pleasurable to you will likely be different from these examples. I encourage you to sense into what they might be.

Sometimes, Nine of Pentacles shows up around areas that are deeply ancestral.

Taking breaks, resting, and pleasure for pleasure's sake were not modeled to most of us for various reasons. For many of us, it might feel uncomfortable, shameful, or even dangerous to make space for pleasure. This can also be true if we've experienced trauma—sometimes relaxing and kicking back is a lot harder than tucking into a project.

The triggers will be different for each of us, depending on how we were raised. Every time I choose to take a nap in the middle of the day, or get my nails done, or paint something when I could be working, I feel a sense of judgmental shame. What a waste of money. What a waste of time. When I feel those things, I know I'm brushing up against an ancestral wound—a place that my ancestors weren't willing or able to go to in their own circumstances. Continuing whatever pleasurable activity I'm engaging in *without* believing the shame helps my body know it's safe to continue. I also believe that it not only helps heal my ancestral line around this wound but also sets my child up for knowing that it's safe to engage in what brings her joy.

Nine of Pentacles is wildly confronting and thoroughly healing. It can be radically disruptive to the Western idea of all work and no play, and it can offer us an opportunity to heal some of our family lineage wounding around these ideas. It encourages us to find play and pleasure in whatever happens to be in front of us, symbolically or realistically, simply because we deserve it. It makes life worth living.

When we get Nine of Pentacles in a reading, we are being invited to make more space in our lives for pleasure—to rest, take breaks, and make space for deliciousness. This can be free and accessible. We don't need to take an expensive vacation to some gorgeous location to touch base with the essence of Nine of Pentacles. What simple things help you to feel like you are enrobed in pleasure?

Nine of Pentacles Reversed

When we get Nine of Pentacles reversed in our reading, we may likely be denying ourselves this need for pleasure, and we want to get curious about why. First, if indeed you do feel a sense of overwhelm/resistance around taking a break, remind yourself that it can be really hard for a myriad of reasons to feel like it's safe and okay for us to open to this idea. It's not your fault. Secondly, what are the barriers? Is it situational—i.e., no space, money, time, ability to access something sweet for yourself? Can you check in on whether that's absolutely true? It might be, but if there's a possibility that it isn't, are you willing to start with baby steps? With something simpler and more freely offered than what you might be considering?

CHAPTER THIRTEEN

CLOSING THE CIRCLE

Tarot Cards for Completions and New Cycles

THE WORLD

KNIGHT OF WANDS

KING OF PENTACLES

THE TENS

THE WORLD

KNIGHT OF WANDS

KING OF PENTACLES

TEN OF WANDS

TEN OF CUPS

TEN OF SWORDS

TEN OF PENTACLES

We experience subtle thresholds and completions all the time. We move through at least 12 new moons and 12 full moons in a calendar year. We watch as the seasons slowly change before our eyes. Our children grow up and ideally become more and more confident and independent. We gain and lose dear, beloved companions. We have a falling-out, or a reconciliation. We discover more about ourselves through the years as parts and aspects of us die away and are born anew over and over again.

When big cycles of completion come to our door—moments when we are closing a chapter in a significant way—we want to be as present with the process as we possibly can. This can feel daunting and challenging for most of us. Goodbyes are difficult, and some prefer not to engage with them at all. Our completions can be clean and simple, messy and beautiful, and/or complicated as hell. We learn a little bit more about what it is to close chapters and honor endings with each one that we experience.

How do we close the circles in our lives? How do we ritualize our endings? How do we say goodbye and honor the people and beloveds that we're leaving behind or are leaving us?

When we're experiencing deep thresholds, strong closings, and soul-led endings of the highest order, we can lean on the wisdom and nourishment of **The World, Knight of Wands, King of Pentacles**, and **The Tens.** These cards can help us move through these big completions and new cycles with as much grace and compassion for ourselves as possible. They can help us engage with these completions ceremonially, finding medicine within them in our own unique ways.

THE CLOSING OF A CYCLE WITH THE WORLD

There are many cards that deal with endings and completions in the Tarot, but none of them are quite like The World. As the last card in the Major Arcana, it is a strong signal that we are wrapping up something quite significant.

The World is the last chapter of the last book in a beloved book series that we've been reading for months, even years. We come to the last sentence and close the book, eyes filled with tears. How wonderful it was to move through this book series, and, even if we reread the whole thing again from cover to cover, it won't be the same. We can't ever go back to the first time we read it. There is only forward from here.

When The World card shows up, we're being invited to know that something in our lives is truly complete, and that we're ready to simultaneously say goodbye to this cycle and welcome in a new one. The ending that The World card typically heralds can be emotional, but mostly, unlike the book series scenario I offered, it's just a huge relief. Once we've reached The World card, there is usually accompanying readiness and even frustration, as if we're energetically checking our watch, tapping our foot, waiting to be birthed into something new already. We're usually beyond ready to bid this parting season farewell, but we can be surprised by how grief weaves itself into that keen desire to move into something new. It is important to hold all the feelings that surround our experience in this card.

It's also important to acknowledge how The World card typically shows up and behaves when we begin to see it in our readings. This card—and the endings that it brings to our door—can be lovely, euphoric, and sacred, but there's often a lot of tedious lead-up to those more welcome experiences. This is by design.

The World card is traditionally ruled by Saturn, which is a planet rooted in the themes of discipline, structure, order, and hard work. Saturn is committed to us, as maddening as that commitment might feel at times. It wants to make sure that we're staying the course, that we're firmly centered on the path that we're meant to be walking in this lifetime. It's here to help us do our soul work. My dear friend Jeff Hinshaw (a brilliant astrologer and Tarot teacher) likens Saturn to someone holding a clipboard, keeping close watch on everything we need to tick off before we're able to move forward and be free. I tend to think of Saturn anytime I'm filling out applications, making sure I have all the relevant documentation needed. This is an important thing to keep in mind when working with The World and, frankly, any major ending in life.

Major endings usually involve cosmic (and often actual) paperwork. We must ensure that our affairs are in order. The World card will not allow us to move forward into the next great cycle of our lives with any outstanding business or boxes left unchecked. The beautiful and often spiritual point of completion that we experience in The World card really comes at the end of our journey with it. Most of our experience in this card is a series of Saturn-like responsibilities, tasks, and initiations. Knowing and expecting that can make our journey through this card much more easeful (and a lot less confusing, especially if we're expecting a quick and glorious shift).

Once we've moved through everything that The World card requires, there is nothing else to do but to leap into a totally new chapter of our lives, one that we're usually truly longing for. We are ready.

The World Reversed

When The World card shows up reversed, we might be experiencing significant impatience around how long it's taking for us to reach that point of sacred completion. Death/rebirth cycles can take a long, long time. The first thing to remember is those feelings are valid and welcome—we are allowed to feel impatient. How can we tend to ourselves in the face of that? Is there anyone we can vent to, or process those feelings with? The other important thing to remind ourselves of is that this ending is coming, even if it feels very out of reach right now.

LETTING IT FEEL GOOD WITH KNIGHT OF WANDS

In Soul Tarot, Knights are ruled by the element of Air. These cards help us get a sense of the aligned timing, pace, rhythm, pitch, and flow of our lives at any given moment.

We can call upon The Knights anytime we want clarity on the movement that would be most beneficial right now. Some of The Knights are a little more centered in the realm of fast/slow, guiding us on whether it can be advantageous to speed up or pump the brakes.

Knight of Wands is less about speed and more about *how* we move. This card wants our movement through the world to feel as good as humanly possible. It encourages us to do our makeup the way we want (if we want to at all), to wear the clothes that make us feel good, and to have pockets of pleasure available to us in easy, accessible ways. Great music in our ears, a delicious snack, a warm mug of a soothing drink—even our willingness to take in the beauty of the weather—is all Knight of Wands' domain. This card isn't about bypassing the challenges of life—it's precisely because life can be so hard that this card is insistent on helping us tether to joy and what makes us feel as good as possible. We don't need to change who we are or have a ton of money to connect with this card. I have found that I connect with Knight of Wands most when I'm willing to be present with what I actually want, as opposed to what I think I "should" do or what I tell myself is expected of me. This card helps us to clear those stories out and fully embrace ourselves as we are today.

When Knight of Wands shows up in a reading, we're being invited to consider whether it might be possible to inject more pleasure, fun, and joy into how we move through our lives.

This card is always helpful, but it can be especially useful amid big completions and clearings. If we're going through a huge World card cycle or are in a death/rebirth process ourselves, extra layers of sweetness are a must. Alongside my work with Tarot, I'm also a budding community deathcare worker, and have been privileged to be of service to folks who are moving through illness, or who are dying. There is nothing like bearing witness to unimaginable grief and loss, or holding immensely tender space for other people, to remind you of your own mortality—to encourage you to eat that slice of cake, to tell that person you love them, to dance, sing, and fully immerse yourself in your life while you're still here, while you still can.

Knight of Wands is truly about living your life to the fullest degree possible in simple, practical, and accessible ways and embracing any opportunity to experience joy—even (and especially) amid life's challenges, completions, and sorrows.

Knight of Wands Reversed

Knight of Wands can show up reversed when we're long overdue for recentering our pleasure-to-work ratio. If it's all grind and no play, this card will show up reversed to have a strong word with us. It's in our best interest, no matter how activating it can be, to sense into ways to allow more enjoyable things to be an active part of our lives.

SERVING THROUGH OUR LIVED EXPERIENCE WITH KING OF PENTACLES

In Soul Tarot, we look to The Kings as leaders, guides, and *contributors* to the world. King energy lives in each of us, whether we are someone who speaks to millions or to a very small circle of folks. The Kings help us get a better sense of our influence, however small it might seem, inviting us to leave a legacy of care, warmth, and tending. The Kings want to be of service, however humble.

King of Pentacles is a very unique energy and easily the most deeply layered of the four Kings. King of Cups is an invitation to care for ourselves as we tend others. King of Wands invites us to blaze the trail, to courageously share our ideas with the world. King of Swords encourages us to express what we're observing and experiencing, even if it feels scary to do so.

King of Pentacles is an invitation to serve from our lived experience, allowing our mistakes, fuckups, successes, and trials—the grit of our lives—to become gold that can help other people through their own journeys.

If you've ever read about someone's story and it's helped you to feel less alone or realize that you're not the only one who feels the way you do, that's King of Pentacles, shining through that person and lighting you up in turn. If you've ever hacked your way through a forest of thorns, brambles, and quicksand and found yourself wanting to help others to not feel so alone in that same journey, that is King of Pentacles singing through you. We come to our own inner King of Pentacles the more we allow our lived experiences to be scars that shine brightly, rather than ones that stay hidden.

This gold that King of Pentacles calls us to center and lift up often feels like our worst quality, or even something that feels shameful or potentially embarrassing. One related personal experience—I live with a chronic illness and pain, and will sometimes need to reschedule a class or a day of sessions because of an unexpected migraine or flare-up. It feels hugely contractive for me to cancel and reschedule on folks who are excited about connecting with me. It brings up shame and "should" and activates my internalized ableism—something I'm still working on, even after so many years of living as a spoonie.

Whenever this occurs in my career, there are occasionally folks who get (understandably) upset and want a refund, which we always provide. But I would say 99.9 percent of folks are not only sympathetic and kind, but reflect gratitude back to me, saying that my willingness to cancel, to acknowledge that my body cannot accommodate our meeting, inspires them to feel permission to not push themselves and cancel when they need to as well. This is King of Pentacles in action, allowing the circumstances of our lives, who we are, and our experience in these bodies to be the catalyst to inspire others to follow their own wise path, too. Grit into gold, over and over again.

King of Pentacles can be a strong ally to us in seasons when we're closing the circle in some way or moving through a big completion or ending. Each and every time we survive a loss or the closing of a door, we can help others to endure their own cycles of completion. Anytime we allow ourselves to be altered, transformed, or changed by a birth, a death, a divorce, a coming out, a transition, a move, a change to our name or our identity, King of Pentacles shines through us. Anytime we get sick and are honest about it, or talk about our pain, or are honest about our regrets, mistakes, and mess-ups, King of Pentacles shines through us. Sharing who we are, letting ourselves grow in front of people, and letting them know where we are today, is living from a King of Pentacles place. May we all strive to see one another in our humanness, and shine in our own.

King of Pentacles Reversed

Are we denying ourselves the gift of being an inspiration to others because of our perceptions? King of Pentacles often shows up reversed when this is going on—when we've told ourselves a story of how people will respond to our experience or choices, we want to really pause and reflect on whether that's true. It might be, but in my experience, King of Pentacles reversed usually points us in the direction of a hidden pocket of gold within us—something so helpful for folks to know they are not alone in, but that we're still working toward feeling comfortable enough to share. Know that you can take your time, but kindly bear in mind that the story your inner protector or mind is telling you might not be the whole truth.

DEATH AND REBIRTH WITH THE TENS

The Tens are our culmination point in the Tarot. They represent the sacred point between death and rebirth, darkness and dawn, an ending and a new rebirth.

We can work with The Tens in much the same way that we might work with the Full Moon: We acknowledge that something has come as far as it's able, express our gratitude for the lessons and gifts that this taught us, and offer it up to the symbolic (or actual) fire. We are making room for much-needed new seeds to take root in our lives when we work with The Tens, but only through our willingness to be present with what's ready to be laid on the compost pile.

The Tens are natural allies to us in seasons of deep and quiet change. These cards live most strongly and presently in shifts to the harvest season, and in the turning of the wheel of the year—in the leaves falling, the ground freezing, and then, miraculously, life renewing itself. It takes tremendous energy to move through these shifts, and The Tens can help us engage gracefully with them. These cards can also assist us in moving through the soul work that is necessary to pivot from death to rebirth. They provide the map, as well as helpful tools to nourish us along the journey.

Necessary Reevaluation with Ten of Wands

Ten of Wands is often spoken about as a card of overwhelm, isolation, and even burnout. This isn't necessarily untrue—Ten of Wands can absolutely show up in seasons like this—but it's not the core essence of the card. We may receive this card and not be overwhelmed, burned-out, or isolated at all, so it's important to gently recenter that as an absolute of this energy.

With Ten of Wands, I tend to consistently see a strong need to reevaluate what we're tending to and responsible for—and, perhaps more importantly, how we're holding it. This happens in life all the time. We pick up things, take things on, manage certain things, and all of a sudden we find ourselves dropping the ball or unable to carry things out as skillfully as we once were. Perhaps the reason for this is obvious: We expanded our family, we have a new job with a higher degree of responsibility, our work has blown up and we need more support than we did a year ago. Ten of Wands signals that it's time for a crucial audit of both what falls on our plate *and* how it's balanced there. True balance is impossible to achieve, frankly, especially for single parents and folks who are working multiple jobs or are caretakers for the elders in their lives (as well as themselves and potentially their children, too). Ten of Wands doesn't ask for perfect order or for us to unrealistically shirk our responsibilities.

This card invites us to lay down every single one of our "wands"—our work, labor, and what we take care of—and strongly evaluate whether each of these wands is still a yes for us. It might be that we have the privilege to pick up only five of the ten wands we were previously holding, fully releasing a few of the remaining wands and allowing other folks to help us hold the rest. Very often, we have to rethink the way we hold and manage the wands we pick back up. Sometimes this reshuffling of our tasks is temporary—only until we've reached a goal or completed a big project, and then we can enfold a few more wands into our arms again. Each situation is different.

Ten of Wands can sometimes feel a little contractive to work with because it often invites us to ask for help, to acknowledge our own limits, and be available to allow others to support us a little (or a lot) more. As activating as it might feel, it is essential that we work with Ten of Wands to the best of our ability. Underneath all of the work it's inviting us to do, it's a clarion call that the way that we've been attempting to manage all that we're holding is no longer working and/or is unsustainable. When this card shows up in a reading, it's not just calling us into that kind of important acknowledgment and subsequent evaluation—it's helping clear the space so fresh, new energy can be welcomed in. Despite how it might feel, Ten of Wands is a signal that we're about to really expand, but we cannot do so without moving through this gentle auditing process.

Ten of Wands Reversed

Ten of Wands reversed is where we can see things like burnout and overwhelm more predictably. The reversal is usually an indication that we've needed to do this energetic evaluation for a long, long time and have either not been aware of it or have actively ignored it out of a sense of discomfort. It is in your best interest to pause and tend to those feelings and work with Ten of Wands. It might be useful to call upon a second set of eyes to be an objective observer a therapist, coach, or mentor would be a great option here. Sometimes we can feel like we "have" to do something, but upon deeper reflection we realize that we have more choice than we might have initially believed. Working with that other party can help us come to that place.

Opening to the Rainbows with Ten of Cups

Ten of Cups invites us to be available for the accessible, nourishing, simple joys all around us: the "rainbows" of life. There's a solid reason that rainbows are present on so many Ten of Cups cards, perhaps most notably in the Smith-Rider-Waite Tarot deck, where a couple is gesturing to a beautiful rainbow in the sky as their children dance and play by their side. A lovely image, one that has undoubtedly influenced the very popular interpretation of this card as one of perfect harmony, happiness, and wishes coming true. I hate to burst any bubbles, but there's very little truth in that interpretation, and it's not ultimately what Ten of Cups brings to our door, at least not in my experience. In fact, even when looking at the

Smith-Rider-Waite image for a little while, some things start to become more obvious: Eventually, the jubilantly raised arms of the couple will get tired, and they will bring their arms to rest. Eventually, the dancing children will have a need, or will take a tumble, or will want to go home. The rainbow will eventually fade.

I don't intend for this to be pessimistic—it is just an acknowledgment of reality. This acknowledgment helps to clear the way for what I believe Ten of Cups really helps us with: the fine skill and art of being present with the beauties and joys of life, knowing that nothing is permanent. We will eventually leave these bodies. We will say goodbye to everyone we love. The privilege and price of wild, unyielding love is to understand that it inextricably accompanies loss. Rainbows are not meant to last. Perfect, beautiful moments are not meant to be gripped on to tightly. They are wild things, meant to arrive and land in our very heart and bones, and then continue on their way. Ten of Cups can, in subtle, transformative, and heartbreaking ways, help us acknowledge that overall losses and endings are an inevitable part of life. This card does not signal a terrible loss or an ending close at hand.

When it shows up in a reading for us, can we open our eyes to the rainbows of life and truly be present with them?

I've noted through my career as a Tarot reader that I tend to see Ten of Cups in challenging seasons of life. It can be useful in any moment, but it tends to be crucial in difficult chapters. When times are unclear, when money is tight, when we're experiencing physical or emotional trials, we often long for clarity on when things will look up. The Tarot cannot necessarily give us this clarity, but if Ten of Cups shows up in a reading, it is offering us beautiful and potent medicine.

So I pose the question to you: What are the accessible joys that make life worth living for you? What helps you to come home to this moment, in the midst of whatever shitstorm is blowing through your life?

As vulnerable and silly as this seems, dappled light in the late afternoon really helps my heart in hard seasons. The sound of the wind. The exquisite perfection and beauty of my child, and the depth of gratitude I have that they chose me to be their mom. I want to leave no kind word unspoken to her, no feeling of love unexpressed. I want to really be present with her, remembering that tomorrow is not promised.

When my beloved cat Wee was alive, he was my strongest entry point into Ten of Cups. No matter how busy or frazzled I felt, everything stopped for him when he wanted a cuddle. *"He won't always be here,"* I would remember, letting my urgency slip away for cheek and chin scratches. Another example is my sweet husband, and how blown away I am that we managed to find one another in this lifetime. No matter what happens, our love gets us through.

Challenges and hard seasons are temporary. Life is temporary. Ten of Cups wants us to love deeply and open our heart to the rainbows of life. This card helps us to shift from an unrealistic expectation of perfect happiness and wishes granted to one of reality, remembering that nothing is forever, for better or worse. May we be present with the joys of life, however fleeting, simple, or practical they may be.

Ten of Cups Reversed

When Ten of Cups reversed shows up in our readings, we are in dire need of some sweetness in our lives, however simple it might be. Try not to focus on the big picture, and instead come home to what's right in front of you.

Shedding Our Skin with Ten of Swords

Ten of Swords is nothing to fear. Quite the contrary, in fact. It might feel somewhat surprising, given its intense, sometimes frightening reputation, but Ten of Swords is a very gentle and beautiful energy. It is so important to remember that we are collectively rewilding The Swords suit in Soul Tarot. When we do this, we move beyond the story that the mind is projecting, and open to what might be happening underneath it, inquiring as to what it might need from us. If we're reconsidering the entire Swords suit, we must reconsider Ten of Swords, too.

Ten of Swords is an indication that a way that we've been approaching something is no longer working for us, and we must take a bold leap into something new. Easier said than done. The Swords suit lives in the realm of the mental and, generally speaking, the mind would prefer that we not change or shift things too much. It wants us in what is familiar and known. Remembering that can be helpful when we're trying to understand why Ten of Swords can feel so activating. This card isn't a harbinger of devastation, desolation, betrayal, or despair, as so many believe. It is nothing short of a rebirth, born of the call to change our minds and try something new. The way that we've been doing things for so long has died—it has become a skin that we must shed because we've outgrown it. It is in our best interest to move out of our comfort zone and do something we've never done before, which is exactly what Ten of Swords invites us to do.

Ten of Swords has often felt like the closest card to The Fool to me, energetically speaking. They are spiritual siblings. They both call upon us to leap into something new, to deal with the churn of death/rebirth themes, and both are absolutely signals that we're ready to evolve and uplevel in some way. Every time I've taken a chance on something terrifying that has brought me incredible success or happiness, I've pulled Ten of Swords repetitively. It is a necessary evolutionary step toward something that the soul is longing for, and that the mind will attempt to protect us from because it's less familiar.

It can feel scary to leap into something new, to acknowledge that an old way that we've become accustomed to no longer serves us, but the freedom, expansion, and clarity that lie on the other side of our work with Ten of Swords is worth every moment.

Ten of Swords Reversed

Ten of Swords reversed is a gentle invitation to trust in the process of this card. After a big soul leap, we don't often get too much in the way of big signs that we're heading in the right direction. In fact, with this card there's usually a big stretch of proverbial road without much in the way of signage to give us the ease and comfort of confirmation. If you know that, it can make your journey through this card so much easier. Trust yourself and your leap, even if it feels scary or makes you want to go back and just hide. It's impossible to squeeze a snakeskin back on after we've shed it, and we can't really undo a leap. Keep going, even if you feel a little shaky.

Honoring Our Harvest with Ten of Pentacles

There is a sweet farm not too far from my house that our family frequents. Unlike some of the other local farms that offer year-round CSAs or produce through the winter and early spring, this farm closes up for the year on October 31. It's honestly a dreamy thing to think about. What might it be like to stop and mark the end of a spiral of growth and output in order to review, rest, reflect, and, eventually, prepare for the next season of offerings to sprout within us?

Ten of Pentacles holds this energetic invitation, a candle at the window beckoning us home after a long night. This card signals a natural and often subtle point of completion for us, an end to a harvest season of the soul. This doesn't mean that we're headed into a fallow period, but it does call us into a kind of seasonality with our work in the world—honoring our own soul seasons requires that we make space for whatever our winter is, that we honor a necessary period of hibernation, review, and ritual. If we work with magic or spell crafting, we can root into the spiral of the moon's phases, planting seeds with the New Moon and clearing things out at the Full Moon. Ten of Pentacles can help us sense into these subtler seasons.

When Ten of Pentacles shows up in a reading, it invites us to gather, reflect, and honor the cycle that is coming to completion for us. What did we grow? What did we compost? What did we keep, store, and enjoy? What did we give away or share with others? What new things did we try? What went great, and what failed, if anything? What would we never do again? What are we excited to try next time? How might we celebrate this harvest season and all the work that went into it?

Working with The Pentacles often involves a significant intersection of the body and its efforts with our soul work. It takes a lot of labor to bring The Pentacles suit to life. Offering ourselves the gift of a soul winter is essential not only for our continued growth and evolution, but for self-love. We are seasonal, spiralic beings whether we want to acknowledge that or not. Ten of Pentacles helps us to come back home to that subtle, gentle current.

Ten of Pentacles Reversed

Do we need a break? Are we pushing past our limit? Ten of Pentacles reversed will usually let us know if that's the case. If we're blowing past these subtle invitations to rest, reflect, and engage with ritual, we might feel tense, pissed, or exhausted. If you can stop what you're doing, please do so. Let yourself hibernate to the best of your ability. If you cannot stop what you're doing, how might you offer yourself some gentle pauses? Even 10 percent more ease in your day will add up and make a difference with time.

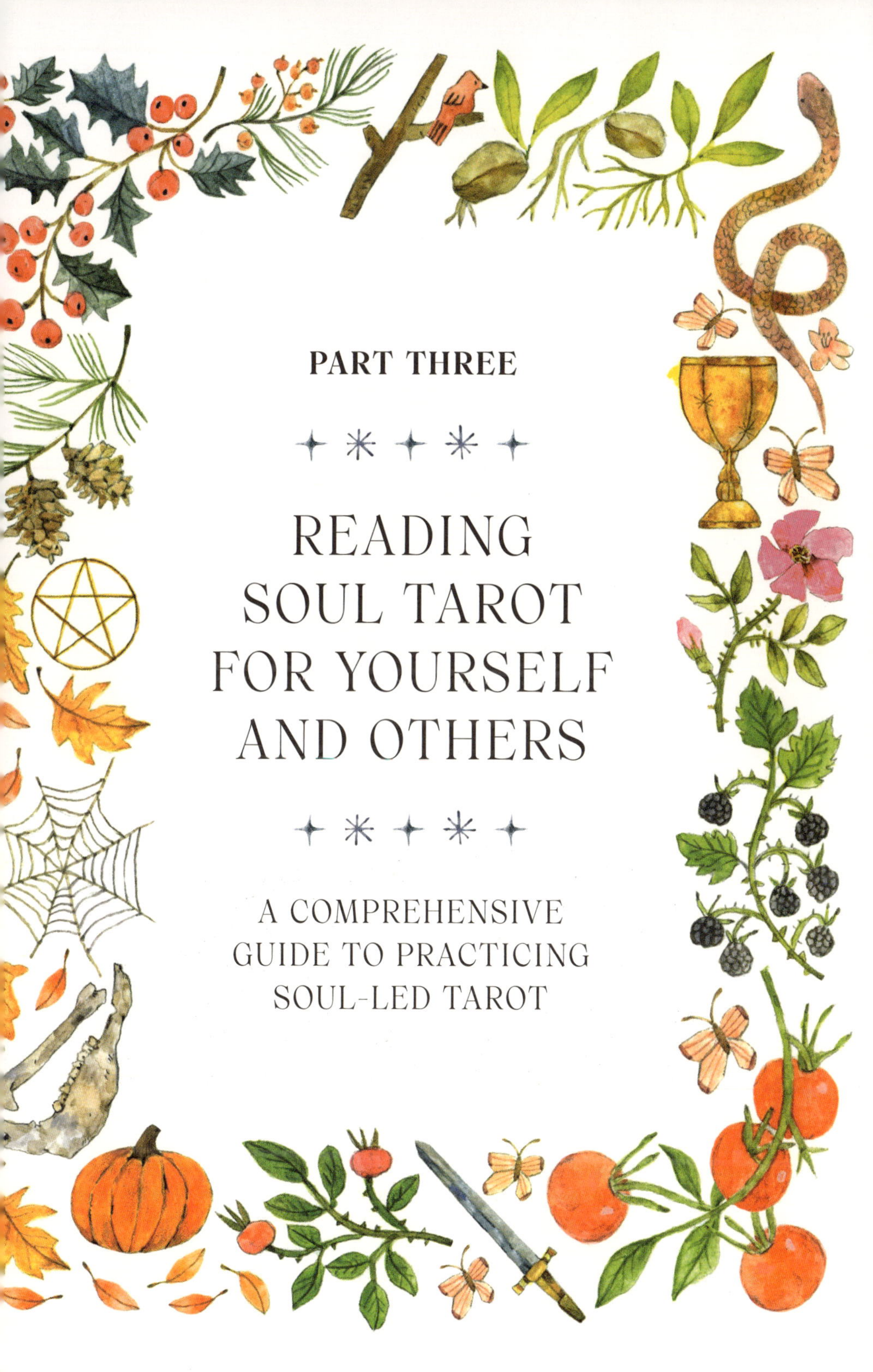

PART THREE

READING SOUL TAROT FOR YOURSELF AND OTHERS

A COMPREHENSIVE GUIDE TO PRACTICING SOUL-LED TAROT

CHAPTER FOURTEEN

GETTING STARTED WITH SOUL TAROT READINGS

Preparing for Your Reading

If you'd like to read Tarot for yourself or another person, you will need a Tarot deck. There is no one right or aligned way to get a Tarot deck. You don't have to be given or gifted a deck (a common myth), you don't have to steal a deck (another common myth), and you don't have to study for a certain number of years before beginning to play around with reading. You can order a Tarot deck from the internet, get one secondhand, or fall in love with one at a shop.

I also want to validate that you might not have your "soulmate" deck right now, or ever. It's okay to work with a Tarot deck that feels like a fine fit but not a completely aligned match. That is quite normal. A great deal of folks are also somewhat polyamorous with their Tarot decks and would never dream of having or working with just one deck. That's beautiful, too. All of it is valid and perfectly welcome. The only thing we want to ensure is that you have a Tarot deck in your hands before you begin this practice.

WHEN YOU HAVE A BRAND-NEW TAROT DECK

If you have a brand-spanking-new Tarot deck, there's nothing special you have to do with it, other than to take the cards out of the packaging and hang out with them. You may cleanse or clear the energy of the deck by using some of the methods described below.

I encourage you to shuffle the deck and get a sense of how it feels to connect with it, perhaps pulling a card for yourself. Whenever I'm working with a new deck, I like to ask, *"What work are we meant to do together?"* It's always interesting to see what cards come up around that kind of inquiry.

WHEN YOU ARE USING A USED AND/OR PASSED-DOWN DECK

Same exact flow as above! Hang out with it, pull a card, get a sense of the work you're meant to do together.

With inherited decks, I always take a moment to talk to the deck (yes, I talk to my decks, and I encourage you to do the same—they will respond to you in their own way) and check in with it: Does it really feel like *my* deck, or are there still traces of the person who owned it and passed it along to me? A simple clearing and conversation with the deck will usually shift that energetically. I have also found that even with those measures, I sometimes have to let the deck be for a bit before I use it. Trust your senses about this.

CLEANSING OR CLEARING A TAROT DECK

My favorite way to cleanse or clear my Tarot deck is to take it outside and ask the air or wind to clear away anything that isn't meant to be a part of my relationship with my deck. Sometimes I will leave my deck out to bathe in the light of the Full Moon, and sometimes it will feel right to brush my deck over my rosemary plant. This seems to do the trick very nicely.

If I need a heavy-duty Tarot deck clearing, I tend to leave my deck overnight in a bowl of sea salt, and sometimes herbs from my garden.

That said, there are many different ways to energetically cleanse and clear a Tarot deck. If one of these doesn't fit or align with you, I encourage you to keep researching until you find the right method for your practice.

THE DROP-IN

In my humble opinion, the Drop-In is one of the most supportive and crucial practices we can engage with when it comes to reading for ourselves and other people. It is a cornerstone of Soul Tarot and provides an immeasurably sound foundation for our Tarot readings, helping establish solid energetic boundaries and ensure that we receive *only* the information that we're meant to know at the time of the reading.

In terms of the realm beyond the veil, this is a free-will universe, and our free will is respected by Spirit. In that Spirit realm, we have to ask for what we want and give our consent to receive it. If we encounter anything unwelcome from beyond the veil that does happen to come in without our consent, we need only tell it to "go away and never come back," and it will. With our Drop-Ins, we also have the opportunity to name who we'd like to speak with energetically, the information we would like to receive, and what we're showing up with today—all before we've even pulled a card.

It isn't the first place that many of us go when it comes to reading Tarot, understandably assuming that "the cards will tell us what we need to know." In my very humble opinion, that's placing a ton of assumption and power on what is essentially just a bunch of images on cards.

We have to ask for what we want. We have to be intentional—even if our question is *What am I being invited to pay attention to right now?* This is our small, unfussy, bespoke window of acknowledgment and preparation before pulling cards—one that is deserved and wholly supportive.

The Drop-In also serves as a crucial checkpoint for us as Tarot readers. I'll offer an example from my personal practice. I was giving a reading not that long ago to someone, and as I listened to them share more and more about their incredibly challenging circumstances, I felt a fire in my belly and a charge in my system on their behalf. I was so sure that it was aligned for them to get the hell out of that situation and never look back. I kept those feelings to myself, however, because I hadn't formally dropped in yet. I finally did a Drop-In, and what I got from this person's Guides could not have been more different from my initial impulse. I had been indignant and outraged for this person, but their Guides were so much softer and more mournful. I started feeling tired in my body, and they let me know how exhausted this person was. They named that it was important that *this* be centered in the reading. The opportunity to leave their current situation would come, but right now they just needed their grief to be acknowledged. And then every Tarot card I pulled aligned beautifully with what I heard from this person's Guides. I centered what they shared, and it strongly resonated for this person. Eventually, they made their way out of the challenging situation at hand, but it wasn't time to clue them in to that. They got there on their own.

I mention this example because it was a very significant experience for me. I felt so relieved that I had waited to check in before barreling forward with what

I was feeling. What if I had assumed that my personal response to their story was automatically on point? I would have completely missed the mark on this person's reading. Sometimes someone's Guides will in fact completely align with the gut check we have as readers, but a Drop-In will help us sense whether that's the case.

To conclude, the Drop-In will provide you with the cleanest, strongest, most beautiful field of protection you could ever hope for. It is a filtration system that allows what's useful to come in and keeps the rest outside of our field.

Drop-In Structure

I believe that everyone can and should create their own structure for a Drop-In, but in case it's useful, this is mine:

1. Close your eyes and take a deep breath.
2. Call upon your supportive figures (Spirit Helpers, Guides, your wise inner knowing, etc.) to be with you as you embark on this reading. By doing this, we are being clear about who we are available to hear from, which is important. We wouldn't ask for advice from just anyone—why would we do so with our Tarot readings?
3. Honor what's happening within you. Make space to name what is present for you or coming up for you, if anything, as you embark on this reading. Name that you have a headache, or that you're feeling jealous. Name that you are showing up in joy, or that you're feeling nervous about getting it wrong. Whatever you've got going on, let it be named and infused into the reading, rather than pushed away. When these things are honored, it is my experience that they soften and shift as a result. When that happens, there is more room in the reading for the actual inquiry at hand.
4. Specifically ask to receive the guidance that is in the highest good for you (or your client) to know at this time from your and their Spirit Helpers and/or wise Inner Knowing ***only***. By naming exactly what we are available for, we create a wildly powerful boundary around ourselves, keeping what's ***not*** in alignment for us out of the reading.

5. From there, name your inquiry or question.

Lastly, an important reminder: We do *not* need to be calm, or in a fabulous mood to read Tarot for ourselves. You are allowed to reach for your tools of support at any moment, but *especially* when you feel contracted or out of sorts. By all means, feel free to meditate, center yourself, and do any kind of ritual you like before you pull, but I want to make sure you know that you don't *have* to, and however you're showing up is okay.

READING TAROT FOR YOURSELF

1. Go to your deck when you feel the need, call, or desire. No need to get centered unless you really feel called to do so. Your pre-pull ritual gets to be exactly what suits and supports you.
2. I recommend that you take a moment to offer yourself a Drop-In (naming what you are available for, who you'd like to hear from, what you're showing up with, and what you would like to receive from this reading) before pulling. Drop-Ins can be very long or very short. Feel free to make this practice your own and play around with what feels good for you. Give yourself permission to keep it really simple. There's no wrong way to engage with this.
3. Once you've picked up your deck and done a Drop-In, you will want to shuffle (if you haven't already been doing so!) and pull a card or cards for yourself.

SHUFFLING

There are a few ways to shuffle and pull a card from the deck, and no one way is wrong or right.

If you have a brand-new deck, I recommend first creating a giant pile in front of you and mixing them around thoroughly, then placing them back into one pile. That will ensure that you are doing a more efficient job at displacing your cards from the order they were placed in when they were manufactured, which is what we want!

In terms of shuffling, you can do a riffle and bridge shuffle if that feels accessible to you. You can hold the deck in one hand and shuffle with the other. You can cut the deck into three piles and then restack with whatever pile feels most like it wants to be on top. From there, you can pull in whatever manner you like—pulling off the top of the deck, tracing your finger along the spine of the deck and then pulling when it feels right, or even pulling from the bottom of the deck. Know and expect that the way you pull Tarot cards will change over time and will be different from day to day, and from client to client, if you intend to read for folks.

1. Once you've pulled cards, hang out with what you've pulled. Notice any judgments, assumptions, mental stories, or worries. See if you can just notice these invitations, rather than necessarily believing them. Open your heart to the card. What might it be bringing for you? What medicine might it want to lay at your feet?
2. Do whatever you like. Pull clarifiers, journal about what you've pulled, refer to one of the helping practices in this book (which are coming up in just a moment) to assist you if you get a little stuck, or just leave your deck and go about your day.

READING TAROT FOR OTHER PEOPLE

BEFORE PICKING UP YOUR DECK

Do what you can to support, nourish, and fortify your being, body, and spirit before you hold space. Only you truly know what that looks and feels like for you, so check in with yourself and tune in to what you might be needing. It might be grounding if you feel nervous, dancing around, listening to music that you love, discharging energy from the body in a way that feels supportive, having a snack, hydrating, or having a sweet chat with a friend before you connect with your querent. Give yourself permission to play and notice what feels really good and supportive for you.

1. Feel free to start the reading off with a simple inquiry to your client. *How can I support/serve you today?* is one of my favorite ways to kick off the session.
2. Listen to your client. Make compassionate, ample space for them to share what's happening in their lives and what brought them to you. Pay attention to what's coming up in your body, what's arising in your heart as you listen to them. Affirm them, honor the courage it takes to share these deep things with you, and when it's time, confirm with them what you're both going to tune in to for their reading.

   If you are reading for someone who is struggling or moving through something activating, it can feel very affirming for the client's experience to consider asking them if there's anything that they prefer *not* to hear in the reading, or if there's any alternative language around something that might feel more welcoming or less activating for them.
3. Drop-In time. I like to tell my client that I'm going to do a Drop-In and listen to their Guides for them, which usually takes one to three minutes. I encourage them to join me in that quiet space by engaging with whatever will be supportive to them. They are welcome to pray or set an intention, look out the window or take a sip from their tea or wa-

ter. Whatever works for them works for me. I always ask if that's okay with them before I begin, and once I have their consent, I go ahead and dive in.

4. Pull cards! How do we enable our clients to pull their own cards in a reading?

    If you're in person, you can hand your deck to your client and have them pick a card. An easy and elegant way to do this is to have them cut the deck into three piles and reorder them in whatever way feels best to them.

    If you're doing a distance/online reading, you can either pull for your client or engage with a practice that my beautiful friend, Julia Inglis of Sacred Familiar, employs: Spread the deck out in front of you, run your hands over it, and have your client tell you when to stop. Wherever they tell you to stop, pull the card that's closest to your fingertips. It's a beautiful way to have your querent "pull" without them being present in the physical space with you.

    Once all the cards are out on the table, look at the song or picture that's forming. What is the reading saying to you? What notes are being harmonized? Feel free to take your time, if you need it, and really sense into the full picture of the reading.

5. Share what you're noticing with your client. Offer them your feedback on what they're being invited to pay attention to, the invitations and medicine of these cards. How can they open to this medicine? What might feel supportive to them?
6. Ask them if they have any questions and thank them for booking the reading. Once they've left, whether that was your only reading for the day or you have several more, nourish and support yourself. Clear the space and your field as you feel called, blessing and thanking the client silently or out loud for their time, courage, and intention.

FREQUENTLY ASKED QUESTIONS

My client won't tell me any specifics at the start of the reading—it's like they want to "test" my skills. What should I do?

I have two potentially helpful answers to this question:

OPTION 1: I encourage everyone (even those who are brand-new to this craft) to have written information on your website or booking site that clarifies your guidelines for a reading with you. In my guidelines, I affirm that I am not a psychic (because I am not) and that these are not psychic or predictive Tarot readings (because they aren't). I also have clients check a box to confirm and affirm that they must have an inquiry for booking with me, and that I will gladly refund them if they do not have a question or an inquiry for our time together. It doesn't have to be a big or well-formed question. It can simply be that they'd like a sense of the invitations of the season or year at hand, or that they are struggling at work and would love some supportive cards to anchor to in the midst of this stressful time. What I do have a gentle boundary around is the following inquiry: "Oh, whatever the cards want to tell me is great." There's nothing wrong with that, and nothing wrong with anyone who regularly says that to a reader. I want to honor that there are some readers who really love to read for folks without a question, so this might work for them. Additionally, there are some Tarot readers who *are* psychic and actively *don't* want information before they pull cards. I think that's great, but I am not one of them. If you are asking this question, you may be in the same camp. Be clear about what you do and what you offer before someone books with you. It will help with this.

OPTION 2: Let's say someone books a reading with you, checks all the boxes affirming that they know your policies, and *still* shows up without a clear inquiry. Maybe they are even being resistant to opening up to you in this way, almost (you believe) trying to test your skills or abilities. You have two options. The first option is to kindly and directly communicate about what this space is. *You know, it's incredible that some folks have such immense gifts with their intuition that they don't need any information around a pull or a reading before they begin! You might have assumed that all Tarot readers are like that, but I am not one of those people. I need a solid inquiry before we get started, and/or a sense of where you are in your life and what you'd like to take away from this reading before we begin. If that doesn't feel possible for you today, I'd be happy to refund you.* Most folks get it and will helpfully provide some kind of source point from which to start the reading. If they push back on this, you can simply say, *I'm so sorry, but I don't think I'm the reader for you. I'm going to refund you.*

I'm a new reader, and I've been practicing with someone who isn't very kind to me. They keep saying things like "That's not what this card means." What should I do?

Folks who feel the need to correct you or point out the "right" way of interpreting a card are not the folks you want to read for—especially as a beginner.

If you get stuck in a reading like this, you can handle it in a few ways. First, you can bring the reading to a close. There's nothing wrong with saying, *I don't know if we are a match. It seems like we have really different perspectives on the cards. I'm going to bring the reading to a close and offer you a refund for your trouble. Thanks!* You can also let their interruptions roll off your back and continue forward. It might be useful to mention to them that there are many different ways of working with the Tarot and interpreting Tarot cards. Are they available to consider that, and to open to the guidance you're receiving? If not, that's okay. You can stop the reading at any point if they are unable to open to a different take.

I encourage you to find a compassionate, open, helpful reading buddy (who might also be a family member or friend) who will practice with you.

Speaking of which, please see the next question!

Do you recommend reading for friends or family members?

It really, really depends on the friend or family member. Some folks are just not available to this kind of practice, especially if they see us as younger, less experienced, etc. Some folks don't realize how utterly naked and intimate a Tarot reading is and can get contracted around the process, taking out their discomfort on us. If you have a very heartfelt, kind, and emotionally available friend or family member who truly understands this, I highly encourage you to practice with them or read for them. Otherwise, my general rule of thumb is to read for folks that you don't have that kind of preexisting bond with.

What kind of Tarot deck should I work with? Is it useful to start with a more standard deck, like Smith-Rider-Waite? What about Oracle decks? How do they factor in?

You are welcome to work with any Tarot deck you like, and it doesn't need to be a standard or classic deck. I think that the most important thing about working with any Tarot deck is the imagery. It must resonate with you. We're living in a true golden age of decks, and you get to work with whatever kind you want.

My only note about potentially working with the Smith-Rider-Waite: It is essentially the source from which a great many modern-day Tarot decks draw. While you might not ever want to read Tarot with the Smith-Rider-Waite deck, I humbly suggest that you consider studying it or having one on hand so you can get a good sense of where we're drawing inspiration from. *Tarot Wisdom* by Rachel Pollack and *Tarot for Change* by Jessica Dore are two excellent books (among many) for deepening our work with the Smith-Rider-Waite deck specifically.

In terms of Oracle decks, they are wonderful, but not the same as Tarot. Tarot decks are a set of 78 images (sometimes more, depending on whether the artist or creator of the deck is offering an alternative treatment of the cards), consisting of the Major Arcana, Minor Arcana, and Court Cards. Oracle decks are decks of cards that allow us to have a much more flexible channeling experience. Oracle decks can have as many cards as desired and don't have to conform to the structure of the Tarot. Tarot and Oracle decks can be used side by side, if desired, in whatever way feels most interesting to you.

When I'm doing a Drop-In for a client or another person, should I invite them to Drop In with me? What if they aren't spiritual or don't want to?

They totally don't have to! As I mentioned above, I like to tell my client what I'm doing when I'm ready to Drop In for them, but they don't have to join me in the process. If you are a more spiritual practitioner, I wholeheartedly encourage you to list that on your website or booking page, so the person you are reading for has full scope and agency to feel for themselves whether you're the right person for them.

I don't typically read Tarot for people with a question or specific inquiry in mind. I like to let the cards just flow and follow the reading from there. You speak a lot about needing to be direct and specific with our readings. How can I approach that advice when it doesn't align with my natural way of reading?

First and foremost, if you have found a way of working with the cards that feels good for you, you can stop there. Nothing more to adjust! Go with what feels aligned for you, no matter what any guide, teacher, or external suggestion might say.

That said, I think rooting our time with a client or with ourselves in a space of intention really helps the reading flower open and be a sturdy, well-boundaried container. This doesn't have to extend itself to being specific around the questions you ask, or the prompts you use for a reading. You might bring this sense of intention and specificity to your Drop-In process: "May I be of service to this person, or may whatever comes through the cards be of value for them?"

Other than that small suggestion (which you are also free to reject!), follow the call and flow of your practice!

You mentioned the possibility of coming to the deck when we're messy and picking a card as a centering practice. Is it okay if the only thing I want or feel able to do is to pull a card and not to Drop In?

Of course! I love and recommend Drop-Ins, but you get to do whatever you want and feel called to—no one knows your practice and relationship with the cards like you do!

I do want to offer (in case it is useful) that I think the point is that you don't always have to be up for a Drop-In. A Drop-In can be nothing more than placing your hands on the deck and naming what is present with you.

I'll share an example with you from my own life. When I'm in a messy space, I'll often pick up my deck and say, "Guides, I want to recenter. If you could give me one card that could help me understand what I need to know to care for myself, to recenter, to know what's going on, depending on what I'm wanting, what would that be?"

It always gets right to the heart of the matter for me. When it doesn't, that's also information for me, but that's its own form of Drop-In.

You do not ever need to feel okay or centered to do a Drop-In. I feel very passionate about emphasizing that. We don't have to feel any kind of way to engage with it.

You're just saying, in your own way, "I'm calling upon everybody who shows up and works for me in my highest and best to help me pull the cards I need to receive in this moment. Only what I need to receive." That's a Drop-In. It's two seconds. There's no special words or feelings that are required.

That said, however, feel free to skip the Drop-In if it doesn't feel accessible!

What if a client brings something to me that overwhelms me, or that I don't feel I can really answer for them/do a reading around?

If your client is asking about something that feels out of the scope of your practice, be willing to say that you're not available to support them with that, and they are welcome to reach out to someone who can. I think many of us start our practice believing that we need to be able to hold anything that comes up for a client (I know I did) when that's simply not true. Don't be afraid to be honest about those boundaries.

Ugh, I have no clue what I'm doing! How can I start reading for people and get that experience while feeling like I'm such a beginner?

If you're a beginner, give yourself the permission to be exactly where you are! Start small and simple. Do one-card pulls for folks, then maybe work up to three-card pulls. Share what you're noticing with your client. Let yourself not know. It's okay! The most important thing is simply to practice, however imperfectly.

How do you shuffle and pull cards?

For a primer in shuffling and pulling cards, see Reading Tarot for Yourself, earlier in this chapter. Right now, I'm finding that what's feeling good for me is to pick up the deck, hold it in my hands, ask a question, shuffle, and run my fingers over the spine of the deck until a card sparks for me, and then I pull from that place. Sometimes, I shuffle until I feel "complete" in some way and then pull from the top.

Of course, there's no one right or wrong way to do this. We can fan the cards out and pick the ones that feel right, we can cut the deck and pull from the top, etc. It's a pretty personal practice, and I encourage you to play with all kinds of ways of pulling to see what feels most supportive to you!

How can we balance engaging with the Soul Tarot framework and a more traditional way of reading? How might I keep Soul Tarot in mind if I'm reading from a guidebook that came with the deck I am using and that has totally different interpretations in it?

The short answer is that you don't have to balance anything!

I would recommend that you keep what works from whatever framework you're using to read Tarot, including Soul Tarot, and leave what doesn't feel aligned for you. Soul Tarot will always be there for you as a resource, should you want or need it. The traditional way of reading Tarot will always be available for you, too. I would advise that you don't have to hold too tightly to anything.

Soul Tarot can be the framework for how we approach the Tarot, and it can also be viewed merely as the "bones" of your practice—a healthy, strong foundation and solid insulation for your continued learning. It may or may not necessarily live in the home of your Tarot practice.

I also think you can take what works and leave what doesn't with guidebooks. As someone who has now written a guidebook, I have made peace with the fact that not everyone is going to align with how I've channeled or interpreted the cards. You will definitely have your own relationship with the Soul Tarot deck (should you choose to work with it) that will diverge from what was in my heart and mind when I created it. In other words, I think it is useful to consider what's written in the guidebooks as *suggestions* for our personal practice, not necessarily as rules we must follow. There might be times when you don't align with the image or traditional interpretation of a card—then Soul Tarot might pop in as a useful leg to keep the table nice and level. For others, Soul Tarot is the table itself.

In short, trust in where you're guided and what calls to you. I encourage you to do this because the longer you practice, the more you will gradually outgrow most of these frameworks, which is not only appropriate but ideal! They will still be a part of the praxis from which you serve or read Tarot, but your own relationship with the cards will outshine everything else, as it should.

CHAPTER FIFTEEN

GETTING UNSTUCK

Resources for Tricky Moments Around Our Tarot Practice

No matter how resourced, centered, or confident we might feel, we will inevitably bump into some tricky spots with our Tarot practice, or when pulling cards for others. This chapter is full of helpful resources that I've created over the years to help get folks "unstuck" and clear again with their Tarot pulls.

THE THREE C'S

When you're stuck in judgment around what you've pulled, consider the Three C's: **curiosity**, **critical thinking**, and **compassion.**

All of us come to the Tarot, and to our Tarot practice, with preconceived notions, judgments, misperceptions, and biases born of the immense cultural influence that looms over these cards. When these preconceived notions, judgments, misperceptions, and biases run unchecked, they can have a really challenging, and sometimes harmful, effect on our Tarot readings.

The Three C's are supportive Soul Tarot touchstones to begin investigating those old paradigms and stories, assisting us in reclaiming a fresh perspective with each Tarot pull.

When might the Three C's be useful to us?

- We have a very binary, black-and-white viewpoint on the Tarot, believing some cards are good and some are bad.
- We feel fear around certain Tarot cards and want to begin to tend to that fear and open to a different way of working with the card at hand.
- We've only ever heard a Tarot card described in a particular, more specific way (for example, Five of Pentacles = financial destitution), and we'd like to widen our perspective on it.
- We pulled a card for ourselves and feel disappointed and like we're in judgment or story about its presence in the reading (*I pulled the wrong card;*

That card shouldn't be here; My situation is really great, so why did I pull a "bad" card?).

CURIOSITY

Curiosity is our best ally when it comes to reshaping and rewilding the way we interpret Tarot cards. When initial judgments and stories arise upon pulling cards in our readings (which are completely normal), we want to pause and get curious rather than get swept into any contractive invitations from the mind. Upon getting curious, we might realize that we're telling ourselves a story about the card we pulled. Is that story true? Is this card "bad"? Is it "good"? How do we know if it's one or the other? Are we consciously or unconsciously expecting a particular card to show up? It's been my experience that when I'm in deep expectation around a reading or am hoping for a particular outcome, I am likely to get my ass handed to me. We can hold a tender space for that vulnerability and disappointment while staying open to the possibility that the card is still bringing something of value. Curiosity will always guide us home, no matter how seasoned or new we might be to the Tarot.

CRITICAL THINKING

Critical thinking is crucial when working with the Tarot because it can be an important recentering when we find ourselves in unlikely, unrealistic, or irrational perceptions about our Tarot card pulls. If we pull Two of Cups and expect to get married, we want to gently pull the threads on that. Is that likely to happen right now? Are we currently partnered? Is it a little more likely that Two of Cups is inviting us to really love on ourselves (especially the parts of us that feel the most challenging to love)? If we pull the Death card and fear that a loss will occur, we may want to pause, get curious, and open to a critically thoughtful perspective. How likely is that? Perhaps for you, it's very likely. For most of us, it's probably not something we need to concern ourselves with. If we find ourselves believing that a financial windfall or disaster is coming, or that we're going to get betrayed, this step of the Three C's can really help. How likely is this scenario that we're working through right now and, more importantly, how might we tend to the fear that's underneath it?

COMPASSION

When we struggle or get stuck in our Tarot pulls, we ideally want to have as much compassion for ourselves as we can muster. It's okay to not be sure, to be scared, or to be worried. It's okay to be learning. It's okay if it takes your nervous system a long while to trust in and be comfortable around a certain card. You're allowed to not know, and to be learning as you go.

THE POWER PRACTICE

If you feel afraid or activated by what you've pulled, consider another Soul Tarot cornerstone, the POWER Practice. POWER is an acronym formed from the words *pause*, *observe*, *witness*, *expand*, and *rewild*.

What happens when we feel triggered by a particular card, or our decks? We can call upon the POWER Practice to help us dive deeper into why, and how we can recenter.

Pause. When you notice stories, anxiety, fear, or what-ifs arising in your reading, offer yourself a gentle pause. Don't try to change anything about your internal state; just be with it and yourself, just as you are.

Observe. Observe the story that is coming up about the card. Try to watch it from a bird's-eye view. See if you can get curious about it without identifying with it.

Witness. Can you offer compassionate witness to yourself around this trigger? What is the root of the fear? What does the fear have to say? Can you make space to really hear this part of you, to embrace and love it?

Expand. Now that you have offered compassionate space to your mind/ego/inner child, check in with your soul. What does your soul know about this card? What do your Guides have to say about it? Can you pull a clarifier? Is there a new download or piece of medicine coming through around this card that is unique to you? Can you make space for this possibility?

Rewild. What has changed since you pulled the card? Can you allow yourself to be on a journey with this card, one that has no beginning and no end? How might you see this card as a friend and helper? What medicine could this card be offering you?

REVERSALS IN SOUL TAROT

A *reversal* is the term for a Tarot card that presents upside down in a reading. Some folks never receive or pull a reversal because of the way that they shuffle and pull (completely okay), and some folks opt to not work with reversals, either because they don't want to or because they don't feel like they are able to fully understand them yet (also completely okay). We never have to work with reversals if we don't prefer to.

Reversals are often, but not always, seen as a warping of the card's original purity. They are often spoken about as a sign that we are out of balance, or in danger of some kind of excess or folly, or that we're not paying attention. Frankly, this hasn't been my experience in working with them.

In Soul Tarot, a reversal is the equivalent of taking the rugged, wild path in the forest as opposed to the marked trail. You are going to arrive at the same place, but you will have a different journey to get there. Reversals help flavor the card's meaning, offering something different and often more complex than the original meaning of the card when right side up.

Reversals can show up for a few different reasons, but the predominant one is that they reflect an aspect of us that's crying out for support on our journey inside a particular Tarot card. I think of a reversal as a heads-up that a part of our being is like a kid frozen at the top of a slide who needs our attention. After receiving our attention, that little kid might feel brave enough to go down the slide—or to climb back down the ladder.

Regardless of why we receive them, reversals are full of beauty and medicine, and opening to that medicine can radically transform and uplevel our readings.

Why might a reversal be showing up for us?

- **A request for self-tending.** Before we leap, do the big thing, shift away from something, or say no, we might need to tend to ourselves or be present with a part of ourselves that's feeling nervous about whatever might be going on. This doesn't necessarily mean that we won't ultimately leap, do the big thing, or shift away from something—it means that in order to do so, we might first need to be with the parts of us that feel trepidatious about it.
- **Something is ready to go or is complete in our lives.** Sometimes a reversal is a signal that we're finished with something, or that a chapter or season is clearing itself out of our lives. This is often really welcome news and tends to be what I observe when the "spikier" cards of the Tarot show up reversed. Nine times out of ten, it is an indication that they are ready to be cleared away.
- **Something is not quite ready yet, and we're being invited to be a bit more patient.** Seven of Pentacles, The Hermit, The Tethered One, and The World are all common examples of this category of reversal. It's natural for us to want to get out of an uncomfortable situation as quickly as possible. Sometimes our reversals will gently clarify for us that we might be rushing things a bit.
- **It's offering us a more internal, subconscious treatment of the card.** I see this category of reversal appear a lot when cards like The Devil and The Tower show up reversed. It's not that we're not going through The Devil and The Tower, even when we see them upside down. But when reversed, they are just a little softer, a little more internal, and a little more subconscious than they might be when right side up.

REPEATING CARDS IN SOUL TAROT

Often called "stalker" cards (a term that I'd like to invite all of us to retire), repeating cards are exactly what they sound like: a card that keeps showing up, again and again and again, no matter how often you shuffle, how often you pull, or what you are asking about.

My students often fret about repeating cards, worrying that they are somehow missing something (which can easily and understandably pivot into annoyance—*I'm trying to understand how to work with this card!*). It's not that repeating cards can't be a heads-up that we're missing something, but the truth is that I don't often experience repeating cards as signals that we're not paying attention. I mainly see them as reinforced indications or reminders of the season we're in. If we're in a deep winter or transiting through a particular season, there's often no new information from week to week. We are just in what we are in.

I like to think of repeating cards as mindfulness bells and opportunities to deepen our relationship with a particular Tarot energy. That's one additional way to reflect on them.

Why might we see a repeater card?

- We're in a season with that particular card and more apt to see it again and again while we are in that season.
- We're being invited to get to know that card a little better (think master class or independent study). When a card repeats, it can sometimes offer us many alternative ways to consider it that we might not have initially thought about.
- It might be offering us a heads-up to pay attention to something that we're neglecting or missing. I think we typically know what this kind of repeating card pertains to when it shows up. When I'm overworked and a little fried, I tend to see the same cards over and over again, gently inviting me to take a little more space and care for myself, even take a tiny break.

Students ask if we can take Tarot cards out of the deck that we don't want to see or receive. I encourage folks to feel free to take specific Tarot cards out of the deck if they are activating and they cannot bear to see those cards in their readings until things in their life begin to shift and change. If you need permission to do this, you've got it.

UNPACKING "SWEET" CARDS IN SHITTY CIRCUMSTANCES

You might ask: Why did I pull Ace of Cups when I'm going through a horrible time?

It can be helpful to remember that Tarot cards don't always "report." This is part of why we can be going through hell but also pull a card like Ace of Cups. When this happens, folks can get understandably upset, feeling that their decks or Guides are mocking them. This is absolutely not the case. The card we pull in cases like this isn't necessarily affirming or reporting on our experience, but in fact is jumping right to the medicine, support, and help that might be needed in a hellish time. Ace of Cups is an invitation to love and regard ourselves with immense kindness. We might not be feeling that way in a challenging time, but pulling this card in the midst of one can be a reminder of how we might respond to ourselves within the challenges.

WORKING WITH "JUMPERS"

Jumpers refers to cards that fly out of the deck while we're tuning in or shuffling the deck. Some folks opt to only work with cards that jump or fly out of the deck and will shuffle in a way that allows for that.

If jumpers don't really resonate with you, you can feel free to place the cards that fly out of the deck back into it and continue to pull in the way that you had initially planned. I wanted to speak to jumpers in this book because I personally love them and adore working with them.

The jumpers I receive for both my own readings and the readings I give to others are usually shockingly resonant, which is why I opt to include them when they show up. I consider them to be an additional, special message from Spirit that pops up as a kind of delightful and helpful surprise as we're pulling cards for ourselves and others.

If a card flies out of the deck while you're shuffling, I invite you to pause and reflect on whether it might resonate with you. If not, no harm done—you can just put it back in the deck and move on.

MESSING UP, MAKING A MISTAKE, OR MISSING THE MARK

As of the writing of this book, I've been reading Tarot for about 25 years and have been doing this work professionally for 11 years. I have a great deal of confidence in my channel, but of course, like all readers, there have been times where I messed up: I said the wrong thing, the guidance I received was proven incorrect, or I didn't handle a situation with client as gracefully or skillfully as I could have.

I want to begin by acknowledging that this is likely to happen on your journey as a Tarot reader. We're ideally going for harm reduction and the safest, most consent-based experience for our clients as possible, but we're humans. We're going to mess up from time to time. This isn't to scare you, but to assure you that you are not alone.

How can we respond if we've made a mistake with our reading, or messed up in some way?

If appropriate, apologize and offer a refund. Acknowledge that you feel or know you messed up. Ask if there is anything you can do to make it right. On rare occasions, our reaching out might be the cause of more harm, so you want to make sure you really consider whether this apology would be in the highest and best good of the client. If your client is courageous enough to come to you to share that their experience with you felt tricky or harmful, *listen to them*. Acknowledge and affirm them. Put your ego aside and offer to repair, if they are available for that.

If apology and repair are not possible for any number of reasons, we can make our Tarot practice a living amends. We can allow those incredibly painful and challenging interactions to be a catalyst for strong reconstruction, improvement, or change to our practice to ensure that it doesn't happen again. I will say for myself (and this is certainly not an excuse, or an attempt to be casual around this subject), I have never made the same mistake with a client twice—part of the reason why is that these experiences stick with me. I know what it is to be in that position, and I want to continually be learning from my missteps.

YES
NO
PAUSE
TEND

CHAPTER SIXTEEN

WEAVING MEANING

How to Interpret Our Tarot Pulls

Anyone can pull a Tarot card—interpreting it is an entirely different thing. Interpreting a card isn't necessarily about knowing an answer or knowing what's to come. It's about being open to communication from a deeper part of ourselves and learning to sense into a different language.

To drop into this deeper layer with our Tarot decks—to bridge the gap between pulling and interpreting—we have to allow the mind to have its opportunity to judge, worry, or project *first*. We can fully open to and honor that experience, tending to the contractions that might arise within that space, letting them be there. Once we've done that, we can shift into our soul knowing, taking the mind with us.

What are some ways that we can do that?

We can root into some of our Soul Tarot pillars, for starters. Remember that the card in question is showing up *for* us, not *to* us. It can also be useful to remember that the cards we pull are merely invitations, not necessarily predictions of what will be or not be. Our nervous systems often need this reminder in order to relax enough to be open to what the card might be calling us into.

It is also quite powerful to remember that the card we've pulled, no matter how spiky or tricky it might seem, is bringing medicine. It is here to help—not to harm, frighten, or forebode. Once the mind/nervous system is quieter, calmer, and less guarded against potential bad news, it is always easier to sense into the wise whispers underneath the surface.

Some other basic ways to begin interpreting are, of course, to allow the image of the card to wash over you. What colors, symbols, or imagery stand out to you? What's drawing your eye? If you aren't able to connect with the cards visually, what smells, sounds, feelings, or experiences come through to you when working with a card?

As a helpful reminder, here is a little cheat sheet for how to consider the three parts of our Tarot decks from a Soul Tarot perspective:

- **The Major Arcana** = macrocosm. We work best with these cards' energies when we *surrender* to them, letting them guide us.
- **The Minor Arcana** = microcosm. We work best with these cards' energies when we *collaborate*, or take *empowered action* with them, letting them show us where we might need to refine our actions or make an internal or external adjustment.
- **The Court Cards** = wise inner teachers. We work best with these cards' energies when we *embody* them, imagining ourselves literally meshing with them, and having them show us the way forward.

We can put this formula into action. Let's say we pull Six of Cups as our card for the inquiry, *What are we being invited to pay attention to?* We've held a space for our feelings and initial response to the card and opened to the possibility of going deeper with this energy.

What do we know about this card right off the bat?

We know that Six of Cups is a Minor Arcana energy and, thus, is one that we *collaborate* with and can work with in an accessible way (as opposed to a Major Arcana energy, which often requires some semblance of surrendering and deeper, soul-led work from us).

We know that The Sixes of the Tarot are often expansive, more interpersonal energies, ones that remind us of the gifts of being in connection with one another.

We know that The Cups are energies that help us reparent ourselves, hold a tender space of loving-kindness for ourselves, and let ourselves take the time it takes to move through our emotional process.

By having an awareness of those structures, we know that we're being invited to expand and open to more interpersonal support (Six) in a way that will likely be vulnerable, intimate, and heart-led in some way (Cups), one that we're being called to take some kind of empowered action around (Minors). That is the beginning of an interpretation.

Let's go deeper. What kind of empowered action could we take around a card like Six of Cups?

Six of Cups shows up after Five of Cups, which is a card of loss and struggle around a change of some kind. In The Fives, we are grieving something that has passed or dried up or run its course. In our work with Five of Cups, we slowly turn from the three empty cups in front of us to the two full cups behind us—life that continues (and in many ways is formed) from our loss. Six of Cups is the heart opening again after a disappointment, grief, or loss. It is an intimate act of sharing, of seeing another (this might be another person specifically, or a community, or humankind as a whole) and allowing ourselves to be seen.

The beginning of a soul-led interpretation of Six of Cups is that it is an invitation to open the heart again, to dance in our vulnerability—to see others and to let them see us. It might feel very intimate, but that's exactly what we're being called to embrace. How might we consider sharing more of ourselves, and who might it feel possible to do this with?

This is only one example, but this approach can be used with any of the cards in the Tarot, no matter the interpretation.

CHAPTER SEVENTEEN

TAROT ANCHORING

An Alternative Way to Work with the Cards

In my anecdotal experience as a trauma survivor, and as someone who has worked with the cards steadily for over 25 years, it is very, very tough (if not impossible) to read Tarot for ourselves in our standard way if we happen to be moving through a five-alarm contraction, transition, or crisis.

When our nervous systems are blown out, when we feel like a live wire, or when we are in the loop of waiting for news in a charged time, we likely won't be able to read for ourselves or absorb the cards that we *do* receive if we attempt a reading. If we want to utilize the Tarot as a tool in these moments, the practice of Tarot Anchoring may be helpful to us.

Tarot Anchoring is a helping practice that I unwittingly developed when I was working with my deck during a particularly distressing time. It is an amazing ritual that can help us become more intimate with certain Tarot cards and assist us in staying tethered to our decks, especially in moments when standard Tarot readings might feel too overwhelming or inaccessible for our nervous systems.

With Tarot Anchoring, we intentionally form a supportive, comforting, or healing bond with a particular Tarot card, calling upon it as a North Star to keep us rooted in challenging moments. We largely opt out of the standard process of the Drop-In and pulling a card with Tarot Anchoring. In this practice, we are empowered to choose the card that we need or want to be surrounded by. If you need to see Queen of Pentacles, you don't have to wait for the deck to give it to you. You can select it and begin to engage with it as you see fit.

ENGAGING WITH TAROT ANCHORING

1. Choose or open to the card that feels like the deepest balm, comfort, and reminder of truth for whatever you're going through. It should feel like a homecoming and a deep refuge for you.
2. Weave in associations. What things make you feel seen, safe, held, and loved? What reminders are most important to you as they pertain to this card? Are there songs, images, scents, deities, memories of beloved dead, or colors that you can braid into your work with this chosen card?
3. Get creative. Maybe you want to rename the card or draw or paint one in your own image. Whatever you choose, this can be a beautiful way to claim and root into the card's energy for your own anchoring practice.
4. Place the card on your altar or call upon it during quiet, calm, or peaceful moments as well as more spiky moments.

CHAPTER EIGHTEEN

SOUL TAROT SPREADS

Inquiries and Prompts for Every Season

A gentle note: You might notice that there are not any visual outlines or directives in this book on particular ways to structure your Tarot spreads. In other words, you are empowered to pull cards and order them in whatever way you wish. I recognize that this is somewhat unusual when it comes to Tarot books, but I feel quite strongly about it.

Some of us don't have the space or ability to support or work with a larger Tarot spread for many reasons. The entire Soul Tarot practice is devoted to empowering, nurturing, and amplifying you—your wisdom, your practice, your capacity. With that comes an added degree of autonomy in terms of how your Tarot spreads look.

Please engage with the Tarot spreads in this section in whatever way you feel called to. You can place, order, and work with the cards however your heart desires.

Some simple, one-card inquiries to ask of our deck:

- What card would be helpful for me for the day/situation/week ahead?
- What would you (my inner wisdom/Spirit) have me know?
- What am I being invited to pay attention to?
- How can I come back home to this moment?
- What support can I call upon in this moment?
- What is the deepest lesson of the day/moment for me?
- What card is showing up as my Anchor at this time?

The Check-In Spread

1. What is present?
2. How can I work with or respond to what's here?
3. What support might I need to call on to do that?

The Soul Tarot Spread

1. What season of life am I currently moving through?
2. What is the deepest lesson of the present moment?
3. What am I being invited to pay the most attention to at this time?
4. What support can I call upon to be with me as I engage with this moment?
5. What is an aligned action I'm being invited to take at this time, if any?

A Dropping-In with Our Inner Voice

1. What is the message from my wise inner knowing?
2. What is this part of me most needing or asking for right now?
3. How can I offer this part of me the nourishment it deserves?

TAROT SPREADS FOR DIFFICULT OR CHALLENGING SEASONS

While Tarot is never a substitute for professional advice, therapy, and/or medication, I believe that it can be a quiet, humble, transformative tool in our toolbox of resources. When we're having a tough time and we just need a little extra nudge of support, these spreads may be of use.

Compassionately Responding to Suffering Spread

1. How can I tend to the pain that's present?
2. What kind of attention can I offer this part of myself?
3. What action, if any, am I being invited to take around this right now?

Tending and Befriending Spread

1. How am I being called to meet myself at this moment?
2. What am I being invited to offer attention to?
3. What supportive energy can I call upon to help me do this?

Tarot for Fear and Anxiety

1. What is present?
2. What is the message of this anxiety and fear?
3. How can I tend to myself and wisely respond to this fear?
4. What is my body needing most at this time?

Tarot for Grief and Big Emotions

1. What is present?
2. How can I tend to the emotions that are showing up at this moment?
3. What is the message my grief, anger, or anxiety is trying to send me?
4. How can I offer my care and attention to these feelings?
5. What can help me move through this experience of deep self-tending?

THE CAIRN TAROT SPREAD: LEAVING AN ANCHOR FOR OUR FUTURE SELF IN THE FOREST OF OUR SOUL

The Cairn Tarot spread is a particular kind of spread that we cast for our future self, specifically around something that presents itself as a consistent trigger, tripwire, and/or activation point for us.

The Cairn spread has no fixed baseline around prompts because it is meant to be responsive and flexible for whatever you happen to need in this moment of your life.

For the purposes of this book, I'll offer prompts around two of the Cairn spreads I've made for myself. You are welcome to use these as a jumping-off point for your own self-tending and care.

Cairn Spread #1

1. When I get triggered by this, what refuge can I come home to?
2. How can I take care of myself amid the trigger?
3. How can I wisely respond to the belief or story that's driving the trigger?
4. What kind of aligned action can I take amid this, if anything?
5. What is the medicine I can take from this?

Cairn Spread #2

1. What card can I call upon to offer support, to help me to be with the feelings but also say no thank you to the roller coaster?
2. What nurturing can I offer the fear?
3. What cards can help me to respond to the trigger in a different and potentially more supportive way?

CRAFTING YOUR OWN CAIRN SPREAD

Sense into a place where you regularly get tripped up or activated that does not overwhelm your capacity to cope. This is what you'll want to center your Cairn spread around.

The best time to pull cards for your Cairn spread is when you are not currently activated. I encourage you to feel into the cards for this particular spread in a moment of relative calm.

Before you pull, it might be useful to make a list of everything that you feel you need in the moments when you get tripped up: Is it comfort or reassurance? An alternative action to take? A different perspective? What would be most supportive for your future self (who will be the one engaging with this spread)?

Make sure you write down what you pull, and any insights that come along with it. As a gentle reminder, there are no bad (or good) cards. It is tremendously helpful when we're able to consider that each card might be bringing some kind of medicine for us—even if that medicine might seem a little bitter or spiky.

TAROT SPREADS FOR SEASONAL THRESHOLDS AND SACRED PASSAGES

Incubating: A Soul Tarot Spread for Gestation Seasons

1. What am I currently nurturing, gestating, or incubating?
2. What kind of nourishment do these tender seedlings need from me?
3. How can I trust in this season of my life?
4. What kind of support can I call upon for this season?

Blossoming: A Soul Tarot Spread for Creation Seasons

1. What is blossoming or blooming in my life at this time?
2. What support can I call upon for this huge creation/birthing season?
3. Where is this deep river of movement and creation taking me?
4. How can I enjoy and open to the bounty of this season, if at all?

Shifting: A Soul Tarot Spread for Transitional Seasons

1. What medicine can I call upon for this deeply transitional time in my life?
2. What am I currently releasing, or moving away from?
3. What am I moving closer to?
4. What is an Anchor that can help me to cross the bridge into this new time in my life?

Resting: A Soul Tarot Spread for Integration Seasons

1. How may I be a gentle guide for this deep season of rest and integration?
2. What message does this guide have for me?
3. How am I being invited to rest at this time?
4. How can I trust in and surrender to this time of rest?

Floating: A Soul Tarot Spread for Liminal Seasons

1. What supportive Anchor card can I call upon to be with me in this void-like, liminal season?
2. How might I be able to rest more fully in the unknown?
3. What gifts might the void space have for me?
4. What card can help me to be more available to these gifts?

The Wild Rose Spread

1. Bud: What is forming and growing in my life at this time?
2. Flower: What is present, in full bloom, longing for my attention?
3. Rose hip: What is ready to be alchemized in my life, transformed from its current state to something new?
4. Thorn: What protective Anchors and energies can I call upon to help me to embark on this cycle?

Solar Return/New Moon/New Beginnings Spread

1. What is an Anchor/Teacher Card for this new cycle of my life?
2. What seeds am I being invited to plant at this time?
3. What kind of tending do those particular seeds need?
4. What kind of support can I call upon for this level of tending?

Completions/Full Moon Spread

1. What is an Anchor/Helper Card for this time of deep release or cycle of completion?
2. What did this experience or cycle teach me?
3. What of this old cycle am I being called to keep or to cherish, if anything?
4. How can I tend to myself through this time of release and completion?

Seasonal Shift Spread: For Cross-Quarters, Solstices, Equinoxes, and New Astrological Seasons Ahead

1. What medicine is there for this threshold?
2. What are the deepest lessons of this parting season?
3. What am I being invited to compost and clear at this time, to not take with me into the new season?
4. What am I being invited to welcome in and make space for in this coming season?
5. What support do I need for the threshold or journey ahead?

TAROT READINGS FOR TIME-BASED QUESTIONS

If the future is not fixed and Tarot is rooted in the present moment, how do we engage with past/present/future readings, if at all? These time-based spreads help to draw the Tarot out of the future and into the present.

Past/Present/Future Alternative Spread

1. What is present?
2. What is the most important thing to know about what brought me to where I am at this moment?
3. What card can help me feel anchored and supported in the next cycle of my life?

From Root to Flower Spread

1. What is the tree of this moment?
2. What are the roots of the tree?
3. What flowers are blooming on the tree?

Passage of Time Spread

1. Where am I now?
2. What got me here?
3. Where is this moment leading me?

FAST/SLOW/YES/NO: A TAROT SPREAD FOR TIME-SENSITIVE SITUATIONS

It can be challenging to get time-sensitive or time-based answers from our Tarot deck, especially in charged moments. The questions or inquiries have to be lined up just so, and even in those cases, it can still be really tricky to get the clarity or direction we might be looking for from the cards. I have personally found that the Fast/Slow/Yes/No spread tends to get the job done in most situations, even if I don't love the answer I receive (which is perfectly valid).

First and foremost, you will need to separate your deck into three piles for this spread:

- Pile 1 is your Major Arcana cards.
- Pile 2 is your four Knight cards.
- Pile 3 is the rest of the deck.

Put Pile 3 off to the side for the moment, as you will be primarily working with Piles 1 and 2.

Once you have your three separate piles, I invite and encourage you to do a Drop-In for yourself. Once you've done a small (or large) Drop-In, you can follow this flow for your spread:

1. What is the season/situation at hand? (Pull from your Major Arcana pile for this one.)
2. What is the most aligned way to move through this season/situation? (Pull from your pile of Knights for this one.)
3. What tools, actions, or resources are needed to assist me along the way? (Place all of your cards back in one pile, with the exception of the two you have pulled for the prompts above, and then pull from that pile.)
4. What Anchor can help me trust in myself, my decisions, my timing, and the cards that are present with me today? (Same as above—pull from your large pile.)

Once you've pulled, look at everything together and see if you can find a pattern, flow, or clarity in it for yourself.

The Why: A Little More About the Structure of This Tarot Spread

We turn to the Major Arcana for the first question in the spread *(What is the season/situation at hand?)* because it can be incredibly helpful to get a sense of the season we are in when trying to figure out what action we're being invited to take in any given moment. If we feel like it's not a great time to do something, but we aren't sure whether that feeling is rooted in fear or a deeper, intuitive knowing, it can provide a lot of insight if we pull The Emperor for this prompt, as opposed to something like The Tethered One. The Major Arcana are our collective, macro, big-picture energies, and specifically energies that we really cannot create or make on our own. We respond to those seasons as opposed to trying to conjure them ourselves. By getting a sense of the larger picture around us, we can get a much clearer understanding of the season we are in, as well as the decisions we can make around that season.

We turn to The Knights for the second question in the spread *(What is the most aligned way to move through this season/situation?)* because The Knights are ruled by Air in Soul Tarot and represent different ways of moving through situations. The Knights establish pace, rhythm, tone, and speed for us, and are the clearest Anchors to us in seasons when we aren't sure how to match the pitch of the moment. We call upon them for this second prompt of the spread because our Knight can offer us guidance on how to navigate the particular waters that we are in at this time.

In terms of the final prompts for this spread *(What tools, actions, or resources are needed to assist me along the way?* and *What Anchor can help me trust in myself, my decisions, my timing, and the cards that are present with me today?)*, we're opening to the wisdom of the rest of our decks to provide some final insight as to the tools that might be relevant and important to our next steps. For example, receiving Ace of Cups (working with a deep intention to love ourselves unconditionally) as the pull for this prompt will likely yield a different response than if we pulled Seven of Pentacles (cultivating patience around waiting). It can offer us that final point of clarity around how we're being invited to gracefully navigate a moment, season, or situation.

IN CLOSING

A PRAYER FOR OUR PARTING

Thank you for traveling through this book with me. Whether you read the whole thing from cover to cover or picked your way through as needed, I am so grateful to you. In honor of this book coming to completion, I'd like to light a candle, make a cup of tea, and offer you a prayer for our parting.

I hope you know that it's okay to be a beginner at the Tarot. It's okay to be learning. It's okay to have decades of practice under your belt and still not have everything memorized. It's okay to be where you are. Where you are can change in a matter of weeks.

I hope you know that the world needs your gifts. When times are horrible, devastating, confusing, and hopeless, we search for deeper meaning, looking more closely for tools, gifts, and helpers. Those things can never be destroyed or taken away from us as long as we continue to be a conduit for the beauty of this work. Art matters. Magic matters. The Tarot matters, and so do you.

I hope you will make a gentle deal with yourself never to pedestalize any teacher, mentor, or guide. Even if you forget that, I hope you will come back to your own immense, wise, glorious knowing, allowing those who support you to be just that—supports—and nothing more.

I hope you know that the Tarot, these archetypes, belong to you. They are of and from you. In learning how to read the Tarot, you're moving yourself back home to them.

I hope you know that it's okay for you to leave this tool behind, whether temporarily or permanently. It's okay to let your practice go to seed. It's okay to be mad at your Guides, to think the deck is bullshit, and to hate this tool. It's not going anywhere, even if you never pick it up again.

I hope you know that mistakes happen, and that you can repair. If you cannot repair, you can aim to let your life be a living amends.

I hope you know how loved you are. One of the greatest gifts of being an intuitive is the privilege of hearing the loving witness and counsel of folks' ancestors, beloved dead, and Spirit Helpers. You have no idea how loved and cherished you are, just by existing. You have no idea how much they are rooting for you.

I hope you know how honored I am to be here with you. Thank you for the gift of your time, your energy, your curiosity, and your tender heart. I love you. We will keep learning and growing together.

ACKNOWLEDGMENTS

I want to begin by acknowledging all the Tarot thinkers, scholars, educators, and readers that paved the way for me to be able to write this book and do this work in the world. Even more importantly, I want to honor the crucial legacy of Romani Tarot readers in the evolution of the practice of cartomancy and Tarot, and the persecution that they have faced throughout history for their beautiful and ancient practices with this tool. To educate yourself on Romani culture (especially as it pertains to the Tarot), I recommend checking out Jezmina Von Thiele and Paulina Stevens's book, *Secrets of Romani Fortune Telling,* as well as their podcast, *Romanistan*.

I would like to thank my beautiful agent, Meg Thompson, for saying yes to me, and for being the most brilliant, sensitive, clarifying champion imaginable throughout this process. I am so lucky and grateful to be working with you.

I am equally as grateful for the immense skill, warmth, and support that I felt throughout the writing of this book, thanks to the incredible team at Running Press: Melanie Gold, Betsy Hulsebosch, Jenna McBride, Elizabeth Parks, Kara Thornton, and Karen Wise. A very special thanks to my editors, Shannon Fabricant and Kate Anderson, for being an absolute dream team. Thank you for being so brilliant, and for making this such a fun and delightful project to work on.

A very special thank-you to Kate Scelsa, for being such a crucial and important ear, sounding board, and voice of reason while editing this book. You are a treasure, and I am indebted to you forever.

Endless, glowing thanks to Chelsea Granger for doing the illustrations for this project, and, by extension, making my wildest dreams come true. Thank you for your brilliance, kindness, patience, and all of those hours spent on Zoom chatting about the images for the deck and the book. You are truly one-of-a-kind, an immense and remarkable artist, brilliant in every way. It is such a gift to know you and to have worked with you on this.

Thank you to everyone who held me up (whether they knew it or not) while I was writing this book: Jenni Gritters, Sheryl, my beloved Beech Street Parenting community, Portland Threshold Singers, Fiona Johnson, and Dylan Pasture. I couldn't have done this without you.

Profound thanks to Michelle Sinnette—there are no words to express all that you mean to me, and all that you have taught and modeled to me. I love you.

Equally profound thanks to Jennifer Benetato, the most skilled and brilliant therapist and coach, and my soul doula for the bulk of this book-writing process. I wouldn't be here without you, and neither would this book.

To all the incredible staff and branches of support at Tarot for the Wild Soul over the years—deepest, immeasurable thanks to Andrea, Valerie, Iris, Rachelle, Annelise, Terri, and Anna. You have made this work and business what it is, and I cannot express my gratitude more thoroughly.

To my beloved Chase—for being everything. The love of my life, my best friend, my greatest champion. Thank you for creating all of the beautiful visuals for the Soul Tarot courses, for editing every podcast episode and piece of audio that has ever gone out to students. But most importantly, thank you for your presence, your love, your amazing advice and feedback. This business, this book, and this life would not be possible without you. I love you so much.

To my beautiful, cherished Lynxie—I love you endlessly and unconditionally, and that will never change. Thank you for choosing me as your mama. This book would never and could never have happened without you.

And, perhaps most notably, to every single Soul Tarot student and client, to the tens of millions of folks who listen to *Tarot for the Wild Soul* podcast—thank you, thank you from the bottom of my heart. It has been the honor of my life to have the privilege and honor of your trust, your time, your vulnerable questions, and your presence. I am profoundly, endlessly grateful, and want to acknowledge that this book would never exist without you. I love you so much.

INDEX